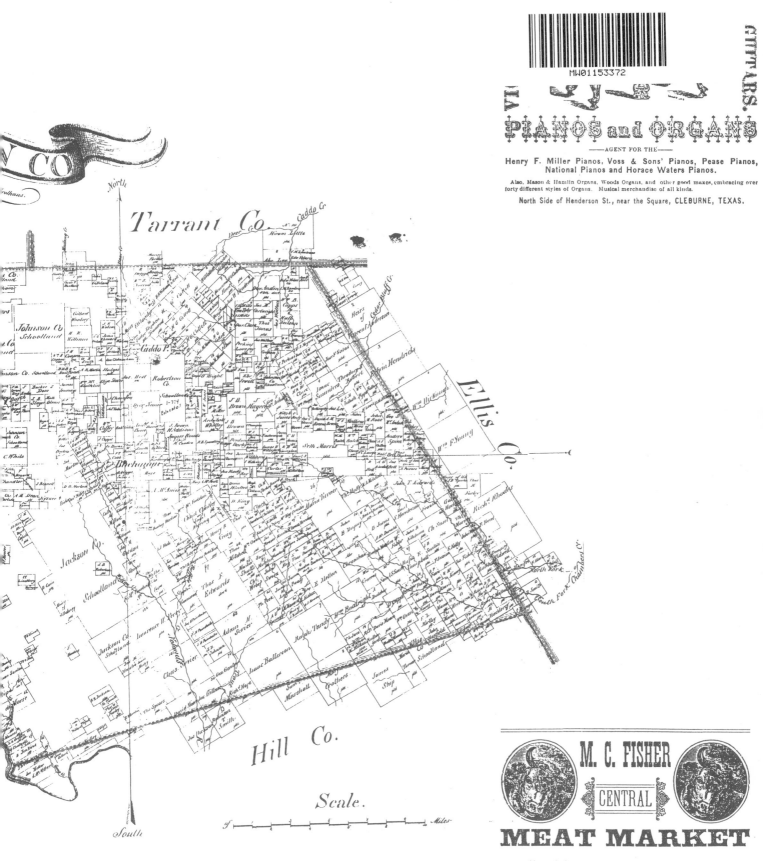

Map of Johnson County in 1859 showing tracts patented and the areas still available for settlement. Originally Johnson County included much of Hood and Somervell Counties. Hand drawn by Frederick Grolhaus. (Texas General Land Office, State of Texas)

Community Bank

*Lending Strength To Our Community*

**THE FIRST NATIONAL BANK IN CLEBURNE**
Member F.D.I.C.

*the* Cowpasture Bank

FIRST STATE BANK in Rio Vista
Member FDIC

Independent Homeowned and Operated Since 1921

Burleson          Cleburne          Godley

**FIRST STATE BANK OF TEXAS**

435 E. Renfro • Burleson, TX 76028
740 S.W. Wilshire • Burleson, TX 76028
Member FDIC

**Historic Burleson**

**Johnson County Heritage Foundation**

**Cleburne State Bank**

**Johnson County Pioneers and Old Settlers Reunion Association**

SPONSORS

Horses, wagons, and buggies crowd the square for "trade days" in 1895 on Cleburne's Courthouse Square. (Dr. Jack Burton)

# JOHNSON
# COUNTY,
# TEXAS

## A Pictorial History

### volume 1

*by Dan Leach and Billie Anne Leach*

*For information write:*
The Donning Company/Publishers
184 Business Park Drive, Suite 106
Virginia Beach, Virginia 23462

Steve Mull, *General Manager*
Bob Jonson, *Project Director*
Barbara A. Bolton, *Project Director*
Paula Foster, *Research Coordinator*
Kevin M. Brown, *Creative Director*
Paul C. Gualdoni Jr., *Graphic Designer*
Jim Casper, *Imaging Artist*
Dawn Kofroth, *Assistant General Manager*
Betsy Bobbitt, *Executive Editor*
Shannon H. Garza, Associate Editor
Teri S. Arnold, *Senior Marketing Coordinator*

**Library of Congress Cataloging in Publication Data**
    Leach, Dan
        Johnson County, Texas : a pictorial history / by Dan Leach and
    Billie Anne Leach.
            p.         cm.
        Includes bibliographical references and index.
        ISBN 1-57864-005-9 (hardcover : alk. paper)
        1. Johnson County (Tex.) 2. Johnson County (Tex.)—History—
    Pictorial works.    I. Leach, Billie Anne.    II. Title.
    F392.J6L43    1998
    976.4'524—dc21                                                97-27971
                                                                    CIP

**Printed in the United States of America**

(JCA)

Gordon Conway and two childhood friends lay on the front lawn
reviewing a picture book at 509 North Anglin, Cleburne, circa
1897.(Courtesy Theatre Arts Collection, Harry Ransom Humanities
Research Center, The University of Texas at Austin)

# CONTENTS

The sound of the fiddle was dance music to the ears of the early Texas settlers. Farm families and friends eased the isolation of frontier life when they got together for an old square dance and caught up on the latest gossip. There was great anticipation if a well-known fiddler played. No one could keep his feet still as the fiddler tuned his instrument, plucked the E string and gave a call, "Partners for the first dance." Note: The woman next to the fiddler lifts her dress slightly as she prepares to step out. The tradition of fine fiddling is kept alive each year at Alvarado by the Johnson County Pioneers and Old Settlers Association. The annual Old Settler's Reunion has met since 1892 and is the premier Reunion event in the state. During the second week of August at the fiddle contests, you can tap your toes and listen as the finest and most well known fiddlers compete for the prize. (AC)

AS WE TRAVEL IN AIR-CONDITIONED CARS down the paved four-lane highway we view Johnson County with our towns and cities full of homes, businesses, and factories. The surrounding countryside is dotted with ranches and farms, all neatly fenced in squares and rectangles; we are kept in or out, depending on our point of view.

The wild west of today has moved into the heart of major cities—gangs of young tough guys ride through town and randomly shoot their weapons. They "paint the town red" with gang graffiti. The pioneers might now be those who bravely live in run-down homes in the aged urban centers and try to civilize, tame, and restore the vacant and abandoned central city. Our modern-day world is turned upside down and inside out. Did we forget the lessons of the past? Must we learn to be civilized all over again?

## The Lesson of History—Lost?

It was not that long ago that Johnson County was the *real* wild frontier at the edge of civilization. Through the early 1840s, Europeans had yet to settle in the county. Johnson County was the Native Americans' home and hunting ground with buffalo herds, trails, and Comanche war parties. Tonkawa and Caddo Indian villages were situated by hills at the edge of the Cross Timbers and near springs and protective cliffs on the many rivers and streams.

After 1845 Johnson County was a border territory . . .with Indians retreating at the advance of the white man. Wild horse hunters, frontier trappers, and traders came along with cruel ruffians and desperadoes. There were no fences and no law, except what could be personally enforced.

Brave settlers by the thousands came with their families as war parties raided from the northwest. There were stagecoach robberies, cruel murders, bank holdups, jail breaks, shoot-outs and vigilante hangings. In the midst of these conditions, settlers lived out their days in pleasure and pain in a courageous struggle just to survive.

Johnson County was a place where the great legend of cowboys and longhorns was born. The "largest forced migration of animals in history" meandered through the center of Johnson County on the Chisholm Trail. Thirty-five thousand traildrivers drove twelve million cattle north during the period from 1866 to the 1880s. Cowboys rode into town for supplies, pleasures, and "wet groceries." Johnson County people knew them on sight, and their outfits were as strange to the townsfolk as those worn by the Indian.

The railroads came and old communities were passed by. New towns developed and there were labor strikes, bank closings, bootlegging, fires, and public hangings. The stuff that fills the pulp novels and movie screens was lived in the towns of Johnson County.

## Legends of the Old West Rediscovered

Visitors come to modern Texas looking for the old west. They ask, "Where is Texas? Can you show me the Texas that everyone has always talked about?" The legends of Texas are now noted only on our street signs: Buffalo Street, Caddo Street, Nolan River Road; or on our schools: Chisholm Trail Academy, Santa Fe School; or our geographic landmarks: Comanche Peak, Caddo Peak, Barnard's Knob, De Cordova Bend, Buffalo Creek, Cross Timbers, Squaw Creek; or place and town names such as Mustang Springs, Caddo Grove, Klondike, Goat Neck, Sand Flat, Island Grove, Fort Spunky, Quicksand, Grange Hall, Rio Vista, Still House Hollow. These names hint of our local history—if we listen to the names, they remind us of their historic meanings.

In careful research, one learns of eye-witness testimony in pioneer journals, diaries, letters, and family stories. Many of these are quoted in this volume, with their original spellings intact, echoing both the accents and attitudes of their times. While they may be flawed by human bias and interpretation, they tell us much about the events and conditions that surrounded the early settlement and growth of Johnson County.

A photographer came by the farm or the family visited a gallery in town, and someone snapped a shutter—a moment of time was frozen in a photograph for

# THE WILD FRONTIER REVISITED

Clarence Victor Leach and his sister Hazel with their teacher studying, circa 1905. (AC)

us. As time passed the images preserved of a well-known person or even commonly known places could not be identified. The photographer had no idea how quaint and unusual the images would become but, for the historian, these photographs are an important, objective, and factual record. Through these preserved images one finds unknown facts and senses a true feeling of the past by looking through the eye of a camera lens from long ago.

## Modern Meanings for Historic Happenings

Perhaps for a few moments as you look at and read this book, learning about our past, you will see the present with new eyes. Martin Luther King, Jr., once said "You know where you are going by looking where others have been." May it be as you view these pages, you will get a better idea about where you are going in this "wild" world of ours.

IT HAS BEEN OUR GOAL IN VOLUME ONE TO trace a historical panorama of Johnson County from earliest times to the beginning of our modern age. What has been revealed to us as we labored is a unique and fascinating heritage whose story is particular to our area, and yet is characteristic of the story of Texas and of the larger American West.

Our hope is that this book will show the basic conditions and shed light on obscure episodes that built our county. For the lifelong resident and the newcomer, knowledge will provide insight, and there will be a better understanding of the forces and events that shaped our communities into what they are.

This book does not attempt to produce a complete detailed history of local towns, communities, churches, organizations, family histories or genealogy. Many fine histories have already been written on these subjects, and that work continues. For further reading there are many wonderful books and periodicals listed in the Bibliography. For more detailed research on particular subjects I recommend books published by local groups involved in preserving our heritage. These people and groups are to be praised for their work in gathering and preserving our county's past.

We are grateful to all who helped and contributed to this work, and have listed those in the credits in the Bibliography. Many fine quotations are included from newspaper accounts, other publications, old letters, and reminiscences, with all the original spellings intact (and frequent misspellings) which convey so vividly the accents and feelings of other eras.

## Sponsors and Financial Institutions

We are sincerely and profoundly grateful to the sponsors and their boards who made this project possible.

Community Bank of Burleson
First National Bank in Cleburne
First State Bank, The Cowpasture Bank of Rio Vista, Cleburne, Burleson, and Godley
First State Bank of Texas
Cleburne State Bank
Historic Burleson
Johnson County Heritage Foundation
Pioneers and Old Settlers Reunion Association of Johnson County, Texas
Anonymous

We recommend to any interested in quality photographic work, The Black and White Works and Lynn Mayes, a top-notch professional. Without their excellent workmanship this book would not have been accomplished. She is chiefly responsible for the sharp appearance of the photographs found in this book. Dr. Jack Burton generously shared his heritage of photographs including some of the most valuable and rare in this volume. The Layland Family established the Layland Museum with the W. J. Layland Collection, the foundation of that fine museum. Julie Baker is now the curator.

The Johnson County Commissioners Court through the Johnson County Historical Commission provided us with support.

J. James (page 167) in the period from 1900 to 1925 was one of the first to encourage the pioneers such as Joseph McClure (page 145) and John Billingsley to record their remarkable stories and memories. Aaron Billingsley, Faye Burton, and Albert Crook left us their reminiscences of the old days; Erlynn Moore and her collection of scrapbooks; Frances Dickson Abernathy, (page 152) Viola Block, Jack Carlton, Raymond Elliott, Mollie Gallop Bradbury Mims, and Mildred Padon, who gathered and published Johnson County histories.

Patricia Boatright, Jim Esely, and Wanda Erickson pushed the book to the final deadline with researching, proofing, computer entry, and caption writing. Wanda researched and copied many documents from the courthouse attic and provided quantities of information from her library and files. Dorothy Schwartz found numerous research items. Mabel McCall and Milly Vaughn labored years assembling scrapbooks on local history. Sandra Osborne helped with research and proofing. Our children Daniel and Benny, spent hours filing, while Eddie and Victoria asked if we needed anything. My parents, Ben and Helen Leach, helped and assisted extensively. We thank them all for the hours they spent working on "the book."

Any omissions that were made in the credits were not intentional, and there must be some, for it would be nearly impossible to remember every one who helped with the vast amount of information. Please contact me, and your name will be included in any future printing.

All profits from the first edition of the book will be invested in local Johnson County historic preservation projects and historic markers, as voted by the Johnson County Heritage Foundation, Inc.

## An Excellent Job!

In 1971 the Johnson County Historical Commission searched for local historic preservation projects. They decided to work on improving the display, housing, and

# ACKNOWLEDGMENTS

Oh yes! We almost forgot to mention those who took the original photographs. We don't often know your names, but we still thank you! (Courtesy Theatre Arts Collection, Harry Ransom Humanities Research Center, The University of Texas at Austin)

availability of the W. J. Layland Collection. These artifacts had been stored and displayed for years on the second floor of the 1905 Carnegie Library Building, 201 North Caddo and in other city buildings. Mildred Padon volunteered for this project and her friends volunteered to help on her committee. The artifacts were soon on display. The museum was open only one afternoon a week,

except by appointment for tours. The caretaker for the building, Floyd Jones, usually opened the upstairs. In 1976, Mabel McCall, volunteered to work an additional afternoon a week.

In the summer of 1978 the Cleburne City Library moved from the Carnegie Library Building to 302 West Henderson. City officials told the volunteer historical group that they could use the whole building for the Layland Museum—if—they could raise the money and do the restoration work, without using city funds. This set Mildred out a second time on the project. A meeting of her friends and volunteers was held at her home and the group organized for the work. Money was raised by soliciting funds from friends and businesses, and all went to work scraping, filling cracks, sanding, painting, and refinishing. The work completed, the grand opening was on March 9, 1979. In October 1979 Mildred became a paid part-time curator; she retired in 1993.

The Research Library started with a few books and grew into a widely known research center on local and county history, Civil War, and genealogy.

Many improvements were made and our beloved museum is regarded as the best small museum in Texas by the Texas Historical Commission.

Mabel McCall

## Reminiscence of a special person:

WEBSTER'S DICTIONARY defines a pioneer as: "One who came first and did great things." Mildred Padon, retired curator of the Layland Museum, born in Fort Spunky along the Brazos River, fits that definition.

I had retired from the Santa Fe Railroad and December 18, 1988, will always be a special day in my memories . . . it was my first visit to the museum, and as a student of history eager to finish research for my book on Texas and Cleburne history. Two little ladies in tennis shoes (their working attire) greeted me and told me about the the only three items in railroad memoral-

Mildred Leona Armstrong Padon (1920–1995) with the Glenda Morgan Award of Excellence in Museums. This is the highest of all official Texas state awards for museum work. The award, signed by then Governor Ann Richards, was presented to Mildred for her many years of exemplary work at the Layland Museum in Cleburne, Texas. Mildred said, "I've enjoyed every second I've been (at the museum) . . . The people make it all worth while." Standing next to her is Dan Leach with his Award of Excellence for Craftsmanship. These awards were presented May 1, 1993, at the Texas Historical Commission's annual meeting in Austin where the state honors outstanding work in historic preservation. Mildred was born at Fort Spunky in 1920 and died in 1995 of cancer. She rests in George's Creek Cemetery beside the other noble pioneers of Johnson County.

Mildred's pioneer spirit, character, and determination is the guide that separates the average from the excellent. Her persistence influenced the publishing of my book, IT TOOK THEIR KIND. It is about people like Mildred who leave something behind for others to enjoy. And some say she was "a legend in her own time . . . " Her monument to another time sits at 201 North Caddo Street, Cleburne.

My memories will be many since that day in 1988, when I met a LEGEND. "I was proud to call her a friend."— W.E."Jack" Carlton, Cleburne, Texas

## Dedication

The authors dedicate this book to Mildred Padon for her many years of thoughtful, tireless work in local historic preservation. Her co-workers say it best—"She did an excellent job!" and "She was LEGEND in her own time." In 1971, when Dan was twenty-one years old, he joined with Mildred on the first committee that set out to organize the museum. You can be sure that she left no stone unturned or any question unanswered. She would open the museum for one child or five hundred people. She never said "no." Upon retirement (for health reasons) in 1993 she received the Glenda Morgan Award for Excellence in Museums from the Texas Historical Commission—the state's highest award for museum excellence. Mildred died of cancer while this book was being complied and written and she assisted in the selection of photographs from her deathbed. This book would not have been possible without her preservation of countless historical photographs and documents over more than a twenty-five year period. Some folks are indispensable when it comes to getting certain things done. She must be included among the pioneers who "came first and did great things" for Johnson County, Texas.

Dan and Billie Anne Leach

bilia they had. These items had already caught my critical eye . . . little did I know that this conversation would end my retirement and I would again be sitting in a caboose another five years.

When Curator Mildred Padon and her assistant, Mabel McCall, explained Cleburne's need for a Railroad Museum, they found in me their recruit. Looking back now, these two would have fared well trading down on the market square during the old days. Maybe they did! Mildred's dream envisioned paying tribute to the railroad families with an annex of railroad artifacts to be housed on the museum grounds in a red caboose. Although, the idea of placing a steel caboose near one of Cleburne's most historic buildings would bring controversy. Mildred's foresight again prevailed when the annex opened on November 22, 1989, to over 1100 guests, increasing the overall attendance each month by 55 percent to the Layland.

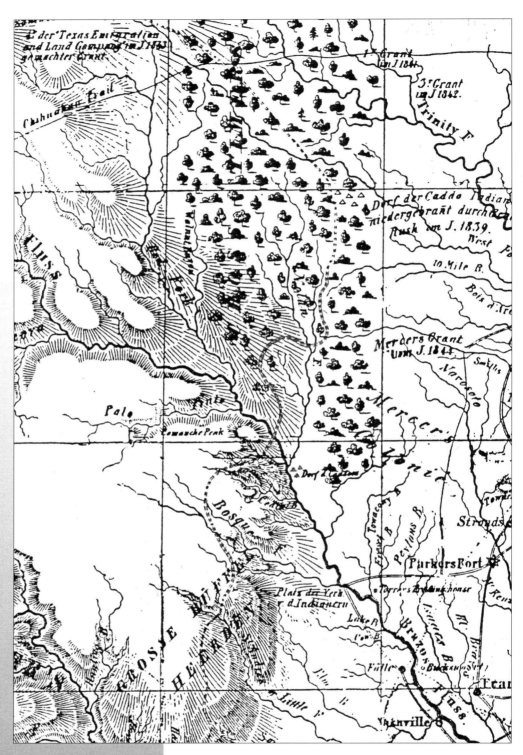

Shown is Caddo Village [Derf] which was burned by General Rusk,
January 1839. Also shown is the Route of the Santa Fe Expedition and
the Caddo Village Roemer visited near the mouth of the Nolan River.
This map insert of Roemer's Texas was published in German in Bonn,
1849, with an English version published 1935 by Oswald Mueller of
Houston, Texas. (AC)

JOHNSON COUNTY'S BOUNDARIES TAKE IN A remarkably scenic and beautiful area of east to west geographic transition. Wide-spreading plains swell into a belt of forested hills where streams flow down to the Trinity and Brazos Rivers on either side.

The range is a rich variety of unique soils and distinct geological areas. East to west, the Blackland Prairie yields the richest of black, waxy clays. In the Cross Timbers it is sandy loam, reddish tan sand, dark red sandstone, iron, and even gold ore. On the Grand Prairie it is tan sand, limestone, fossils, and petrified wood. At the end of the thirty miles you can see dinosaur tracks in the creek and river beds of the Brazos River Valley. The vivid divisions among the unusual geological areas are found only in this particular part of Texas.

## Cross Timbers

The Cross Timbers is a gently rolling high ground which divides the Trinity and Brazos Rivers. Tributaries of these two rivers flow out of the county in all directions. The Cross Timbers belt runs north and south in a strip four to twelve miles wide through the center of the county. There is an almost equal division between timber and prairie, all of which is blessed with an abundance of water. Two noteworthy Texas prairie types, the Blackland and Grand Prairies extend from either side of the narrow timber belt.

The geographic features in our county created natural borders and barriers. The Cross Timbers terminate in the brakes and hills of the Brazos River Valley in the southwest corner of the county and in Hill County to the south. In their natural condition the Cross Timbers stand as a dense thicket of trees overgrown in layers: post oak, blackjacks, live oak, pecan, cottonwood, elm, hackberry, willow, mulberry, honey mesquite, bois d'arc, cedar (Ashe Juniper) and sycamore. Under these larger trees are layers of bushes and shrubs. The layers are embedded with a thick, impenetrable undergrowth of greenbrier, mustang grapevine, privet hedge, and Virginia creeper.

The Cross Timbers was a landmark clearly shown on all early maps. It deserved special attention from the explorer and settler. Washington Irving in his A TOUR ON THE PRAIRIES wrote in 1832: ". . . we beheld a beautiful open prairie country before us; while, to our right the belt of forest land called Cross Timbers continued stretching away to the southward as far as the eye could reach."

In 1841, George Wilkins Kendall, one of the over 320 men who were part of the Santa Fe Expedition, crossed

1

## FRONTIER TO 1860:

# CROSS TIMBERS, PRAIRIES, AND RIVERS

the Brazos south of Comanche Peak (route shown on map, page 12) and described the Johnson County area. *Our next day's march was along the high ridge of prairies which divides the waters of . . . Nolan's River from those of the Brazos. The prospect on both sides was romantic to a high degree. To the east, for miles the prairie gently sloped, hardly presenting a bush to relieve the eye. In the distance, the green skirting of woods, which fringed either border of a large stream, softened down the view . . . To the west of the ridge, the immediate vicinity was even more desolate, but the fertile bottoms of the Brazos, with their luxuriant growth of timber, were still visible, and the Comanche Peak, rising high above the other hills, gave grandeur and sublimity to a scene . . . far from monotonous. This peak is celebrated as a looking-out point for the Comanches, commanding, as it does, a complete view of the country around as far as the eye can reach—and hence its name.*

Kendall considered the Cross Timbers the western edge of the United States. *An afternoon's march brought us to a noble spring in a grove of post oaks—a grove which turned out to be on the outskirts of the celebrated Cross Timbers . . . On the eastern side of the Cross Timbers the country is varied by small prairies and clumps of woodland, while on the western all is a perfect ocean of prairie. The belt, therefore for whatever purpose it may have been fashioned by the Great Creator of all things, appears to be an immense natural hedge dividing the woodlands of the settled portions of the United States from the open prairies which have ever been the home and hunting ground of the red man.*

Army Captain and explorer Randolph B. Marcy said the Cross Timbers *seem to have been designed as a natural barrier between civilized man and the savage.* His 1852 observation was made as permanent settlement was being established along the edge. The wild and fierce native tribes freely roamed the Grand Prairie on the west side of the Cross Timbers.

"A Deer Drive in the Cross Timbers." Frontier hunters and their dogs drive game. The Cross Timbers was full of animals and had been a hunting ground for the natives for centuries. The Indians ran mustangs and buffalo off the prairie into cul-de-sacs in the timber. From the mid-1840s frontiersmen came to the area to hunt for game. Bountiful springs flowed along the edges of the Cross Timbers creating lovely places for settlements and a ready source of timber for fuel and building materials. The adjoining prairies were used for pasture or put to plow for farming without the work of clearing timber. Later, pioneers who settled further from the edge of the timber on the prairies bought small tracts of timber from which to cut firewood and building materials. (HARPER'S WEEKLY, 1874. AC)

Indian signals by sign or smoke gave the camp news of a buffalo herd or other information. Indians did complicated things with smoke—unusual shapes, strange rising patterns, clouds disappearing in a puff—each had meaning. After contact with Spanish traders, mirrors were used to flash signals over the great distances from high peaks. The message received was as clear to the receiver as any given over telegraph lines by Morse Code. Comanche Peak was an important communication point for the fierce warriors of the plains. Indians communicated how many were in a group and where they were located. The western part of Johnson County was Comanche country for 150 years prior to white settlement. (HARPER'S WEEKLY, March 23, 1873. AC)

## Prairies

Native Americans used fire to hunt and herd animals on the Grand Prairie. The ash from their burnings acted as natural fertilizer. The new green shoots of grass were a favorite of the buffalo. These manmade fires, as well as those set naturally by lightning and summer heat, kept the brush and trees off the prairies and restricted them to ravines and the rocky bases of hills. The Grand Prairie was the land of the buffalo and mustang herds. It became excellent ranching as well as farming country. The prairies originally were covered by waving seas of grass which grew as high as stirrups on the horses ridden through them. When dew settled on the grass, the boots of the riders became soaked as they rode through the wet grass. The varieties were buffalo grass, bluestem, gramas and mesquite grass. One pioneer memory recalled seeing a group of riders on horseback that appeared to be on foot, their horses lost in a sea-like mirage of waving grass.

The native grasses remained until about 1879 when overgrazing and cultivation of the land had largely destroyed what had been a basic natural feature of the prairie. New types such as Johnson Grass and Bermuda were planted as ranching experiments to replace the lost native species.

HARPER'S WEEKLY.
JOURNAL OF CIVILIZATION.
VOL. XVII.—No. 847.]    NEW YORK, SATURDAY, MARCH 22, 1873.    [ WITH A SUPPLEMENT. PRICE TEN CENTS.
Entered according to Act of Congress, in the Year 1873, by Harper & Brothers, in the Office of the Librarian of Congress, at Washington.

## Blackland Prairie

Early Texas maps describe this as a "great body of excellent land." The rich level Blackland Prairie on the east is considered the richest soil in Texas and is famous for its farming capability. "Up to the Civil War this was mostly a stock country and comparatively little attention was paid to farming. Thousands of horses, cattle and sheep roamed over the prairie and there were deer, antelope, turkeys and prairie chickens innumerable." Over the first century of modern Texas history, 75 percent of the wealth of the state was based on this narrow belt of rich earth, and much of this wealth by then was in cotton production.

## Grand Prairie

The gentle rolling plain of the Grand Prairie is fine grazing land. The Grand Prairie breaks up in the western part of the county into hills, ravines, creeks, and cliffs. These "brakes" are filled with cedars, live oaks, willows, elms, post oaks, and blackjacks which lead down to the Brazos River. The area has huge, ancient live oak trees growing alone or in groves. Early maps indicate that great herds of buffalo and mustang horses roamed here.

## Natural Borderland

Johnson County was an area of natural crossroads for animal and man. The mighty buffalo herds of the west Texas plains came annually to drink the mineral rich waters of the Brazos River. The paths made by these great herds cut down the steep banks of rivers and streams creating easy paths for man to follow. The forested sandy rolling hills of the Cross Timbers captured water for thousands of years creating a high water table, with springs flowing onto the prairies along the creeks. A few dramatic artesian springs bubbled up along the edges of the higher rolling tableland. During times of severe drought wild animals instinctively sought out the pooled water near the forest. Herding animals such as the buffalo and later the wild mustang established migratory routes that took advantage of the springs and the rich prairies at the edge of the timbered hills. The trails followed along the natural barriers of the land leading to water, sheltered clearings, high prominences, and natural river fords.

Springs and creeks were campsites for native semi-nomadic tribes. There were five springs at the Caddo encampment that preceded the town of Alvarado. Cleburne was founded at one of the largest of the reliable springs on Buffalo Creek. Two of the most beautiful spring locations in the western part of the county were Fern Cave and Still House Hollow flowing to the Brazos. It was not until the close of the 1880s and 1890s that many of the springs began to run dry. The water table of the entire area had been permanently lowered by the digging of deep wells and using windmills and pumps to bring water to the surface.

The Native Americans followed the animal paths for their hunting and trade noting the dependable watering holes along the way. An east-west "Historic Buffalo Trail" went through a narrow place in the Cross Timbers in the southern part of the county. In the north a Spanish era trade route called the "Comanche Trail" cut east-west from Nacogdoches in East Texas to the "Comancheria," the lands west of the Cross Timbers. The natural highways would later be used by Spanish explorers, trappers, "Texian" expeditions, Rangers, surveyors, fort supply wagons, settlers, and cowboys on the Chisholm Trail.

## Comanche Peak

Comanche Peak rises 1229 feet above sea level, originally in Johnson County, now Hood County.

Other names for Comanche Peak are *Loma Alta* and *Monte Grande*. The Comanche Indian name for the mesa is *Que-tah-to-yah*, or *Rocky Butte*. The Comanches held the ancient mountain to be sacred; it was a landmark guiding them in their travels and serving as a base camp. Sentinels were placed there to report approaching enemies. It was a signaling point for their communications and could be seen over 40 miles. Provisions and supplies were stored at this stopping place when they raided into Mexico and Texas. The Comanche left their women and medicine men camped by the creeks near Comanche Peak. When pursued after a raid, they dispersed into small groups or scattered individually to confuse the enemy, knowing they were to meet later at the "Rocky Butte." After successful raids their ceremonial victory or scalp dance was held on the flat top of the mesa. The Comanche believed that greater and lesser spirits inhabited great hills and mountains. There they held the eagle and the sun dances. Comanche Peak was a place where young men, warriors and medicine men went to communicate and receive special powers and visions. To the Comanche, these supernatural experiences revealed a message, a mission, a taboo, or their special medicine from nature or the spirit world.

## Caddo Peak

Shown on early maps as *Peak, Pilot Knob, Caddo Mound*, and *Signal Hill* in north central Johnson County, two miles northwest of Joshua, at an elevation of 1,065 feet above sea level, is Caddo Peak the highest point in Johnson County. The Caddos used this hill for signaling, which could be seen from Comanche Peak twenty-four miles to the west and beyond it to Chalk Mountain. In the 1860s and 1870s the hill became an important landmark on the Chisholm Trail as the herds passed one mile to the west. Cattlemen could spot Caddo Peak and Brushy

Knob near by, soon after crossing the Brazos River, twenty miles to the south. They would drive their herds along the Nolan River towards the peak for one or two days. A number of inscriptions have been recorded on the red sandstone of the peak over the years, the oldest bearing the date 1836. It is also reputed to have been a burial ground for the Indians.

## Brazos River Valley

The Comanche name for the Brazos River was *Puh-che-o-qua* which means *Clear running water.* The Caddo name for the Brazos was *Bahatsi.* Another Native American name for the Brazos River was *Tockanhono.* The Spanish named the river *Los Brazos de Dios* meaning *The Arms of God.* This name reminds one of the protection found in God's arms, but in the early 1800s the Brazos River Valley was "the roughest frontier in the world," and the major raiding route of the Comanche going south. In those days it would be much easier for the unwary to be gathered into "The Arms of God" through a random violent death, which was lurking around every corner. As European contact and settlement reached into Johnson County, this frontier was recognized and described as "a disputed country . . . in the middle of a common battleground."

## European Exploration

Louis de Moscosco, the leader of the survivors of the De Soto expedition, crossed the upper parts of the Trinity and Brazos Rivers, documenting aspects of Caddoan settlement.

He visited a Caddoan town named Guasco, some believe to have been on (Caddo) Village Creek south of the Trinity River and explored into Johnson County. One writer states, "No doubt they passed right by Comanche Peak in 1542." Governor Diego de Pealosa of New Mexico Territory made an expedition to the Brazos and Comanche Peak area in 1622. Between the years 1611 to 1634, Catholic missionaries such as Juan de Salas, Diego, Ortego, Estévan Perea, Didaco Lopez, and Alonzo Vaca visited the Indians along the Brazos River. Missions and presidios were established in East Texas and western Louisiana between 1691 and 1721. The Spanish objective for the Caddo Indians was: "to convert him, to civilize him, and to exploit him."

In 1772 De Mezieres left Natchitoches on an expedition to the vicinity of Palestine, Texas. They visited the Tonkawas on the Brazos River near Waco. His party followed the river to the village of the Wichitas.

Spanish explorer Pedro Vial visited the springs of Buffalo Creek in 1788, the first recorded European to see them. He was traveling with his Comanche guide from Santa Fe to Louisiana. After crossing the Brazos River he wrote: "I set out at six in the morning on said cross and at a space of four leagues arrived at a forest, very beautiful, which they called El Monte Grande, and which they say is two hundred leagues long and only three leagues wide. There I stopped at a spring and made camp." He spent two days at the spring, now thought to be Buffalo Springs near the edge of the Cross Timbers. By 1790, immigrating American Indians and Anglo-American settlers began moving into Louisiana and Texas quickly outnumbering the Caddoan inhabitants.

### Philip Nolan (1771–1801)

There was a fabled land of "milk and honey," great riches to the west—a land with endless prairies, beautiful river valleys, and streams. This prairie land was brimming with wildlife and overrun with great herds of buffalo, wild horses, and cattle, all there for the taking. Back in the United States—the nation was on the move—the demand was great for just such animals. Negotiations were made between Philip Nolan and the Spanish governor Miró, and passports were given for the entering of this territory and the taking of horses. Nolan was possibly the first American to begin this trade. Nolan was bringing horses back to the states for the use of the military. General James Wilkinson, who raised Nolan, was a leading senior military officer in the U.S. Army and eventually commanded the entire U.S. Army.

As Nolan initiated his work in 1791, the Constitution of the United States was only two years old, the country was only twenty-five years old, and there were fifteen states in the Union. He made maps during several successful expeditions over the next ten years to the Brazos River Valley and the area which is now Johnson County. The commerce in mustangs became a dangerous business for the Americans as well as the Spanish. For the Americans it was an unknown land with no maps and wild native tribes. The Spanish had a colonial system which was in decline. The greedy Americans would covet this lovely wide open land filled with great natural riches but few occupants.

In the summer of 1801 rumors spread through the American border city Natchez, on the Mississippi, home to westward adventurers. Three men from Nolan's latest mustang expedition struggled back across French Louisiana from the Spanish province of Tejas. President

Thomas Jefferson wished to speak with Philip Nolan about what he had learned. But Nolan was dead from a mortal wound to the head received during the opening shots in a fray with Spanish soldiers. At their small stockade near a tributary of the Brazos River, Nolan's group was attacked at dawn and persuaded to make a conditional surrender allowing them to return home. Instead, the crafty Spanish took the survivors and their weapons, put them under arrest, and took them for trial deeper into Mexico. After the surrender, Nolan's slaves, Robert and Caesar, were given permission to bury their master. Before burial the Spaniards took Nolan's ears and sent them along with his maps, papers, and diary to the Spanish governor at Bexar de San Antonio.

During the forced march a few Americans escaped and made it home. The remaining prisoners began what was to be a twenty-year captivity and death. One of the Americans was hanged, the rest were sent into solitary prison slavery throughout Mexico. After years of servitude, two of the captives rose through service in the ranks of Mexican society to positions in the military and fought Spain for Mexican Independence in 1824. Ellis Bean was one of the imprisoned men who escaped the Spaniards. He joined the Revolutionary forces of General Morelos and became instrumental in helping Mexico obtain Independence. He made two trips back to the U.S. and fought with Andrew Jackson at the Battle of New Orleans on one of these trips. Bean became a full colonel in the Mexican Army.

During the American War with Mexico (1846–1848) Nolan's diary was found in the archives of Monterrey by an American soldier. José Agustin Quintero of the staff of New Orleans' DAILY PICAYUNE, quoted from it, but later the diary was lost in Louisiana and again waits in obscurity for rediscovery.

Joel Pierce died in captivity in Mexico. Before he died he wrote to his family in North Carolina, telling them how to get to Nolan's beautiful pasture land in Texas. The Pierces later came to claim a large ranch in Johnson County near Goat Neck, following the instructions in Joel's letter.

Nolan's association with General Wilkinson is significant. The brash horse trader may have been collecting information for General Wilkinson and even Jefferson.

Jefferson's interest in Nolan, as a result of Wilkinson's correspondence, implies that Nolan may have been doing more than horse trading. At Jefferson's request, Wilkinson had Nolan scheduled to meet with him for an interview. Nolan's letter of introduction is in Jefferson's papers. With Nolan's death, Jefferson selected another protégé of Wilkinson, Merriweather Lewis, to explore the Louisiana Purchase in 1804–1806. If Nolan had survived his last expedition into Texas, the history books might now be referring to the Lewis and Clark Expedition as the Nolan and Bean Expedition. Lewis and Clark were themselves pursued by the detachments of Spanish soldiers with Comanche Indian guides who failed to intercept Jefferson's latest exploration group.

Another Wilkinson protégé, Captain Zebulon Pike, of Pike's Peak fame, was surveying the West for the U.S. Army in 1807. Captured by the Spanish and in Santa Fe's prison he met Solomon Cooley, David Fero, and Caesar of Nolan's ill-fated group. Cooley and Fero were prisoners but Caesar had been freed at Chihuahua. Nolan's death in 1801 began the great mistrust along the borderland between the United States and Mexico.

"The First of the Race." In 1519 Cortez, the Spanish Conquistador, subdued the Aztecs of Mexico with horses brought from Europe to North America. The Pueblo revolted and drove the Spaniards out of New Mexico around 1680, leaving many thousands of horses behind to roam free. Mustangs from the Spanish haciendas near Santa Fe were a pivotal influence on the history of Texas. The Comanche were on foot until the Europeans arrived, now they captured wild mustangs in Colorado and bartered or stole them from the Ute Indians. The Comanches' dogs had provided meat and were used to haul travois. These tasks now became functions of the horse which they named "god-dog." After mounting the horse the Comanche was transformed— he knew the horse had been created just for him. (AC)

Mexico believed that a buffer of Anglo settlers might prove worthwhile, if placed between themselves and the raiding Comanche. An uneven process of granting colonization was allowed with various restrictions. The first empresario grant for the colonization of North Central Texas, including much of Johnson County, was issued April 15, 1825, to Robert Leftwich, agent of the Nashville Company in Tennessee. Stephen F. Austin received the third grant in 1832. This grant was executed by Sterling Robertson. Overlapping claims between these colonies brought legal action and internal trouble in the land companies. This along with Mexico's bitter controversy over the Anglo's settling Texas, contributed to the ten-year delay in the settlement of North Central Texas. Preparations for the war for Texas Independence ended the long Robertson Colony controversy. With the confusion of war, the Texas Assembly passed a decree closing all land office business in Texas until a permanent government was organized. With the declaration of Texas Independence in 1836, all grants and contracts with Mexico or the State of Coahuila became null and void. From this date until the last year of President Lamar's administration in 1841, there was no law governing colonization contracts.

## Native Americans in Texas

The rich well-watered lands running through Johnson County supported varied tribal lifestyles. Many Native American tribes on the frontier were civilized by white man's standards; they could read, write, and record their history. Tribes such as the Cherokee, Chickasaw, Choctaw, Biloxi, Creek, Kickapoo, Delaware, Seminole, and Osage were forced to leave their homes in the North and East. The Indians were pushed into Texas by overwhelming European settlement. The accounts of these tribes in our county are fleeting. They were often in an area only a season or two before being pushed on. Pressures put upon these tribes caused them to encroach upon the hunting and camping grounds of western tribes. Many small bands of Cherokee, Choctaw, Chickasaw, Creek, and Seminole, who came to live in north Texas, became attached or absorbed into other local tribes. These displaced tribes had been exiled from their ancestral homelands mainly in the southern states. Exceptions were the Delawares who were driven to the Texas frontiers from the east coast, and the Kickapoos from the Great Lakes. The Caddo lived here since the 1830s, being expelled from their homes in East Texas, Arkansas, and Louisiana. The Tonkawa lived and hunted

"The Last Shot." (HARPER'S WEEKLY, September 14, 1867. AC)

here long before the Spanish came in the early 1500s. Some Wichita tribes lived south of our vicinity. These Native American tribal groups living on the Texas frontier became victims of the raiding Comanche bands.

### The Plains Indians
#### Comanche

The name *Comanche* is a Ute Indian word meaning *Enemy* or *Stranger*, or more exactly *Anyone who wants to fight me all the time*. The meaning was learned with dread by the Spanish in Santa Fe. The resourceful Comanches stole and traded horses from the Utes and other tribes. The Comanche became superb horsemen, unrivaled on the plains. More horses were taken as they swept out of northern Colorado around 1700. They stripped and ravaged the Spanish settlements of New Mexico and Texas. The Spanish Mission system failed and many cloistered Texas tribes returned to their former lifestyles.

Comanches and their allies, the Kiowa and Kiowa-Apache, developed a horse based, nomadic culture. The numerous Comanche called themselves *human beings*. Comanche warriors pursued buffalo with spears, arrows, and later the gun. The horse allowed them to chase and hunt migrating buffalo over great distances. A better supply of food led to an increase in the Comanche population. The possession of the horse became paramount to the Comanche. For two hundred years trading and raiding activities revolved around further acquisition and possession of horses. The horse and the warring nomadic lifestyle of the Comanche fit perfectly the open and sparsely timbered prairie lands of the Southwest. After 1700 there were great numbers of escaped mustangs grazing on the prairies of Texas. The mustangs wintered along the protective edge of the Cross Timbers and foraged for food. The Comanche rode from their ancient homeland of Colorado and Wyoming trading and attacking for horses, this new and important source of wealth and power. The campaign eventually led through New Mexico, Kansas, Oklahoma, Texas, and finally deep into Mexico.

### The Lipan Apache

The Lipan were a small tribe of Apache Indians the Comanche had driven off the plains to the edge of the Cross Timbers. They were located just to the southwest of our county and are mentioned at the tribal councils, parleys, and peace conferences along with other North Texas Indian tribes.

### Tonkawa

The Tonkawa had their own distinctive language and were not closely related to other North Texas tribes. They foraged and followed the buffalo to the northern plains of Texas. Tonkawas lived in the Bosque and Brazos River Valleys from north of Waco to Fort Worth. This brought them into direct conflict with the Comanche for whom they developed a deep tribal hatred. The powerful Comanche considered anyone who lived in their path "fair game" and drove the Tonkawa south from their ancestral land.

Friendly Tonkawas fought alongside the whites. They went with them as scouts and troops to fight the Comanche. The Tonkawa had an unusual custom that made them abhorrent to other tribes. They often cannibalized parts of their slain enemies. This ritualistic practice may have been to acquire the powers of the defeated foe. After battles Tonkawa warriors were observed shouldering the hacked off limbs of Comanche warriors toward their camp. As a tribe though, they claimed to have never killed any whites.

### Wichita

These distant Caddoan relatives migrated to the plains about 1500 B.C., developing a plains culture dependent on the buffalo for food. They lived in grass lodges like their Caddoan relatives. The two tribal groups separated so long ago that they could not understand each other's language. Some of the tribal names were Tawakoni, Waco, Taovaya, and Kichai (Keechi). As the tribes' numbers diminished from disease, their remnant tribes joined with the Caddoan people.

In the 1700s, a Spanish captain from the garrison at Nacogdoches was sent to East Texas to persuade the natives to stop trading with the Louisiana French. After being told they should only trade with the Spanish, a Keechi warrior said the French were giving ten instead of five musket balls per pelt. The captain went into a violent rage, and the Keechi told him never to come to his house again. At this, the captain announced to the Keechi that all the land on this side of the Red River belonged to him. The warrior picked up a handful of dirt and threw it at the captain saying, since all the land was his, he should take it all with him as he went home.

## Woodland Mound Builders

### Caddo

The three Caddoan confederacies were the Hasinai, Kadohadacho, and Natchitoche. From the year 1200, tribes of the confederacies lived in North and East Texas, layer trading with the Spanish, French, and Americans in turn. Caddoes acted as middlemen between the whites and the plains tribes such as the Comanche who, because of their warlike lifestyle, rarely established peaceful relations. "The Caddo understood and spoke Castilian Spanish" as well as their own language.

The area that would become Johnson County was a hunting ground to many of native tribes. In the 1830s the Caddo tribes fled west because of the advancing white settlers. The Caddo's original homeland was centered where the corners of Arkansas, Louisiana, and Texas meet. The Cross Timbers in Texas served as a natural barrier from the raiding Comanche.

Caddo lifestyle combined agriculture with the hunting of game; they relied less on the buffalo and more on agriculture. Their thatched houses were located in natural clearings along streams in semi-permanent villages. As an area was depleted of wood and game, the tribe moved a few miles up or downstream.

The Caddo were often considered a friendly tribe. The Caddo Indians are credited with unintentionally giving Texas its name. Between 1500 to 1700 brought the first European contacts from the Spanish and French. LaSalle and the survivors of his expedition lived with the Caddo for a time in the late 1680's. They were greeted with the Caddo word, *Tejas*, so the Spanish called them *Tejas* Indians and sent reports from *Tejas* land. The greeting word meant *friend*. Later reports furnish different information calling Caddoes "the greatest threat on the frontier."

### Caddo Raids After Texas Independence

A month after Texas won its independence from Mexico at San Jacinto, the most notorious Indian raiding party in Texas history organized. The band of five to six hundred marauders, consisting primarily of Comanche and Kiowa with a few Wichita, Caddos, and Keechi,

"Caddo Indian Celebrities." These Caddos are thought to be tribal leaders among those who had lived near Johnson County until the 1850s. Exiled from areas in East Texas in the 1830s, during the 1850s many camped near Barnard's Trading House along the Brazos River Valley. In 1854–1856 pressure by European settlement forced them onto two upper Brazos River reservations. Large numbers of their tribe served as scouts and troops in defense of whites against the wild Indian bands, but 1859 brought their thankless expulsion from Texas into Indian Territory. (Travis and Vivian Morris)

struck Parker's Fort, May 19, 1836. After showing a white flag, the Indians killed several settlers and captured women and children. One of these captives was Cynthia Ann Parker. It is thought that Wichita or Caddos in the raiding party initially captured Cynthia Ann. She was traded to the Comanches, probably at the Comanche Peak scalp dance held in celebration of the successful attack on Ft. Parker.

In January of 1839 one Caddo village paid a terrible price for their involvement in this and other raids. The anger of the whites over accumulating raids was allowed vengeance. Sam Houston, president of the Republic of Texas held a conciliatory attitude toward Indians which contributed to his defeat for another term of office. In 1839 General Rusk was sent into North Texas by newly elected President Lamar to punish the Indians and drive them out of Texas. Lamar launched a campaign to rid Texas of all Indians. He addressed Congress saying, "*The white man and the red man cannot dwell in harmony together. Nature forbids it.*" It was the official policy of the President of Texas that these U.S. Indians did not belong in Texas. The Texan Army traveled to North Texas and

up the Trinity River. They found a trail leading along Caddo Village Creek (now Village Creek) and followed it to a Caddo village close to present-day Burleson. The Texans attacked the Caddo village and captured most of the "troublesome" band encamped there. The village was burned and the animals were divided among Texans. The captive men, women, and children were carried to the U.S. officer at Shreveport, Louisiana.

## The Barnard and Torrey Brothers

George Barnard, age twenty, and John Torrey, age twenty-one, came to Texas in 1838. The Hartford, Connecticut, boys had been schoolmates. Soon Charles Barnard, as well as the Torrey brothers and their father, followed. The Torrey family served with Sam Houston as mediators to the Indians at treaty parlays. Thomas Torrey and George Barnard joined the Texas Santa Fe Expedition of 1841. During July this group of over 320 journeyed through Johnson County. (route, page 12)

Kendall wrote:

*July 16, 1841:*

*[T]he joyous intelligence that a large cool spring had been discovered but a little way off of our course. The line of march was instantly broken; for those who had good horses dashed madly forward, . . . In small straggling parties we reached the goal of our hopes. A ledge of rocks, from which cool and limpid water was gushing in all directions, formed the head of the spring, and a few yards below the different branches fell into a common basin some twenty yards in width, and filled to a depth of eight or ten feet with the transparent element . . . Our thirst was slaked at the very fountain-head—the basin was converted into an immense bathing-tub, where all hands enjoyed the invigorating luxury of a bath . . . The next morning, after enjoying another bath, we left this delicious spring with regret, and pursued our journey with no prospect of water before us.*

The expedition may well have been at the Buffalo Springs on Buffalo Creek in Cleburne. When the "flowing wells" just north of the crossing of West Henderson and Buffalo Creek were first seen by settlers they were large and deep enough to swim a herd of 100 horses.

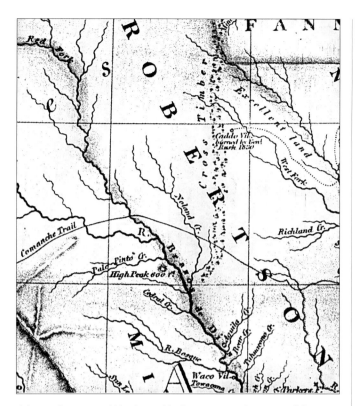

Johnson County would be located in the area near the center of the map. Detail of "Map of Texas, published April 17th, 1841. Compiled by John Arrowsmith, 10 Soho Square, London. Recorded in the Land Office of Texas." The map shows the Comanche Trail; Cross Timbers; High Peak, 600 ft.; Comanche Peak; Robertson and Milam Land Districts; and Caddo Village (burned by General Rusk, January 1839); Waco Indian Village; Brazos, Nolan and Trinity Rivers. (AC)

In the early years herds of wild horses frolicked in the springs causing some to call the waters "Mustang Springs." Earlier the Spanish may have called the springs "Painted Springs," because of Indian story pictures on the ledges above the springs.

On the prairie near the location of the Johnson County springs, Kendall wrote:

*At sundown a drove of Mustangs, or wild horses of the prairie, paid us a visit. They were first seen ascending a hill at the distance of a half mile, and as they were coming towards us were taken for Indians. When seen on a distant hill, standing with their raised heads towards a person, and forming a line as is their custom, it is almost impossible to take them for anything but mounted men. Having satisfied their curiosity, they wheeled with almost the regularity of a cavalry company and galloped off, their long thick manes waving in the air and their tails nearly sweeping the ground. They are beautiful animals, always in excellent condition, and although smaller than our American horses, are still very compact, and will bear much fatigue.*

*Many were the stories told that night in camp, by some of the older hunters, of a large white horse that had often been seen in the vicinity of the Cross Timbers . . . the 'White Steed of the Prairies,' for he is well known to trappers and hunters by that name, that he has tired down no less than three race-nags, sent expressly to catch him, with a Mexican rider well trained to the business of taking wild horses.*

The expedition crossed the Brazos on the 14th of July somewhere between Nolan River and Comanche Peak, possibly at Kimball. They traveled along a ridge where both the Brazos and the Nolan River Valleys were visible, a situation which occurs only in Johnson and Hill Counties. Their "spies" (scouts) learned of a large encampment of many tribes including Cherokees, Caddos, and others who at the time were hostile toward Texas.

Kendall reported:

*July 18, 1841:*

*The skull of a white woman, but recently killed, was found in the vicinity, and large and fresh Indian trails were discovered running in the direction of the Brazos . . . At first it was determined . . . to attack this party in their stronghold . . . but after thought it was feared that the detention would be too great, and the adventure was given up.*

The expedition traveled, keeping a close guard on the livestock at night, then decided to cut east through the Cross Timbers.

*In that portion through which we passed, and we spent nearly a fortnight in the Cross Timbers, we found the face of the country broken, and full of gullies . . . We had been buffeting about during the day, cutting away trees, crossing deep ravines and gullies, and turning and twisting some fifteen or twenty miles to gain five . . . The growth of this range is principally small, gnarled post oaks and black jacks, and in many places the traveler will find an almost impenetrable undergrowth of brier and other thorny bushes. Here and there he will also find a small valley where the timber is large and the land rich and fertile and occasionally a small prairie intervenes; . . . It was thought that by sending a large fatigue party in advance with shovels and axes, . . . we could cut our way through . . . For two or three days we journeyed through the middle of the belt, every attempt to find a passage out proving futile. On one or two occasions, distant fires were seen upon the hills at*

Wichita grass huts of the kind described by Dr. Roemer with a Plains Indian teepee in the background. From an original Irwin Smith print, "Near Anadarko, Indian Territory". (Silver Horse Gallery Collection, Donna Davidson, Cleburne, Texas)

*night, but we were unable to get a sight of the Indians who were encamped by them . . . I had previously traveled many weary miles, over the worst roads, and by the worst conveyances; I had thought my sufferings great these different journeyings; but . . . all those sufferings were cakes and gingerbread compared to . . . a fortnight in the Cross Timbers. . . . "I've seen the elephant." . . . I have heard swearing in many quarters, but for originality, deliberate utterance, and deep wickedness, I have never heard that of some of the drivers on the Santa Fe Expedition equalled.*

The exhaustion, loss of time, and depletion of supplies contributed greatly to the mission's eventual failure.

As the group neared Santa Fe, Governor Armijo sent lancers out to besiege the worn-out remnants of the force, accusing them of treason against Mexico and con-fiscating their goods. Many died in chains during a forced march of a thousand miles to Mexico City. Thomas Torrey and George Barnard survived it all making it back to Texas in 1842, after cruel treatment and a stay in Mexican prisons.

The Cross Timbers was a preferred camping and hunting area for American Indians from ancient times. During the 1830–1850 period it was known as "a favorite range for many of the Texas Indians and their usual home in the winter." Prominent hills at the edge of the timber and prairie provided choice locations for villages and campsites. As the white man approached it was along the Cross Timbers and the timbered bottoms of the Brazos River and its tributaries that the remnants of once numerous Texas Indian tribes became pressed between "two fires," the Comanche and the whites.

Caddo villages were probably the encampments encountered by the 1841 Santa Fe Expedition in our area. Dr. Ferdinand Roemer, the father of Texas geology, traveled and studied Texas for two years from 1845 to 1847.

His work describes a Caddo Village near Johnson County on the Brazos River near the mouth of the Nolan River (see the map [Derf] page 12):

*[W]e saw . . . from the top of a hill the destination of our excursion—the Caddoe Indian village lying before us. A more suitable and pleasant place could not have been selected by the red sons of the wilderness. The village lies in the center of a plain two miles long which on the one side is bordered by the wooded banks of the Brasos and on the other by steep precipitous hills. A beautiful clear creek flows diagonally through this plain on a smooth bed of limestone and on its banks are     several large live oaks.*

*The huts of the Indians stood on both sides of this creek in picturesque disorder and near each was a cornfield. Between the hills from which we looked down and the village proper, about a thousand head of horses were grazing on the plain, among which a number of naked, long haired Indian boys rode back and forth yelling. Thereupon we descended to the village. At the various huts which we passed we were welcomed in a friendly manner by the inmates, as my companion was well known to all of them.*

*Just after sunrise the following morning we took a walk through the village. The home of every family consisted of several huts of diverse form. There is always a large conical shaped hut present, about fifteen feet high, which is enclosed on all sides except for a small opening at the bottom. It is thatched with long grass and therefore at a distance resembles a haystack of medium size . . .*

*. . . the following morning . . . the thought involuntarily came to me how long it would remain in peaceful possession of the apparently harmless sons of nature, and if perhaps even now a land-hungry Yankee had cast his covetous looks upon it. My companion disillusioned me in a hurry, in that he assured me that not only this land, several days distant from the settlements, but also many other parts higher up on the Brasos, had been surveyed and for some time had been the property of individuals. He also told me that the latter even now had the intention of asking the government to move the Indians to a more distant place.*

## Cynthia Ann Parker

Cynthia Ann Parker was captured at the age of nine on May 19, 1836, along with her brother, John, at Parker's Fort, sixty miles southeast of Johnson County. The captives were brought through Johnson County to Comanche Peak.

A quarter of a century later in 1860, orders from Governor Houston sent a command after a band of marauding Comanches. The group was under the leadership of Captain Sul Ross (future governor of Texas). Among the men in the force were a sergeant and twenty troopers from Fort Belknap, a detachment of Texas Rangers including "Den" Richardson, and sixty volunteer citizens including Charles Goodnight. Captain Ross and his men went through Alvarado and bought a crop of corn from Joseph McClure to supply food for the combined force and Barnard's Trading Post supplied other provisions.

Cynthia Ann Parker and her infant child, Prairie Flower, were recaptured after an attack on a group of retreating Comanches December 18, 1860. She was forcibly brought to the Johnson County home of Charles and Juana Barnard. Juana Cavasos Barnard, who had once been a Comanche captive, was unable to comfort her. Cynthia did not want to return to her white relatives who lived near Fort Worth. She never adjusted to white civilization and grieved, wanting to be returned to her Comanche husband and sons. She attempted daily to escape her new captors and was locked in her room nightly. Her husband, Chief Peta Nacona, died soon after her capture. Prairie Flower died in 1864. Cynthia Ann mutilated and starved herself to death the same year. As a child and as a mother, Cynthia was kidnapped from her family twenty-four years apart. Both times she was taken off through Johnson County in the shadow of Comanche Peak, a silent sentinel to her sorrow.

## Nations Meet at Comanche Peak

The United States annexed Texas as a state in December 1845, and chose to announce the fact to the Indians of Texas at Comanche Peak. Many presents were promised for those who would come to the council. The government wished to make treaties with the Native Americans who inhabited north and west Texas. The U.S. hoped the Indian tribes would not take sides in the coming war with Mexico. There were many unlicensed Indian traders on the frontier who did not want the council to take place. They told false stories that those who came would be killed or poisoned, and that the Americans had smallpox.

In 1846 the American government arranged for an expedition to make a treaty with the Texas Indians. Government agent P. M. Butler, worked through guides and interpreters for months urging the tribes to meet at Comanche Peak. There were thirteen interpreters, run-

Comanche Chief Quanah Parker with a painting of his mother, Cynthia Ann Parker. Her tragic life and death were mourned by both her white and red relatives. The portrait of his mother was located after Quanah advertised in the Fort Worth newspapers. Quanah was successful in getting the government of Texas to release her remains to him for reburial in Indian Territory, later he would be buried at her side. (Photo by H. P. Robinson, Ft. Sill, Oklahoma; Archives and Manuscripts Division of the Oklahoma Historical Society, No. 705)

ners, and messengers including Jesse Chisholm, a Cherokee-Scot. The Comanches had refused to attend the meetings in November of 1843. Captain Nathan Boone, Daniel Boone's son, arranged for an earlier meeting with the Indians at Tawakoni Creek where chiefs of several tribes made a tentative agreement with commissioners. Captain Boone and the Indian painter George Catlin were delayed, and the Indian guides refused to wait until Boone came.

On January 29, 1846, difficulty was experienced in locating Comanche Peak as well as the Comanches. The

party divided into four groups to locate the Comanche. Early in February, Kickapoo, Caddo, Lipan, and Tonkawa gathered at the peak.

In April, Jesse Chisholm and his oldest son George were finally successful in persuading a large number of Comanches to come to the rendezvous at Comanche Peak in what was later Johnson County. Chisholm was one of the few people on the frontier who had any influence with the warlike Comanches; they knew him to be honest. He traveled safely among the Indian tribes as a trader and diplomat and was valued by all.

Several Comanche chiefs came to the council. Among them was Comanche Chief Buffalo Hump who claimed those lands in Texas west of a line from the Clear Fork of the Trinity and Brazos Rivers to Comanche Peak and then on to San Saba. The gathering was unique in frontier Texas because of the many antagonistic tribes who came together for exchange of captives, festivities, gifts, and celebration.

## Chisholm's Legacy

Twenty years after Jesse Chisholm helped arrange the great meeting at Comanche Peak which soon freed John McLennan and others, portions of the Military Road in Texas became a major cattle trail from Texas. Just before 1868, the year of Jesse's death, cattle drovers connected this old fort trail through Johnson County to a trade road Jesse had marked off in 1865 with his wagon from his home in Indian Territory to a government post in Kansas. The whole route from Texas to the Kansas railheads would bear Jesse's name, The Chisholm Trail.

## McLennan—From Scotland to the
## Plains of Texas and Comanche Peak

In May of 1846, at Council Springs near present Waco, a followup treaty council meeting was held where all agreed to bring their captives. Among the captives returned was young John McLennan, then about twenty years of age. "Bosque John" as he was later known, became a frontier scout and Indian fighter. John's uncle was Neil McLennan for whom McLennan county is named. According to Patricia Ward Wallace,

*Neil McLennan emigrated from Scotland to the United States in 1801 when he was fourteen years old. McLennan and his brothers, John and Laughlin, settled in North Carolina. A few years later the three brothers and their families left for Spanish Florida. The McLennans cut wood from Florida forests and built a small schooner to sail from Pensacola to the Gulf of Mexico. On the way brigands captured the McLennans and fastened their schooner to the pirate ship by chain. Helpless, the McLennans were being towed toward they-knew-not-what when a night storm nearly capsized both ships. To keep their ship from being battered by the schooner, the pirates cast the McLennans adrift and by morning light they learned that the storm had blown them out of sight of their captors.*

*Neil McLennan was forty-eight years old when, after six weeks at sea, he reached the mouth of the Brazos and proceeded northward to Pond Creek. His family had barely settled before Indians killed Laughlin, burned his cabin, and captured his wife and children.*

*Vance Maloney concludes it was about 1836, Laughlin McLennan was splitting logs on Pond Creek, near its conjunction with the Brazos, when he was attacked and riddled with arrows by a band of Indians. The Indians then rushed to the log cabin, took his wife and little daughter and two sons prisoner, knocked his mother down and burned her in the cabin. Mrs. McLennan and young daughter soon died from the harsh treatment. One of the boys was ransomed, but the other remained with the Indians and grew to manhood as an Indian brave.* Some years later after his redemption he gave the account of his capture.

*I saw the Indians killing my father. They run to the house, knocked my grandmother down, took my mother, brother, and myself prisoners, robbed house, gathered horses, set the house on fire and burned grandmother up in it. My mother died at Comanche Peak.*

It is probable his little sister died at the landmark as well. Neil's brother, John, was later ambushed and killed by Indians after the surviving family had moved closer to the Texas coast in 1838. It seems so tragic that after coming across the Atlantic Ocean and providentially escaping the pirates of the Carribean, that so many of the McLennan family should ironically fall victim to the pirates of the plains. The earth by Comanche Peak contains the dust of Scottish Highlanders, Clan McLennan.

## Juana Cavasos Barnard

In 1846 the Comanches kept a Spanish girl just a few miles away from the U.S. Government Council mission with Texas Indians at Comanche Peak. Juana Cavasos' captors did not take her to any of their councils where white traders were gathered, keeping her and a squaw medicine woman some distance away. Later that year the Comanches took the girl to the Torrey Trading Post No. 2 near Waco at Tahuacana Creek, where George and Charles Barnard worked. As a prelude to the actual trading, the braves held competitive

Jesse Chisholm (1805/6–1868) was an important emissary of Sam Houston to the various Indian nations. In 1846 he guided and interpreted for the United States Mission to the Indians at Comanche Peak. Jesse was Sam Houston's nephew by Houston's marriage to Tianna Rogers. Will Rogers, the talented showman and American folklorist, was Sam Houston's grandnephew. Jesse was the Cherokee-Scot trader whose wagon trail across Indian Territory into Kansas was later called Chisholm's Trail. His original trail was from his trading post at Council Grove, Indian Territory (Yukon, Oklahoma) north to the government provision point at Wichita, Kansas. Texas cattle drivers ultimately gave Jesse's name to the entire old cattle trail from San Antonio, Texas to McCoy's cattle pens in Abilene, Kansas. (Courtesy of the Archives and Manuscripts Division of the Oklahoma Historical Society, No. 1757)

festivities showing off their various skills. Juana's riding skills were such that the Comanche braves respected her. She decided to risk great danger for a chance to be seen while the Comanches were performing. She made a showing of her admirable horsemanship and then rode back to the Comanche camp. George Barnard noticed the maiden was not Indian and urged the tribal chief to trade her. The chief insisted he would not, but soon the pile of goods amounted to $300 in horses and merchandise, including a huge amount of valued sugar.

Charles Edward Barnard (1823–1900) was born in Hartford, Connecticut. His finely tailored suit would soon be traded for frontier buckskins. He came to Texas on the advice of his older brother George who arranged for him to set up a state-approved Indian trading house a half mile east of the southern most point of DeCordova Bend. He traded with the remnant tribes living in DeCordova Bend area: Caddo, Anadarko, Ioni, Waco, Tonkawa, and Tawakoni. Known both as "Uncle Charley" and the "Baron of the Wilderness," he soon accumulated great wealth from the hides he received from trade, becoming the wealthiest man in antebellum Johnson County.

This Connecticut Yankee Indian trader met and ransomed the daughter of a Spanish aristocrat on the wild frontier of Texas; they fell in love. Charles built their wedding cottage as a multi-roomed log trading post on the frontier that became Johnson County. The Barnard Trading Post was located east, across the Brazos River, from Comanche Peak, a place where Indian tribes had traditionally gathered. The post was stocked in autumn of 1847, but not until October 1849 did they make it their home. Juana and Charles were married one year later by a traveling priest. Their adventurous tales were handed down through their large extensive family. (George Barnard Papers, The Texas Collection, Baylor University, Waco, Texas)

Around the age of 17, Juana Josefina Cavasos (1824–1906) was captured by the Comanche Indians while visiting friends on the Texas side of the Rio Grande. After three years of captivity, George Barnard saw her among the Indians near his Waco trading post and bought her with a "fabulous price in sugar." When Charles Barnard met Juana they fell in love, married, and moved to his trading post near DeCordova Bend. Juana Barnard pictured here late in life. She rode a horse every day until the day she died. She was born in the Canary Islands off the coast of Africa. Juana and her twin brother Juan's mother was Maria Josephina, who maried the son of Don Narciso Cavasos. In 1792 the king of Spain gave Don Cavasos the largest Spanish land grant ever extended to one person in the New World. It amounted to just under 1,000 square miles on both sides of the Rio Grande River. (John and Fredda Arney)

The chief could not resist, Juana was traded and left behind, standing in silence at the post.

Earlier fate had intervened in what might have been the gracious life of a landed Spanish aristocrat in Mexico. In August of 1843, Juana left her home in Matamoros and crossed the Rio Grande into Texas to visit with Anglo friends who lived on one of her family's cattle ranches. The settlement was warned of a Comanche raiding party in the area. Most of the ranch hands rushed to intercept the warriors. Juana's intuition

made her want to leave, but the other women would not allow it. At 11 AM on the 15th, the women heard the thundering hooves of the attacking Comanches racing towards them. Juana ran quickly and hid in the brush. However, she and a friend Mary Alice Andersen were discovered and captured by the Comanches. Her pleading friend's throat was cut right in front of her eyes. Juana defiantly exposed her throat as the bloody knife was brought to her—she would have welcomed death. The Comanches admired this lack of fear, the chief complimented her, "Brave, like Comanche; you go with us." As she was taken deeper into Texas she longed for escape as the chief made her test river crossings and exposed her to other dangerous situations. Juana was made the helper of an old squaw medicine woman who taught her herbal and medicinal cures.

Dr. Ferdinand Roemer saw Juana at Torrey's post just after her ransoming by the Barnard's. She cooked wild game for the men and experimented by adding tiny "chilies" she had found growing on the prairie. The United States' War with Mexico was eclipsing all other events, preventing a reunion with her family in Mexico. Roemer also observed two ransomed Mexican boys who were masterful at roping chickens by the legs—future vaqueros (cowboys), no doubt.

Charles Barnard became entranced with the ransomed girl. And so a Connecticut Yankee and a daughter of a Spanish aristocrat found each other on the wild frontier of Texas and fell in love. Charles built their wedding cottage as a multi-roomed log trading post in the wilds that became Johnson County. The Barnard Trading Post was located east, across the Brazos River, from Comanche Peak, a place where Indian tribes had traditionally gathered. The post was stocked in autumn of 1847 and in October 1849 they made it their home. Juana and Charles were married one year later by a traveling priest.

By coincidence years later Juana was reunited with her twin brother Juan at Barnard's Trading Post. Juan was herding cattle with a group of cowboys. They crossed the river at the trading post because Kimball, the usual crossing place, was flooded. Juana thought she heard a famil-iar voice and recognized the vaquero from Mexico. Juana returned to Mexico in a carriage and brought all of her remaining relatives in a caravan to live near her in Texas. Her parents and grandparents had died still grieving for her. Juan brought with him a 1792 Spanish land grant which was kept in the Barnard's safe for many years. Juana became the midwife and frontier doctor of the community on the Brazos River.

## Texas Trading Posts

The Texas Legislature approved a trading post system in 1844 and required the Indians to trade at these posts. The Torreys and Barnards became involved in

The Barnards operated one of Texas's most important and successful trading posts in Johnson County before the Civil War. Scenes similar to this were common at Barnard's Trading Post of the 1840s and 1850s. Charles's wife, Juana, had been a Comanche captive as a young woman, and did not fear the Indians. She and Charles were respected as straightforward, honest people. Even the fierce Comanche and Kiowa honored Charles's word and traded pelts to him. Trading posts became an important part of Indian life as hunting grounds and game became scarce. The trading post would convert Indian pelts for lead, gunpowder, guns, food, beads, and ornaments.

Tonkawa Indians were among the tribes who traded at "Barnard's Trading House." This group posed for George Rinehart in 1898. Their

nomadic way of life had drawn to a close and traditional ornament and clothing to be discarded in favor of Western dress.

During the frontier years of the 1840s to 1860s, Tonkawa Chief Placido, friend of General Edward Burleson, led his tribe into many fights against the Comanche on the side of the whites. Eventually there was no room for him in Texas. He was forcably removed to Indian Territory where his former enemies, the Comanche, assassinated him near Ft. Sill in revenge for his service to the whites. Those whites who knew him said that he was "brave to the upmost," "a soul of honor" who "never betrayed a trust." (National Anthropological Archives, Smithsonian Institution #1205)

the Indian trading post enterprise which had Sam Houston as a regular visitor and stockholder. Sam Houston for his part assured the Indians they would receive honest treatment and fair prices. The Comanches particularly insisted on a line delineating a separation of red and white hunting grounds as a part of this trading agreement. The trading agents were to be men of truth and honor who would, in turn, be given safe passage over lands claimed by Indians.

After their return from Mexican captivity, the Torreys led in the forming of a company to operate trading posts. George Barnard encouraged his brother Charles to emigrate quickly from Connecticut. Members of both families were eventually managing stores or hauling goods from post to post. In 1847, only a year after the U.S. Mission to the tribes of Texas, the Barnard brothers started their own trading post on George's 1840 land grant across from Comanche Peak. Sam Houston had some shares in this enterprise as well. In 1848 the Barnards bought out the Torreys' interest in all seven trading post locations.

Charles Barnard's Indian trade made him Johnson County's wealthiest antebellum citizen, in 1860 he was worth $119,400. He continued to trade with the tribes as they were rounded up for removal (1854–56). In 1856 Charles followed the Indians to set up a trading house near Fort Belknap when the Native tribes were moved to the Upper Brazos Reservations. Barnard came back to Johnson County when the tribes were removed from Texas to Indian Territory in 1859. He built a mill at the future site of Glen Rose (1860–64) where he and Juana lived for a time.

## Fire on the Prairies

On July 14, 1841, as the Santa Fe Expedition was venturing into what would be Johnson County, George Wilkins Kendall recorded:

*I saw for the first time the magnificent spectacle of a prairie on fire. All night the long and bright line of fire, which was sweeping along the prairie to our left, was plainly seen. The next day it was climbing the narrow chain of low hills which divided the prairie from the bottoms of the Brazos.*

When George Barnard first brought his brother Charles up from Galveston they saw fires at night burning across the prairie. They looked like a string of pearls to Charles who asked his brother about the cause of the fires.

*"It's a grass fire set by Indians, they kill the animals as they run from the fire,"* said George.

*"Do they enjoy killing or kill only what they need?"* Charles asked.

*"The only thing they kill without eating is a rattler— or a settler,"* quipped George.

The Billingsleys reported the great prairie fire in 1847–1848 that came in front of a blue norther scorching the countryside. John Billingsley described it:

*This country had never been surveyed. The settlers all made claims to the land that suited them best and went to work to improve their homes without titles, as titles could not then be obtained, and it was a great task to improve a place then, there were no lumber or shingles or wire for fences . . . so we made rails to fence our fields. And for doors and floors for our cabins we had to hew slabs, . . . It was late in the fall and a dense coat of grass from hip to waist high covered the prairies. Everything was dry and there was a high wind from the south. All day we had seen smoke boiling up in the north. In the late afternoon I started to the timber for a load of wood and my father started to the field to fire around it as a means of protection. But before he got to the field, and just as I reached the timber, there came a puff from the north then a calm, then another rush of wind that made the timber bend under its force. A regular "blue norther" had now saluted us, not with sleet, and snow but with a sweeping raging fire. The fire came in abreast and many miles wide, roaring and curling, swirling and dashing in wreathful flames, leaping and catching sometimes as much as fifty yards ahead, then on again with the speed of the wind. When I got home our fences were all in a light blaze. The branch and bluff with the naked place about our cabin had saved the house and family, but the fire went on, . . .These devas-*

*tating fires would sweep from river to river, leaving a blackened world of destruction behind them.*

This fire was so devastating that in the aftermath many settlers believed it had been set by the Indians to drive the settlers out. However, the Indians had used fire when hunting to herd animals on the plains from ancient times. Following the disastrous fire of the late 1840s the settlers between the Trinity and the Brazos Rivers of North Texas came to rely heavily on the game found in the Cross Timbers and on the plains nearby. Ultimately many of them moved their families to live in what would become Johnson County, becoming some of the first Europeans to live here permanently. They homesteaded along the edge of Cross Timbers, the rich source of food and dependable springs.

## "Mitchell's War"

The Billingsleys departed their homes in Missouri in December 1843. On May 4, 1844, they pitched tents in Texas. Nine Billingsley families had come by 1845. Soon after arrival they began to build individual cabins for the families:

*Round logs, dirt floors, board roofs held on with poles, and not a glass window to be had this side of Shreveport. Most of the time was spent in the chase killing buffalo and deer for their meat and hides. Deer and buffalo hides was our produce then, as cotton is now. We would bale up our hides and take them to market on Red River, a hundred miles away, and buy our groceries, bread, corn, and ammunition. Our crop failed the first year; some had to go to Red River in the fall for bread.*

After hauling the corn a hundred miles, they beat the corn into meal in the mortar. Five miles a day was the average rate of travel for an ox wagon in the 1840s:

*As for dry goods, we had to make our "hunting shirts" and everyday wear of dressed deer skins. Buckskin pants, hunting shirts and moccasins was the garb of the frontier man, and the women had to spin and weave their own clothing.*

In the spring of 1845 the *Texas Rangers were put on our frontiers to keep back the Indians. The line for our division was from the head of Richland Creek, and up Chambers Creek to where it entered the Cross Timber(s), then up the eastern edge of the Cross Timbers to the Trinity, this line passing where Alvarado now is. Scouts passed over this line twice every day but sometimes the Indians would slip through and steal our stock.* (John Billingsley)

Map of Johnson County showing Barnard's Old Trading House. Indian trade made Charles Barnard the wealthiest antebellum citizen in Johnson County. Barnard continued to trade with the tribes as they were rounded up in 1855 and escorted to the Upper Brazos Reservations. He came back to Johnson County when the tribes were removed from Texas to Indian Territory in 1859, and built a mill in 1864 at the future site of Glen Rose. The location of "Barnard's Old Trading House" now lies over the Hood County line. (Johnson's New Map of the State of Texas, by Johnson and Ward, n.d. AC)

The intricacies of trading with Native Americans in a barter economy often led to awkward and delicate situations. Misunderstandings grew out of language barriers; these could readily turn deadly as in the "Mitchell's War" incident described by John Billingsley:

*This year, 1849, we had an Indian raid to come down among us . . . An old Chief and about 30 of his tribe passed through the Ranger line at some unguarded place and made their appearance at the home of one of our neighbors, a Mr. Mitchell, who lived two miles from our home. The Indians demanded supplies and, leading Mitchell around, pointed out such as they wanted. When they received a good supply of eatables and tobacco they went into camp near Mitchell's home and had a gay time, judging from their merrymaking. Mitchell was the postmaster on the Austin line, the same John (David) Mitchell who was the first postmaster at Alvarado. The mail carrier, a lad of sixteen, came along about the time the Indians were leading Mitchell about, so he, being scared, came bolting to our house, seeing Indians in every ravine and thicket passed. He told the news in a hurried and excited* way and passed on, spreading the alarm as he went on to Bonham, making it worse at every post station.

We had been living in quiet and peace so long, and the game had been driven out to a great extent. We had turned our attention more to improvement and farming, so our guns, from disuse had become out of fix, and some entirely useless, but something must be done, so my father who was always calm and ready for any emergency, snatched up his gun and hurried to the scene of danger. It was just at night and I mounted a mule and started for the settlement seven miles up the creek. The news soon reached every door, although they were few and scattered in those days. I found few who were prepared for fighting, but all were ready to respond and they began to rub up their guns, getting them ready for defense.

Two men were sent to the Rangers' camp that night on Chambers Creek at the edge of the Cross Timbers about thirty miles away, and two went with me to Mitchell's. Neither of us had a gun. It was a stirring time with us that night. While the men were gone to see about the Indians and learn of their plans, the women and children were running from house to house, and some of them took to the thickety bottoms, hiding in darkness of the night. The next morning about sunrise, six of us armed with but one gun and an old home made sword, with some smaller and less dangerous weapons, sallied out from Mitchell's house to the Indian camp.

The Chief was on his horse, and we took possession of him, and held his horse by the bits. We demanded pay for what they had taken, but he feigned to not understand what we wanted, and tried to pull loose, but we held him fast. He then gave a whoop and his men formed on horseback with bows, guns and spears, ready for action. We saw that our best policy was to keep the Chief safe while we had him, and he knew if a gun was fired he would go by the board. Although we had but one gun; it was held in reserve for him. He then gave another command and his men dismounted, laying down their arms, and came up to shake hands with us. We did not shake hands, but we saw that we could not force them in to measures. So we turned the Chief loose and retreated in good order to the house. Just then we saw some more men on the high prairie, a mile or more away, coming from the settlement above. The Indians saw them too, and in a few minutes they were mounted and going across the prairie in a rapid gait, and as soon as our men came up we found that we could muster eleven guns for use. So that many men mounted on as many of the best horses and joined the chase. The Indians struck a beeline to the southwest

and had about forty horses with them which made a plain trail. We ran them about 15 miles, full drive, but they gained distance on us, and at the gap of the Mountain, where Chambers Creek passes through, we halted. We could see them about four miles away, making for the Cross Timbers, at a rapid speed. We then turned back, but soon met the Rangers coming on their trail. Some of our crew that was best mounted, joined them and they gave chase again. The Rangers ran them to the breakes of the Brazos River where the Indians set fire behind them and scattered.

Aaron Billingsley ends the story in this way: . . . The Dragoons or Texas Rangers came too late to intercept them here but took up their trail and followed them to the Brazos River, where they were in camp and partaking of a hearty meal of Mr. Mitchell's beef cows. They ambushed them on the river, killing several of them, chased them across the river about five miles and the Indians took refuge in a cave on a small creek. The Rangers shot all dead—except one Squaw who made a get away up the creek but was chased and captured. They named the creek Squaw Creek which it still is called. It empties into the Paluxy River just east of (the) town of Glen Rose, Texas.

These wagons at a family reunion about 1900 in Erath County are pulled by horses and mules. Pioneer families typically traveled in wooden hooped covered wagons pulled by oxen. The Balches had the words, "Texas or bust" on their wagon. Fashion at the time dictated that women also wear hoops—under their skirts. Albert Crook remarked about the similarity in appearance: that "to see her coming looked like a covered wagon." In 1860 a hooped skirt cost $3 to $5 in Johnson County. (Jack Morton, Cactus Jack's Boot Country, Alvarado, Texas)

John Billingsley recalled how important their rifles were to them:

> We carried our guns, wherever we went, weekdays and Sunday, too, for we never knew just when we would need them . . .
>
> Alone and in a frontier land
> Where savage Indians roamed
> We were united and ready to stand
> In defense of our western homes.
>
> With our rifles always ready
> We feared not the savage foe
> For we knew how to hold them steady
> And just when to let them go.
>
> . . . We were a band of brothers and neighbors all along the border line. We had no law. We needed no law or officers of the law to keep the peace. Our motto was peace and friendship with everyone, and everyone was our friend. The pioneers who lived on the borderline of civilization . . . rescued Texas from the savages and the wilderness so that others, who were yet in the rear, might march after years and find the way opened and made easy . . .

## José Maria and the Red Fly-Net— "A Frontier Reminiscence"

From the GALVESTON NEWS, October 1, 1879:

*This is my first visit to Cleburne since it became a local habitation and was graced with a name, although 28 years ago I was introduced to the then wilderness of this section in a very lively manner—chased through it by old José Maria's band of semi-civilized Indians, all of whom were stone-blind drunk. The writer, in 1851, was "green from the States," and, being possessed of a top-buggy, the only one, perhaps, in the State of Texas, he undertook a cruise through this wilderness of a country, accompanied by a negro boy only. The buggy horse was covered over from his head to the other end of his longitude with what was aforetime a fashionable as well as useful article called a fly-net. Our fly-net was a brilliant red in color, the most fascinating of all colors to the savage eye, and when José Maria and his villainous-looking followers caught sight of it from an eminence in the rear of us, . . . he and his forty or fifty braves incontinently went for us; and the first the writer knew of the chase was from the negro boy who generally lagged behind on the pony he rode. The negro came tearing past me, . . . I tried to rally him, thinking he had suddenly gone crazed. His only response was a punching movement of his arm toward the rear of us. At this I turned my head rearward, and I—well, I felt my heart sinking within—experienceing sensations similiar to those of a greenhorn on taking his first raw oyster. . . I came to the sage conclusion that there would be no use trying to get away from the red devils by running any further than I had—about a mile—so I called a halt and began to collect my senses, which were much in need of mobilization. In a few minutes I was completely surrounded by as ugly a pack of human hounds as ever beset anyone. Excepting the aboriginal clout, the Indians were all naked. Their faces were daubed over with red and yellow ochre, with huge brass rings pendant from their ears and noses; long black, coarse hair, parted in the middle and hanging unkept about their shoulders and backs, and all armed with rifles and bows and arrows. On being surrounded, I was shivering like an aspen leaf with fear, but almost instantly I felt relieved when I discovered the Indians riveting eyes on the red fly net, and summoning courage enough to speak, I saluted them in Spanish with, "Good morning!"*

*At this old José responded in a deep guttural tone, "Yes."*

*Recalling the fact that I had two bottles of whiskey in the buggy, I made haste to haul them out, and holding them up with the remark, "Good whisky," I drew their attention from the fly-net. Handing one of the bottles to José and the other to another one of the outre crew, I reined up my horse to move on, when the old chief stopped me, as he said, to drink and dance to my good health. I said to them, "All right," and "On with the dance!" Those infernal rascals kept me waiting in the big open prairie two mortal hours, and at the conclusion of their jamboree insisted on my presenting old José with the red fly-net. At this I shrugged my shoulders a la Frenchman, as though, I was loth to part with the fly-net, yet, in truth, I would have given them horse and buggy and fly-net and the negro boy, if he had not ran away to get clear of them.*

*However, I gave old José the net, and thanking me, he said: "You tink me wild Ingun, and you run like the devil. Me good friend; live at trading house with Charley Barnard," and then the whole pack of them broke into an excruciating howl, which they meant for laughing, and for the first time the fact dawned upon me that I was sold by a drunken party of friendly Indians.*

The writer might have valued his escape more had he known that Special Federal Indian Agent Stemm considered José Maria the "most influencial chief on the Brazos." José Maria was a veteran of many deadly fights with whites. José Maria and his band had taken the scalps of numerous surveyors, frontiersmen, and settlers during the previous sixteen years. About 1851, the year the writer was confronted and within ten miles from where it took place, a family of settlers was killed and scalped during a general Indian uprising. The flynet and refreshments may well have saved his life.

The Caddo entered into a treaty with Texas in 1837 which the Texas Senate ratified on August 21. Sam Houston was not re-elected in 1838 and a new President, Mirabeau B. Lamar, took office who had no qualms about exterminating Indians. "Strangely the treaty with the Hainai and Anadarko was lost from the files and never found."

In 1839 the Mexican government commissioned their military leaders to enlist Texas Indian tribes to attack settlers all along the Texas frontier. José Maria as chief led his warriors against the the whites near Bucksnort (Marlin), where two notable battles occurred known as the Morgan Massacre and Bryant's Defeat. At the Falls of the Brazos (Bucksnort), José Maria and his warriors stormed a cabin at nightfall and slaughtered the adults of families named Morgan and Marlin. Five men, women, and children died in the massacre; only four children escaped and fled to nearby cabins to tell of the butchery. Everyone in the area forted up, and ten days later forty-eight men thought they were ready for a second attack, but ten more settlers were killed. However, Chief José Maria recieved a bullet in the chest, and at least seven of his braves died.

In these early days José Maria showed a special bitterness towards surveyors who located land for white settlers marking the trees with letters that cut up the Indian hunting grounds with invisible lines. His group attacked many surveying parties, killing the hated land thieves. One story has it that José Maria's band captured a four-man survey party southeast of Waco. As his men were about to kill them, José Maria spared the life of one named Taylor after accepting from him a masonic sign. José Maria is said to have told the man he was a Master Mason from a French lodge in Canada. A local story from the Harrell family has José Maria returning a missing paint horse, saddle, and bridle belonging to J. J. Gathings through the efforts of Sam Houston.

Carter explains in CADDO INDIANS: WHERE WE COME FROM that: "For more than 150 years after the first white man came to live within Hasinai territory, there were peacefull friendly relations. It was only when the American population began to outnumber that of the tribes and the white settlers began to overrun the land that the relationship became fragile and distrust destroyed the peace."

José Maria, the notable Anadarko chief, and a group of his tribe chased a would be settler in a "top-buggy" across Johnson County in 1851. The buggy's horse was adorned with an attractive red tasseled fly net, which fluttered in the breeze. The settler pulled to a stop, "shaking like an aspen leaf with fear" as the pack of fifty-odd Indians surrounded him. ("The Charge on the Sun-pole," drawn by F. Remington; Fly net from "Mosemans' Horse Furnishings" 1889. AC)

José Maria (1800–1862) was the caddi or political chief of the Anadarkoes and Ionies (Iron Eyes) for nearly thirty years. He also was the key advisor to the other Caddo tribes at councils with the whites. Toweash chief (caddi) of the Hainai was José Maria's "second chief." José Maria's pragmatic reasoning held the Caddo tribes together during the desparate decades as they were driven from Texas. His small stature did not prevent him from being one of the "most impressive chiefs in Caddo history." José Maria was "The chief of the Nadako tribes, usually called Anadarko, after 1835, he rose as the principal leader of the Hasinai tribes that settled along the north forks of the Trinity River after being pushed out of northeast Texas. José Maria's name was Aasch (also

spelled Aaisch and Iesh), but the Mexicans and Americans called him José Maria. Aasch was probably born in the Anadarko village on the east bank of the Angelina River or on the Sabine River. He was christened José Maria by the Spanish missionary who was serving the mission of the Guadalupe de Nacogdoches."

José Maria had been wounded in several battles, eventually realizing the futility of warring against the whites. In 1844 José Maria spoke at council,

*As I, myself, small in size, my words to fit me shall be few, long talks admit of lies; my talk shall be short but true. Captains and chiefs, . . . I want you now to listen to me. The Big Spirit above is watching all now here, young men you all look happy. Captains, if you love your children, advise them not bad, but good; show to them the white path . . . we are all made alike, all look alike and are one people, which you must recollect. The Great Spirit, our father, and our mother, the earth, sees and hears what we say in council . . . I hold the white path in my hands (a string of wampum beads) . . . the white people gave it to me. To you . . . I give it. Stop going to war with the white people. I give to you this piece of tobacco to smoke, and consider of the white path, when you return to your village, then smoke this tobacco, think of my words and obey them.*

After the 1846 Comanche Peak meeting between the U.S. and the Texas tribes, José Maria was one of the chiefs invited to Washington, D.C., that summer. José's treaty document was signed by U.S. President James K. Polk. The Caddo preserved the document and proudly handed it down through the generations:

*Know all men by these presents, That José Maria, a Chief of the Ano-dah-kos and the tribe to which he belongs are by treaty on terms of Peace and Friendship with the United States of American.[sic]*

*José Maria has in person visited Washington City, the seat of Government of the United State and conducted himself according to the terms of the treaty to which he was a party.*

*The paper is given in testimony of the Friendship existing between the two countries.*

*Done at the City of Washington this the twenty fifth day of July one thousand eight hundred and forty-six.*

The story in the "Frontier Reminiscence" of the red fly net took place five years after José's Washington visit. José had his only known portrait painted by J. M. Stanley in 1843, while living north of Comanche Peak. The painting was later destroyed in a fire. José Maria's tribe and other closely related groups moved their encampments up and down the Brazos River. They hunted and raised crops on favorite bends along the Brazos between Johnson, Hood, Hill, Bosque, and Somervell Counties. About 1848 José moved to Barnard's Trading post near Comanche Peak establishing a village on De Cordova Bend. Fort Graham was established in 1849 across the Brazos from where José Maria's village had been.

Sam Houston, Governor of Tennessee, was in line for the U.S. presidency among the members of Andrew Jackson's political group. Instead he gave it all up, resigned as governor, and came to Texas on the rebound from the sorrow of a failed marriage. While on this rebound, he and a few other Americans, Mexicans, and other newly arrived "Texians" just happened to change the course of the Western history at San Jacinto. Sam Houston visited Johnson County on many occasions. (Matthew B. Brady, photographer, HARPER'S WEEKLY, March 30, 1861, AC)

In 1855 the bands were being rounded up for relocation on two small reservations near Fort Belknap. As José and his band were forced from Johnson County, he spoke at a council. The words of the near sixty-year-old chief reflect his crushed hopes:

*I know the Great Father* (U.S. president) *has the power to do with us as he pleases; we have been driven from our homes several times by the whites, and all we want is a permanent location, where we shall be free from further molestation, . . . Heretofore we have had our enemies, the whites on one side, and the Camanches on the other, and of the two evils, we prefer the former, as they allow us to eat what we raise, whilst the Camanches take everything, and if we are to be killed, we should much rather die with full bellies; we would therefore prefer taking our chances on the Brazos, where we can be near the whites.*

## Confusion on the Texas Frontier

Settlers were arriving in response to the offers of "free land" and the promise of a warm, healthy climate. They scouted the remote lands of the frontier to make claims. The common settler was pitted in battle against roving bands of superb horsemen born of a savage warrior society. Even with constant vigilance, the odds were not in favor of an isolated settler.

The Comanche tribes and their allies the Kiowa were the most feared and hated of the natives. Their reputation was well deserved. As warriors they were barbaric, they often savagely tortured their captives. They could mislead, elude, and conceal themselves. They were expert hunters—skilled and cunning.

With the Texas frontier embroiled by the continuous and confusing circumstance of change, there was much confusion about "who was who" on the frontier. Many settlers were foreigners and could not speak English. Rarely could the new settlers differentiate between the various Indian tribes. White renegades and outlaw gangs would use native tribal dress and wigs when stealing livestock or committing acts of violence. Stories abounded of trickery and treachery by Indian bands using the white flag or signs of friendship before an attack.

### A Massacre

During the years 1850–1851 an Indian uprising developed, the result of several influences. The Federal Indian Commissioner for Texas was doing a poor job. He stayed in his office and did not supply the Indians the provisions promised under treaty. Wild Cat, a wily tribal chief of a hostile group of Seminole and Kickapoo, was stirring up trouble and threatening the peaceful tribes with assault if they did not join in an attack on the whites. In the autumn of 1850 a rumor spread that George and Charles Barnard had abandoned their trading house because of threatened danger from the Indians. Federal Indian agent John Rollins reported that he believed that the Barnards were stirring up trouble because the Rangers had not held profitable councils near Barnard's posts. The Barnards countered by pointing to Indian conditions. General Brooke threatened to remove the Barnards from their property if they didn't leave on their own "and that in haste." The Barnards reminded him that the federal government had no authority over law-abiding Texas citizens.

The rumors spread as all the settlers ran back to "the Mountain" (Midlothian) except for Sam Myers and the Barnards.

"An Indian Foray," (HARPER'S WEEKLY, May 10, 1873. AC)

The Mountain was considered safe since patrolling Texas Rangers kept a camp at the point where the Chambers Creek cut through the escarpment. Settlers who built beyond the Mountain, were on land claimed by the Indians. As the Indians came through they burned all the settlers cabins except for the Barnards and the Myers.

During this 1851 Indian scare, legend says a family was massacred about three miles west of Godley, within the present-day boundaries of Johnson County. Little is known about the family of immigrants or the horrible end that came to them. Perhaps they received no warning because of language barriers or their isolated location. It is thought four or five members of the family were killed and scalped at their log cabin. The site of the tragic event is now marked only by a windmill. The deed record to their land was burned along with their cabin. A later replacement deed referred to the earlier deed that was destroyed in the cabin fire during the massacre. Another cabin and windmill were subsequently built on the spot. The members of the family were buried four hundred yards northwest near a creek, marked only by surface rocks a few of which had initials. In 1920 there were about fifteen graves discernible in the location. One of the rocks was inscribed: "Mrs. Wels."

**Pioneer Heroes on the Frontier**

". . . [N]one of them ever turned a back on his friend or an enemy."

The state organized "Ranger" forces and equipped regional "Home Guards" who went on forays against marauding Indian bands. The Tonkawa and Caddo were often called upon to serve as scouts, guides, interpreters, hunters, and troops.

Middleton Tate Johnson was looked upon as a rescuer by the settlers of Johnson County, and later they asked that the county be named after him. Capt. J. C.

The log cabin inside the planking was the first home of Samuel Houston Myers. He settled three miles north of Alvarado, Texas, arriving on August 21, 1851. On several occasions Myers entertained Sam Houston in this cabin; they may have been related. In 1870 the cabin was moved back to this site and a larger log house built. It was torn down in the 1970s. (Cleburne Pubic Library)

Terrell said Johnson was "grand . . . physically, morally and mentally . . . weighed 225 pounds and was physically the strongest man I ever knew. . . . We loved (him) for the manifold good he did . . . To us old settlers (he was a) veritable hero."

Settler, blacksmith, and scout Sam Kirkham was one of the first settlers to build west of the Cross Timbers. Arriving in Johnson County around 1850, he built one of the first houses between the Red River and Fort Graham; he lived on Caddo Village Creek one-half mile south of Burleson until 1878.

In 1853–1854 Kirkham assisted in organizing the county. In 1856 he claimed to have paid the county's first taxes to E. M. Heath. During the Civil War he reluctantly served in the Army of the Confederacy.

As a youth, Kirkham was captured and tortured by Indians who cut his ear. Through the years he fought in several more skirmishes with hostile Indians. One

Middleton Tate Johnson (1802–1866) was the first permanent settler of Tarrant County. As the admired leader of north Texas frontier guards and Texas Rangers, he became a hero to the citizens in Johnson County whom he protected and rescued from raiding Indian bands. Johnson's Station in southwest Tarrant County served as headquarters for his troops. When Johnson County organized in 1854 the settlers asked that it be named after "Tate" Johnson. He was a candidate for governor in 1857 but lost to a successionist. He personally was against succession but agreed to raise a large troop after Jefferson Davis promised him an appointment as Brigadier General. After inducting his troop in Arkansas he went on to Richmond only to be denied the appointment after Confederate President Davis learned about his reservations. Later he agreed to supervise blockade runners for the CSA. He died in Austin while attending the post–Civil War Constitutional Convention as a delegate. (J. W. Dunlop, Arlington, Texas)

Samuel Bonaparte Kirkham was born in Kentucky in 1829. He was one of the first settlers in the Johnson County area. He was a farmer and a blacksmith and scout—always working with his weapon nearby. He was a trusted guide for the Indian fighter, Col. M. T. Johnson, and assisted him in selecting the most suitable site for a new fort, which became Fort Worth, Texas. Kirkham died April 2, 1919, and is buried in Prairie Spring Cemetery. His descendants still thrive in the county he helped to establish. (Wilma Kirkham Reed)

notable battle took place in a grove of trees just south of the spring, about where the old Cleburne High School building stands. Indians often hid in willow trees next to the fresh water of the Buffalo Spring to kill deer and buffalo as they came to drink. In this confrontation he took three Comanche scalps and narrowly escaped death from an arrow which struck him in the front of his body. An old Kiowa medicine man dressed the wound which left a large scar. In 1998 Kirkham's great-granddaughter lives adjacent to the site of the fight.

Courageous scouts and rangers like these endeared themselves to the settlers of the county by coming without question when called.

## "Well Suppose We All Go to Texas"

An 1858 letter shows the spirit that led many of these pioneers to Texas. The elderly patriarch of one family in Kentucky is quoted by his daughter in a letter written to family members already in Texas:

*. . . I would be glad if we were all in Texas & well fixed, but I am afraid to go for fear that we would not do well. Father is anxious to move there, but he is old & mother is old & they hate to break up* [house] *but he often says, "well suppose we all go to Texas . . ." I remain your friend and niece,*

*Mollie Dinquish*

The Tidwell family at their log house thoughtfully built in the shade of some ancient oaks. On the porch is the mother who shows off her very modern pedal sewing machine while the father sits near the children and their toy wagon. (Layland Museum, Cleburne, Texas)

During the nineteenth century the boasts of land boomers and speculators' outlandish claims were common. It became the safe practice of prospective settlers to investigate the grand claims of promoters by corresponding with someone who had gone on ahead and settled the land.

## Trails to Texas

The Brazos, Trinity, and Red River Valleys formed natural corridors for the settlers to travel. They journeyed along timbered valleys where fresh water abounded and the trees sheltered game. Emigrants followed buffalo trails through narrow places and cut down the banks in timbered river bottoms. Others rafted down the Ohio and Mississippi Rivers to the river towns of Shreveport, Louisiana, and Jefferson, Texas. A number came up from the coast near Galveston riding riverboats as far as the boat could travel up the shallow Texas rivers, and then proceeding to their destination by wagon.

Often families struggled across a thousand miles of rivers, woods, and prairies in covered wagons. The pioneer stories of immigration to Johnson County have a tragic but common thread that runs through them—the death of a family member while traveling to Texas.

"Texas is hell on women and horses," some people warned others. Tom Borden wrote to Moses Lapham back in Iowa, "Don't bring a wife to Texas." "Wait and find one here. Then she'll be used to the climate." Pioneers on the journey faced the "three big I's—

Samuel Billingsley and his wife, Temperance Davidson Billingsley, came to Alvarado, Texas, in 1852. Eight of the Billingsley families moved to the community. The Myers, Balches and a few other families were already settled there. The Billingsley families swelled the population by fifty people, doubling the population within the county. They helped establish the first school at Alvarado and built a horse-powered mill. (Cleburne Public Library)

Indians, Insects, and Illness." Many almost made it, dying just short of reaching their land. In the first few years after arrival, six wives and mothers from the Myers and Balch families were laid to rest in the Balch Cemetery in Alvarado.

*Our path often lay amid rocks and crags instead of among the lilies. The web of life was drawn into the loom for us, but we wove it ourselves. We threw our own shuttles and worked our own treadles, and as it was a new year, something new must take place. The usual round of business, such as improving our places, and getting a living out of the ground, and the woods, still we went on.—* John Billingsley, 1847

Many who came to Texas had experienced personal misfortune and loss. The initials GTT became widely known for "Gone to Texas." It became a familiar postscript for tax collectors and constables out on their rounds back in eastern states. The words were often painted on doors of houses abandoned by settlers moving to Texas.

## Settlements on a New Land

When the settlers arrived they found a wild open land, rich and unspoiled.

The first of the Billingsleys came in a family caravan of wagons that included over six brothers and cousins, the eldest being Samuel. The Billingsleys had some more of their clan join them in 1845 who brought with them their "old frontier veteran" mother, who:

> . . . *saw the men retreating from the first battle that was fought with the "red coats" and heard them singing as they passed, "He that fights and runs away, will live to fight another day." She had passed through the hardships, troubles, and trials of the Indian wars and massacres, in the early settling of Tennessee and Kentucky and in the year 1811, she came with her family to the Arkansas River. That was then a wilderness country. She had passed through all the troubles, trials, and vicissitudes of raising a large family in a frontier land, where it tried women's souls as well as men's, and besides the cares of a mother, she had been a nurse and a physician in her children's families, as well as in many others, and she was 75 years old, she was strong and full of life and energy . . . After spending about twelve years here among us she passed on to her reward.*

Emigration to Texas slowed dramatically during the Mexican War. Johnson County's first permanent settle-

The Alamo in 1852 before the familiar top was built on it by the Texas Military. "Ruins of the Church of El Alamo," (GLEASON'S PICTORIAL DRAWING-ROOM COMPANION, February 18, 1852. AC)

ment occurred simultaneously with the 1849 California Gold rush only a year after the end of the Mexican War. In 1851 Samuel Myers' caravan to Texas had a number of their men continue to California gold fields. Joseph McClure's stepfather got the bug, and left after stopping here for only a short time. He came all the way back to Alvarado with "three belts of $20 gold pieces around his waist," and went again with a second group to California, never to return.

By 1850 many pioneer families established claims and temporary homes or campsites with tents for part of the year in what would become Johnson County. They used their claims much as the Indian had, living in tents in hunting camps to kill and smoke buffalo meat for the winter months.

Through the Mexican War, the Mountain or White Rock Escarpment at Midlothian was as far as settlers could safely venture. Between the Mexican and Civil Wars the influx of Anglo-Americans to Texas would push the western frontier into and past the Cross Timbers of what is today Johnson County.

Grave of Elizabeth Crockett, widow of Davy Crockett, who died in Johnson County, January 31, 1860. Her monument was dedicated on May 13, 1913. The grave site in Acton Cemetery was designated a state park in 1945, and is the smallest state park in Texas. (AC)

## Famous Pioneer Texans

While Texas may have attracted more than its share of people who had to look back over their shoulders, it also attracted larger-than-life heroes.

Sam Houston visited Johnson County often. He used the Indian trails through Johnson County on his way back home through the "Falls of the Brazos" from his council with the peaceful tribes in 1843 at Bird's Fort in present Tarrant County. Sam was a partner in the Barnard Trading Post (1847–1856) near Comanche Peak and consulted with the Barnards about Indian affairs. Sam Houston visited the Myers' Settlement and stayed with the Sam Houston Myers family near Alvarado on several occasions during 1851 to 1860.

### Davy Crockett

David Crockett caught the vision of Texas. Davy was a nationally famous personality in his own time. Before he came to Texas, he was widely known as a legendary frontiersman, who had risen to be a Tennessee congressman. Books, an almanac, and many stories were written about him and by him.

One local family legend says that on his way to fight for Texas, Davy came through parts of what would become Johnson County. On January 9, 1836, from St. Augustine, Texas, he wrote these final words to his family in Tennessee:

*David Crockett to his Daughter Margaret and her husband, Wiley Flowers*

*My Dear Son & Daughter This is the first time I have had an opportunity to write you . . . I must say as to what I have seen of Texas it is the garden spot of the world and the best prospect for health I ever saw is here and I do believe it is a fortune to any man to come here Theare is a world of country to settle it is not required here to pay down for your League of Land every man is entitled to his headright of 4000-428 (4428) acres . . . I expect in all probability to settle on the Bodark (Bois d'Arc) or Chactaw Bayou of Red River That I have no doubt is the richest county in the world. Good land Plenty of timber and the best springs and wild mill streams, good range, clear water, and every appearance of good health and game aplenty. It is the pass wher the buffalo passes from north to south and back twice a year, and bees and honey plenty. I have great hope of getting the agency to settle that country and I would be glad to see every friend I have settled theare . . . I have taken the oath of the Government and have enrolled my name as a volunteer for six months and will set out for the Rio Grand in a few days with the volunteers from the United States but all the volunteers is entitled to a vote . . . and I have but little doubt of being elected a member to form a constitution for this Province. I am rejoiced at my fate. I had rather be in my present situation than to be elected to a seat of Congress for life I am in hopes of making a fortune for myself and my family . . . do not be uneasy about me I am with my friends I must close with great respects your affectionate Father Farewell David Crockett*

Davy died during the fall of the Alamo, but the hopes and dreams he had for his family and Texas lived on. Davy's family followed his instructions to come to Texas.

Right: "The Land Merchant of Texas" was Jacob de Cordova for whom a large beautiful bend of the Brazos River extending into Johnson County is named. He promoted Texas colonization all over the U.S. and Europe through speeches and pamphlets. He was described as handsome, ready with a smile and jest. His cosmopolitan wit made him a favorite among the early-day Texans. After death his body was reburied on the state capitol grounds. (Archives Division, Texas State Library)

Below: The ferry at Kimball Crossing traversed the river by the swift current and a cable. The cost was 50 cents per wagon and team, 25 cents per buggy or horseback, and l0 cents per person on foot. Pictured on the ferry are: J. C. Jiles, John Bochoper, Walter Cleveland, and T. E. Luck. (Layland Museum, Cleburne, Texas)

His wife, Elizabeth Crockett, Davy's son, and other relatives came searching for the beautiful land that Crockett spoke of. They settled in Johnson County in 1854 receiving the first of several tracts for Davy Crockett's service and sacrifice for Texas. Elizabeth Crockett's headright grant was near Barnard's Trading Post close to Ft. Spunky. The Crockett land grants lie within the boundaries of today's Hood and Johnson County. A number of his descendants, some bearing the famous Crockett name, still live in the area.

## The Winter Garden of the World

In August 1849, as Henry Briden and his wife came up the Brazos from Galveston and viewed the Nolan River Valley. He turned to her on the wagon seat and exclaimed, "Why it's the winter garden of the world." They built a cabin on the west side of the Nolan River three miles north of Rio Vista. They soon discovered they had built their cabin alongside and in plain view of a well traveled Indian trail. They received warning from soldiers to hide because of rumored Indian uprisings (1850–1851). They moved south to Fort Graham for two years. Upon returning they found their cabin burned. They rebuilt on the secluded east side of the river.

## An "Oddfellow" Comes to Texas: Kent

Jacob de Cordova (1808–1868), a Jew born on Jamaica, is considered the Father of the Independent Order of Odd Fellows in Texas. He was commissioned as the instituting officer and brought the charter for the group to Texas March 12, 1841, as the first lodge outside the United States. He became one of early Texas' great promoters. In 1850–1851, a group of thirty English families founded a colony with a capital called Kent. De Cordova had arranged their locating on land near the Kimball Bend of the Brazos. The English Immigration Company sent thirty families from England in the 1840s to twenty-seven thousand acres in the midlands of the Brazos. Lieutenant Charles Finch MacKenzie led the group to establish the town of Kent. These idealists were so unprepared for the wilds of Texas that a few of them served food on solid silver dinner pieces while they lived in tents and brush arbors. They planted crops but neglected to put up rail fencing or hedges to keep out their grazing livestock. After fattening on the crops, the animals were stolen by Indians. During the first winter many of the settlers died, the others scattered or went home. A family or two recouped and moved closer to the settlements back down the Brazos sixty miles. By 1852

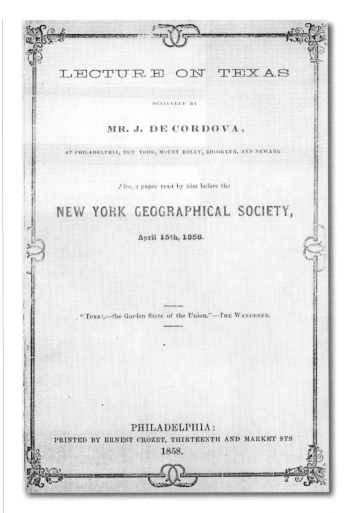

Printed form of Jacob de Cordova's "Lecture on Texas." A pamphlet used to lure settlers to the area. It contains his glowing speech before the New York Geographical Society and many other cities in which he touted the wonders of Texas. His 1858 edition contains a new admonition not seen in some earlier printings. After his Kent experience, Jacob tempered the speech with a warning for those caught up in the romance of Texas. ". . . —although Texas is the finest State in the Union, and may be literally regarded as a "land flowing with milk and honey,"—it is necessary for them to milk the cows and gather the honey before they can enjoy either one or the other: neither can be obtained without labor. (Bosque Collection: Elizabeth Torrence)

the colony was gone, only one man and his family from the original group stayed on to continue farming.

### Kimballville

Richard Burleigh Kimball was born in New Hampshire in 1816 and died in New York City in 1892. He practiced law in New York where he became financier and advisor of Jacob de Cordova, the land merchant of Texas. As partners, Kimball and de Cordova

William Love Clifton is pictured after the Civil War. Clifton destroyed a sheepskin Texas Land Grant he inherited from his father and his step-mother to thirteen acres of downtown Cleburne—this because he had not worked and improved the land as required by his traditional Irish beliefs. (Bill Lemens)

owned about one million acres of Texas land, including a cotton plantation known as Kimball's Bend. Richard Kimball was president of the first railroad in Texas, the Houston, Galveston, and Henderson Railroad.

In the 1840s Richard B. Kimball acquired land on the Brazos River by buying up script and having the land surveyed and patented in the general land office of the state. This land included a bend of 2,720 acres which was almost completely encircled by the river. It is still known as Kimball Bend.

Jacob de Cordova influenced Kimball to come to that area in 1853–1854. They chose a place on the river that was shallow and free of quicksand for the site of a city. Soon after 1854, a town developed with stores, churches, schools, saloons, and residential areas.

In the bend, Richard B. Kimball built a house with a gallery which commanded a seventeen-mile view of the Brazos River. He subdivided his land so each of his slaves had his own portion to work. The slaves were rewarded in proportion to individual production. Each plot of land had its own cabin, a gardening area, and a poodle dog to keep rabbits out. The plantation had its own cotton gin. The town of Kimball flourished during the Chisholm Trail cattle drives just after the Civil War.

## "Get with the Wild"

*On our arrival in Johnson County in 1851 it was over run with Indians, buffalo, mustangs, deer antelope, panther, cougar, black bear and hogs. These were pests to the would be farmers as their different kinds of stock would get with the wild and take days of chasing to separate them.*—Joseph McClure

*Wild, is a disease easily contracted by gentle cattle.*—Joe Evans, trail driver of Johnson County

The Billingsleys hunted the great herds of buffalo which ranged the prairies on both sides of the Cross Timbers until the late 1840s. These early visitors in Johnson County reported ten thousand visible from one point, spread across the wild open prairies as far as the eye could see. Within a few years they were gone forever, receding to the west. The last local wild Buffalo was seen in Hill County south of here in 1852. From a high of fifty million once on the plains only about a thousand would remain in 1880.

## By Metes and Bounds

Texas retained its public debt and lands as it entered the Union—the only state to do so. Texas formed the General Land Office to record existing titles and manage the project of giving the public lands away. Texas was generous with its land because it wished to encourage continued immigration and settlement. Today 97 percent of Texas is privately owned, 2 percent is public, and 1 percent is road right-of-way.

Surveyors were the vanguard of the settlers. The native tribesmen observed surveyors marking trees and stones and placing "invisible lines" across their homelands and hunting grounds. Recognizing that this activity resulted in eventual loss of their lands, the warlike tribes repeatedly targeted the surveyors and tortured them to death horribly. Known peaceful tribes might attack a survey party without provocation or warning. Several parties of Robertson Land District surveyors were killed by Indians. For the great risks there were great rewards. Many of our county's founders and their family's fortunes were based upon the work of the member who was at one time a surveyor. In our county the names of some early surveyors are: B. J. Chambers, Jacob De Cordova, Henry Briden, James E. Patton, D. R. Mitchell, Richard Bell, B. S. Jenkins, George M. Pierce, G. H. Cunningham, S. G. Graham, and the Heath brothers. Joseph Philpot's old sorrel horse, Buck, could step off a piece of land as well as the average chain carrier. Robertson Colony later became a land district and then several counties. B. J. Chambers was deputy-surveyor from 1836 to 1850 and acquired his Cleburne land while working for the Mercer Colony part of the Robertson Land District in 1847.

## Land Grants

Anyone who signed up for a land grant had to pay to have their land surveyed and registered with the state. The claimant was also required to pay the cost of surveying a second and nearly equal amount of land for the state for assignment to various school districts, businesses, and governmental subdivisions. Many claims overlapped and eventually had to be settled in court. Even Davy Crockett's widow and her estate had a lengthy litigation over her headright claim ending in the loss of some of the land by her heirs. These deed holders would then sell the land for hard cash as a means of raising funds. Early county maps show many counties, school districts, and railroads which had been given land and took their scrip in surveyed Johnson County land to sell for cash. In 1860 Charles Barnard negotiated with Milam County for the tract where his mill and the future site of Glen Rose would be.

One of the earlier grants filed was that of George Barnard. On January 11, 1840, he registered his claim to a headright of 320 acres: one-half a square mile, surveyed on a creek later to be known as George's Creek in Johnson and Somervell Counties. This was surveyed a year before the Santa Fe Expedition and six years before Dr. Roemer visited the Caddo Village near the mouth of the Nolan River. Native American tribes were firmly in control of the area at that time. Because of Barnard's involvement in the trading post, he would ask for and receive permission from the Comanches to travel through the area. Still the Comanches would check his wagons for women or plows, either of which would have cost the lives of the freighters. The Comanches hated settlers because they took the land.

### Indian Claims

Native American people had an especially difficult time registering and keeping claims to land. After 1859, by law, North Texas tribes were not even supposed to be in Texas.

On the journey to Texas, Loving Clifton lost his wife Hannah in Lamar, Red River County. Loving and his son, William Love Clifton, immigrated here during 1854–1856. While coming through Buchanan the lack of water was observed at the new county seat and they moved on. Loving met a lone Indian woman, believed to have been

Joseph and Losada J. Moyer McClure of the Myers and Balch settlements. Joseph McClure arrived as a child of seven and recorded his childhood experiences when the Caddo Indians were his neighbors in 1852. (Joe Ann McClure Sladovnik)

Choctaw, who lived in a log house by an abundant spring. Their arrival occurred about the time of the removal of many tribal groups camped along the Brazos River in Johnson County. Loving fell in love, and married the woman by the spring on Buffalo Creek. She had received a sheepskin (vellum) grant from the State of Texas to the thirteen acres east of Buffalo Creek by the Buffalo "Big" Spring, land that would later become downtown Cleburne. The fateful union lasted only a short time, for the Indian bride died within a year. Loving resided at the spring with his son for several years and died about 1860, the year before their home place became Camp Henderson. The camp was the gathering and training encampment for the volunteers going off to the Civil War. Loving's young son, William, was left alone in the world and never bothered to probate or to press his survivorship claim. William did hold onto the sheepskin and the memories he had of his parents. As the years passed, William married and had a family. Occasionally he would tell them the story of his coming to Texas and he would show the old document to his daughter and later to her son Bill Lemens. Bill, his grandson, examined the vellum land grant asking why they didn't make a claim to the land, by then the valuable downtown section of the bustling city of Cleburne. William explained to his family that people in Cleburne had purchased their land in good faith, and that according to his Irish traditions, a person was not entitled to land unless that person had worked and improved the land. It was certainly fortunate for many, who had invested and built in downtown Cleburne, that William

Meredith Hart brought his family to Johnson County in 1855 locating on the Mustang Creek seven miles south of Cleburne. Hart owned three ranches. The family lived in a small log cabin until the completion of the permanent home which was begun in 1859 and finished in 1861. The foundation and the bases of the chimneys were made of large white rocks found on the land, hewn into shape, and sunk deeply into the ground. The sills and joists and framings were from post oak trees from the Cross Timbers and hewn down to the heart. Holes were mortised into the sills, plates and tenons cut in the scantlings and put together with draw pins without a single nail in the frame. Every part of the woodwork was made by hand, including the doors and window sashes. The roof was made of hand-split shingles of post oak timber, shaved down to the heart and smoothed with a drawing knife. The kitchen floor was made of flag stones held together by jointing and sunk into the dirt that had been filled in up to the level of the other floors. (Pat and Beverly Patman)

Love Clifton held such beliefs. Many cross claims of this type were still being filed in the local courts through the turn of the century and being won! William Love Clifton eventually destroyed the sheepskin grant, preventing anyone from making the claim.

There were tribes in our area that refused to leave during the 1854–1856 Indian removal to the upper Brazos Reservations. Some Indian people refused to be pushed any further despite persecution and stayed to become a part of the community. Bill Lemens witnessed a conversation at the dinner table of a family he was working for as a field hand near Glen Rose. The topic came up between the elders of the family, one accused another of being involved in the slaughter of an Indian tribe that had lived on their land. The tribe had been massacred in order to get the farmland that they lived on.

There is local legend of a Biloxi tribe living along a spring-fed stream that fed into the Brazos. Whites who coveted the land attacked and massacred the tribe. That stream is said to be the Paluxy River, *Paluxy* being a superstitious renaming of the Biloxi name. When the citizens of the area that is now Somervell County, originally petitioned to form the county in 1875, they requested the name of Biloxi County. It seems they may have remembered the tribe that was there before they came. However, Somerville was the initial name given the county on March 15, 1875, and changed to Somervell in September, 1875.

During the Civil War, the able-bodied men enlisted and were ordered to the front. With the ranches and

"The last Indian baby born here" before this expulsion to the reservations was in a thicket at the Lonnie Wilbanks place. The squaw dropped out of the group when she came to a thicket. She tied her horse, which was pulling a buffalo hide travois, cleaned out a place under a little hackberry and hung a papoose bag on the tree. Some men working out this way saw her and then they went to the house and told Mrs. Wilbanks. She went down to help, but the Indian woman sent her away saying she would have the baby okay without any help. Mrs. Wilbanks worried about her all night and went back at daylight. The Indian woman had all her belongings loaded and the baby strapped on her back. She got on her horse, waved goodby to Mrs. Wilbanks and took the trail of the other Indians." The Tonkawa and Caddo were reported to have been the last to leave. "Population of an Indian Village Moving," drawn by Theodore R. Davis, (HARPER'S WEEKLY, May 21, 1870. AC)

farms defenseless, some wilder tribes began to raid and pillage the frontier. A home guard was raised from the few remaining men and boys. The home guard attacked a Choctaw village near the present day intersection of Highway 144 and Highway 67 in eastern Somervell County. Most of the members of the tribe were killed except for a few children who hid under a bluff near a flowing stream known as Squaw Creek. One of the young survivors was Mellie Cholt, who was taken in by another tribe.

Another time near this area, William Thomas Junell ran away from home with his dog and very little food. One night he came upon an Indian village along a stretch of the Brazos River that would eventually be in eastern Somervell County. While attempting to steal a melon from the Indian garden he was caught and taken to their camp. He was later adopted into their tribe, raised by one of the families, and ultimately married an Indian maiden. Thomas and his bride moved near Ft. Spunky, close to Barnard's Trading House where they later had a child named Tom. In 1871 this Tom Junell met and married Mellie Cholt, the young Indian maiden who had survived the massacre near Squaw Creek. These Native American parents would bring eight children into the world living in a dugout home built into the side of a mountain overlooking the Brazos River. The children grew up, married, and made their homes in Johnson and Somervell County communities. Two of them became barbers and one of these children, Bob Junell, was Chief of Police in Cleburne by 1947.

## Indian Neighbors

Joseph McClure arrived as a child of seven and describes his childhood when Caddo Indians were his neighbors in 1852:

*I played with the Indians and would run foot races and shoot bows and arrows; and when I was large enough to hoe corn I would get them to help me for awhile then would go play with them . . . I can show spots where they used as camp grounds . . . families were all on hand before a house was started, so we joined hands, cut logs, and built cabins. Robert Billingsly having a broad-axe did the hewing while others did the scoring. I can hear the ring of that broad-axe today. I can also see the Indians standing by enjoying the work going on . . . I remember many times when Indians or wild animals would get after our dogs and run them through our bed quilt door shutter after night, and many times they would kill our dogs . . . So during the year 1852 many more settlers had arrived, and more cabin smokes shown over the hill tops, and more cocks crowing for day. That tickled our Indian neighbors, to hear cocks crowing for day . . . Now in those days there were few white settlers in the area. But, there were thousands of Indians and wild animals were plenty. The Indians loved us better than their own tribes until the Eastern pack horse traders ravished their women and madly killed an Indian warrior. Then they began to kill our people but they never scalped one until an Indian was scalped first by the white man . . . I was in three runs from the Indians from Alvarado land . . . By 1853 most of these pests . . . had emigrated west to the Brazos River which was a great relief. However the Indians made trips back trading until about 1860 when they began killing and robbing which caused more state troopers and volunteers to go to the west.*

## Expulsion of the Indians from Texas

Between 1854 and 1856 the peaceful tribes in North Texas were removed to Fort Belknap on two reservations containing an area of 53,136 acres. The Upper Brazos Reservations put the remnant tribes of Caddo, Anadarko, Tonkawa, Wichita, Waco, Tawakoni, and Keechi on one plot: and the Southern Comanche on another. These two reservations were in what is Palo Pinto and Throckmorton Counties.

These reservations and their inhabitants became embroiled in controversy; the object of retaliation, revenge, and ambush. Enemy tribes and certain whites made trails to the reservations from the scene of local raids to implicate the reservation Indians. After being attacked and accused of various local crimes, many fled to Indian Territory. In 1859 all the remaining tribes in North Central Texas including the Southern Comanche, Caddos, Wichitas, and small remnants of others—were removed from Texas. They were escorted by military guard to Indian Territory land leased from the Choctaws and Chickasaws. After the tribes realized that they were losing all their hunting grounds, homelands, and reservations in Texas, the most hostile, angry, and resentful warriors banded together for continued raids into North Central Texas. Indian attacks increased during the Civil War and Reconstruction, ranging as far south as their traditional hunting areas and even Mexico until about 1874.

In 1859 a nephew of old José Maria was killed in an ambush by some whites and soon he and his band were escorted along with all the rest from Texas to "The Nations." Major Neighbor's census listed a remnant of 218 Anadarko and 244 Caddo.

While at the Upper Brazos Reservations these tribes joined the Texas forces in raids against the Northern Comanche. They fought bravely and supplied many warriors. The Tonkawa and Caddo were called upon to serve as scouts, guides, interpreters, hunters, and troops. Afterward, when they were of no more use to the Texans, they were casually shipped off to Indian Territory along with the Comanche they had hunted down.

Indians in the state of Texas had faced a unique situation: Texas controlled the land, and the United States the Native Americans. The removal of the Indians from the Brazos Reservations ended all "impractical theories" about friendly Indians and the idea that the two races could live with amicable relations. After 1859 Native Americans were not to be in Texas, except the Alabama-Coushatta on their reservation in East Texas.

Knowing personally of the tragedy that had befallen the American Indians, Sam Houston's words before the U.S. Senate are a requiem:

*As a race they have withered from the land. Their arrows are broken and their springs have dried up. Their cabins are dust . . . Slowly and sadly they climb the mountains and read their doom in the setting sun . . . They will live only in the songs and chronicles of their exterminators. Let these be faithful to their . . . virtues as men and pay tribute to their unhappy fate as a people.*

## Johnson County Organizes

The Billingsleys were of the Presbyterian denomination and seemed to have been a church group migrating en masse. After all the Billingsleys arrived in the county, the population almost doubled. As the yard of William Balch filled with camping settlers, his place became known as "Sprawls Hotel." Many other new settlers arrived in 1852. Among them was Major E. M. Heath and wife, Sophia, a daughter of David Mitchell. Beginning in 1853 E. M. Heath was among the leaders of a movement to bring government closer to the people for the convenience of deed recording and legal work:

*During* [the winter of 1853–] *1854, E. M. Heath canvassed on horseback the surrounding territory and secured the names of 107 qualified voters to a petition to the state legislature for the organization of the county, which was duly granted (February 13, 1854). An election was held in August in the new store house on the north west corner of the square of Alvarado. 120 qualified voters cast their ballots for the organization of the county of Johnson named for Colonel M. T. Johnson.*

*After the first full set of elected officials the elected candidates together bought a barrel of whiskey and divided it into two barrels in Alvarado. One barrel was set at the south of the store and the other north of the Larrimore store. There were no voluntary candidates, they were selected by the people and their names placed to the public for election.*

During an 1856 vote,

[Joe Shaw:] *. . . would not quit his plowing to come to the election. Shaw was a good man. I was sent to the field to notify him of his being elected . . . it seemed to sadden him.*—Joseph McClure

Wardville, the first county seat, was located on William O'Neal's land after several votes of the citizens. On April 26, 1855, the county court ordered the sale of lots there. The location of Wardville was on the west side of the Nolan River. It now lies beneath the waters of Lake Pat Cleburne near the southwest end of the Highway 67 bridge over the lake.

The log courthouse also served as a community church, and as whiskey was accepted in payment of fines, Johnson County's bar of justice may have served as a bar of another kind on occasion. These early county officials recognized the value of alcohol offered in payment of fines as legal tender. This was not a new idea; liquor and spirits were "negotiable" commodities in America since Colonial times. Robinson County, Kentucky, whiskey was the standard of the day; it was thirty cents a gallon with a red corncob stopper and was quickly accepted as ready cash on the frontier.

In 1856 there was great excitement in Wardville when a bear came up to the home of Mrs. Lewis. The misguided bear paid the ultimate price for the trespass, as the townsfolk did not wish their fair city to be known as a place where bears freely walk the streets.

More excitement came with the accidental burning of Wardville's log courthouse. E. M. Heath described the spaces between the logs in the walls of this courthouse as being large enough to throw a horse collar through. During a "heated" court session, a blue norther took advantage of these cracks as it raced across the prairie. The primitive courthouse caught fire from a blaze which the occupants were using to keep warm. In the middle of the fire fighting, the presiding judge abruptly halted the efforts by ordering, "Let it burn—maybe we'll all get warm."

On October 4, 1856, it was voted that the county seat be moved east to Buchanan, but not because of the fire. It was determined that Wardville did not meet the state requirement that all county seats be within five miles of the geographic center of the county. Buchanan, the new seat of government, was named for then U.S. president, James Buchanan. The old fort supply road went down Buchanan's Main Street later becoming the Chisholm Trail.

Buchanan was a lively enough place when court was in session and during the cattle trailing season, when it was the scene of at least one saloon killing. A tornado swept through town in 1858 killing two; one person being thrown down a well. Buchanan had one unforgivable shortcoming, a chronic shortage of water. It would have been better for the people of Buchanan if the state legislature had required a county seat be located within five miles of reliable water. Many potential settlers moved on, after traveling through the "dry" town on the rolling plains.

On the right is Horatio G. Bruce. In 1861 the First Company of Confederate soldiers was organized in Johnson County by Gen. W. H. Parsons. W. J. Neal was elected captain; W. R. Shannon was elected captain of the Second Company; A. J. Frizzel, the Third Company; J. A. Foomwalt, the Fourth Company; H. C. Bruce, the Fifth Company; H. C. Childress, the Sixth Company; Sam Caruthers, the Seventh Company; W. Cathey, the Eighth Company, and H. A. Hart, the Ninth Company. Bruce's Company became Company H, Twentieth Texas Cavalry, Bass Regiment. Bruce was captured at the battle of Honey Springs in 1863 and spent the remainder of the war in Federal prison camps in the north.

Elbert Monroe Heath, on the left, was six feet tall, broad chested, carried himself erect, and a fine looking man in appearance. Eight years before, in 1854, "Major Heath" was appointed by the fifth legislature of the State of Texas as the commissioner to organize Johnson County. In 1861 he volunteered in the Twentieth Cavalry, commanded by Colonel Bass. His coat pocket hangs heavy with the papers that accompanied his position as a high private and acting adjutant of the regiment. An accident threw him in the way of the Federal forces at Elk Creek, Indian Territory, and he was made a prisoner in July, 1863. He was imprisoned sixteen months in the worst prison in the North, the old "Picay Cotton Press" yard. On April 9, 1865, he was exchanged at the Red River. He worked his way home on foot to Johnson County. One year later, Major Heath was elected sheriff of Johnson County and then was forced to resign during Reconstruction because he had served in the Confederate Army. (Layland Museum, Cleburne, Texas and his great-granddaughter Hattie Lou Harp Alfrey of Godley, Texas)

## Trouble Between the States

THE PERIOD OF THE CIVIL WAR WAS A defining time for the United States. After the war there was no longer a loose group of independent states with a weak association in federal government. We became one country—and it was paid for with a great price.

The ancient practice of enslaving people was still a curse to Texas and the Southern states a little more than a century ago. The economy and the wealthy class were dependent on it.

The largest number of slaves listed as held by one person in the 1860 Johnson County census was twenty-five. This "owner" was William Powell who, on his 1640-acre farm, produced fifty bales of cotton. To dispel any misconception that a slave's life on Johnson County plantations or farms was any different from other parts of the South, the Texas Slave Narratives, recorded in 1936, contain two accounts of local people born or sold into slavery. The memories are not carefree, pastoral, or picturesque. Terror was an essential tool used to force people to remain in bondage. These frightful experiences became folklore in the black community.

Auntie Thomas Johns was born during the Civil War (1862–1863) near Burleson's future location. She recalled the stories that her mother and husband recited from slavery's gloomy days:

*One of Major Odom's slaves was whipped by a man named Steve Owens. He got going to see a slave woman Owens owned, and one night they beat him up bad. Major Odom put on his gun for Owens, and they carried guns for each other till they died, but they never did have a shooting.*

*Colonel Sims had a farm adjoining Major Odom's farm, and his slaves were treated mean. He had an overseer, J. B. Mullinaz, I remember him, and he was big and tough. He whipped a slave man to death. He would come out on a morning and give a long, keen yell and say, "I'm J. B. Mullinaz, just back from a week in Hell, where I got two new eyes, one named Snap and Jack, and the other Take Hold. I'm going to whip two or three slaves to death today." . . . He wouldn't give his slaves much to eat and he'd make them work all day, and just give them boiled peas with just water and no salt and cornbread. They'd eat their lunch right out in the hot sun and then go back to work. Mama said she could hear them slaves being whipped at night and yelling, "Pray, Master, Pray," begging him not to beat them.*

# 2

## 1861 TO 1878:

# CIVIL WAR, COWBOYS, AND THE WILD WEST

*Other slaves would run away and come to Major Odom's place and ask his slaves for something to eat. My mama would get word to bring them food, and she'd start out to where they were hiding, and she'd hear the hounds and the runaway slaves would have to go on without nothing to eat.*

This narrative may indicate that there was a route through Johnson County that escaping slaves used to reach Mexico or the Indian tribes. (In the preceding narrative, the word *slave* has been substituted for a derogatory racial term.)

In the 1860 census, Simeon Odom was a forty-one-year-old Methodist Clergyman who owned a farm of 1262 acres. The native Mississippian listed three slaves and produced one bale of cotton with his major crop being Indian corn. No "Sims" is listed among the slave owners in 1860, but he may have arrived with the many who came during the war.

## The Right to Secede

Were it not for a Southern sympathizer named General Twiggs, the Civil War might have begun in Texas. Two months before Fort Sumter was attacked, the U.S. armory and garrison at San Antonio was surrounded by Texan secessionists. Twiggs turned over the Federal arms and supplies, resigned his commission, and soon joined the Confederate Army.

After Fort Sumter was attacked in 1861, Federal soldiers were gradually recalled from frontier forts in the states which joined the Confederacy. In February 1861, Texas citizens voted in a referendum of 46,129 to 14,697 to secede from the Union. The legislature acted on March 2, 1861.

A number of families from Johnson County were among 120 wagons and as many as 500 voters returning north across the ferries at Coffee's Trading House at Preston and Colbert's Ferry on the Red River. Spies sent among them said that they were "returning north to their old homes having failed in the ballot box."

Among others who chose to return north rather than be forced into the Confederate service was Campbell Dickson. In 1858 "Cam" had driven a flock of sheep to Texas with several other shepherds hoping to establish a ranch in the West. After three difficult yet profitable years of shepherding in Hill and Bosque Counties, he'd had enough. He, like Sam Houston, felt strongly that the breaking up of the Union should never occur and besides it was getting a little too "hot" in Texas for him:

*Saturday, August 4, (1860)*

*A man by the name of Black, who had committed several murders and depredations, and who had fired the town a few days ago, was caught . . . When the prisoner reached this neighborhood, he was identified as a man who had murdered young Barnes, whose father had sworn vengeance on him. A man was sent to let Mr. Barnes know that the desperado was a prisoner here. Early the next morning an old gray haired man rode into Hillsboro. Learning that Black was in jail, he secured an ax, took with him his gun, went to the jail, knocked the door in, and discharged both barrels of his gun into the poor cuss's side. There have been no less than ten men hung near here in less than a month besides those strung up at Dallas and Waxahachie. A young gentleman of my acquaintance was recently murdered—a sheep man. Never has there been so much theft and robbery committed in Texas. The summer has been very hot. The thermometer has been, for many days 110 and 112. I am in for a change . . . Cam.*

Campbell Dickson sold his sheep a short time after Texas seceded, escaped from the vigilantes and set out alone on a lonely journey north carrying in his belt all the gold from the sale of his sheep. Upon reaching New York he volunteered and was mustered into the service as a second Lieutenant of Company I, Ninth New York Cavalry.

Johnson County voted 50 against and 500 for Texas to secede from the Union—well above the state average. By comparison Tarrant County voted for secession by a majority of only 27 out of 800 polled. Most local citizens were not slave owners; in Texas only about 10 percent of the population owned slaves which was the same percentage found in Johnson County. The economies of most Southern states were based on cotton production and huge profits were made from the money invested in slaves by a relatively few citizens. Yet the remaining population offered their wealth and lives to fight for the right of their state, or "country" as they called it, to keep the institution of slavery a local or state issue. On June 3, 1861 the Johnson County Police (Commissioners) Court recognized that:

*. . . war now exists between the United States and the Confederate States and the President of the former Republic is raising a large army for the purpose of invading our country . . . Johnson County is situated near the northwestern frontier of this State and it is without arms with which the people could defend their homes from the invader . . . our enemies will endeavor to bring on the*

*inhabitants of these frontiers the merciless Indians savages whose known rule of warfare is an undistinquished destruction of all ages, sexes, and conditions: & . . . Johnson County ought to be armed for the emergency: qualified voters . . . may express by ballot whether they are willing for the court shall levy a tax . . . for the purpose of arming the county.*

The commissioners organized two battalions of home guards under the authority of an act of the Texas Legislature, February 15th, 1858. The battalions, made up of six cavalry companies of citizen volunteers in Johnson County, were gradually absorbed into other commands and sent to the war front states.

### First Battalion

Johnson County Independent Mounted Infantry Companies:
Grand View Cavalry—Grand View Mar. 30, 1861
Grand View Mounted Infantry—Grand View Mar. 30, 1861

### Second Battalion

Johnson County Home Guards Companies:
Rock Creek Guards—at Rendezvous May 25, 1861
Johnson Cavalry—Buchanan Armory June 3, 1861
Stockton Cavalry—Buchanan Armory June 3, 1861
Alvarado Rifle Company—Alvarado Armory June 15, 1861

*When . . . Texas seceded I joined the Southern cause and enlisted in the Confederate Army for three years, or during the war. I was in Captain H. G. Bruce's Company H., Col. T. C. Bass's Regiment, Twentieth Texas Cavalry . . . Then we marched off leaving our loved ones not knowing whether we would ever see them again. Some of our company never lived to return.*—Abe Onstott.

Joseph McClure said:

*January 15, 1862 . . . I joined the army and went to war in Company A, 18th Texas Cavalry, Dasher's and Granbury's Brigades . . . Mustang (Buffalo) Springs where Cleburne now is was our cavalry drilling grounds.*

A grand Fourth of July picnic and dance was held for the departing soldiers of Childress's Company in Stone's Brigade at Camp Henderson. *The coffee was made in great washpots: and all the night before, the negroes had been at the grounds barbecuing the beef. There were roasting ears and all manner of good things to eat . . . I remember the long teams of Mexican carts, by droves, loading wheat for the Mexican government. . . . in January, 1862 . . . a Mexican train of carts was there (in Alvarado) and we Confederates took all their revolvers from them . . . When my company had formed to start to*

Campbell Dickson (1836–1911), not wishing to fight against the Union, escaped from pro-secession vigilantes in Hill County and set out alone on a lonely journey back North. Upon reaching New York he volunteered for service and eventually became a captain. "Cam" was in many battles including Gettysburg, where his "company fired the first shot, lost the first man that was killed, and took the first prisoner and Captain Dickson himself was so severely wounded in the face, thigh, and hand that after his dismissal from the hospital, he was ordered to be honorably discharged to recuperate his health." After the war he returned to Texas, bought out a Cleburne hardware store in 1878, and ran Dickson's Hardware which was among the first stores to bring barbed wire to Texas. (Cleburne Public Library)

*war and was circling around the Balch house for our farewell to friends and relatives, Miss Martha made us a fine talk, and she presented to our company a handsome silk flag of her own make. Not over fifteen out of 126, that she hoped to return did so.*—Joseph McClure.

### The Soldier's Farewell

*I've left my home and friends to go*
*Where the blood from bravest hearts will flow*
*Where the cannons roar on the field of strife*
*And many a brave man parts with life.*
*To fight for my country in deep distress.*
*May God my efforts bless.*

Howell A. Rayburn was twenty-four years old when he rode into Des Arc, Arkansas, early in 1862 with Parson's Twelfth Texas Cavalry, CSA. The Confederates planned to transport troops by boat down the White River. Rayburn was slight of stature, weighing less than one hundred pounds, and had shoulder-length blond hair. After arriving in Des Arc, he was stricken with "malignant fever" and remained when the other troops were transported. When he recovered in 1863, he could not rejoin his unit because of the position of Federal troops. Rayburn organized fifty "local boys of like adventurous spirit," aged sixteen to twenty, into a guerrilla force and he was elected their captain. These partisans were participants in Price's Raid into Missouri early in 1864 and harassed Union installations at DuVall's Bluff. One memorable evening the droll Rayburn, disguised as a woman, attended a Federal military ball on Christmas night at DuVall's Bluff. After dancing with a Union officer, he strolled to the corral, selected a fast horse, and drove away the mounts of the Federal garrison. (Layland Museum, Cleburne, Texas)

*. . . God bless the dear ones left behind*
*And O may (His angels) ever kind*
*Watch over and keep them from all harm*
*And shield (them) from adversities storm.*
*(Pray when at last this war is done)*
*(We'll) meet again in peace at home.*
Written for Miss Susan E. Shropshire
By Esq. D. N. Shropshire, Company C, 12th Texas Dragoons—Edited by the author
Elisa Jackson wrote to her husband George on June 28, 1863:

*My dear Husband.*
*. . . I told you a short time ago that Sam Kirkham was shot, but I learned since that it is a mistake. There are so many reports circulating that a person can't tell what to believe, but it was generally credited here as Kirkham acted so badly before he left. I wrote you just as I heard it. Mr. Hawkins was here today on his way to his command. Old Joe was with him going down to take Mr. Hawkins place. . . . Hawkins gave him 10 head of horses and 5 head of cattle which is everything on earth he posesses, and his note for 350 dollars . . . It looks hard for a person to give all they have for a substitute, but it is still worse to be deprived of a husband's society so long, and I am perfectly willing to give what we have for one for you if you can get one and are willing for one to stay in your place . . .*

Sam Kirkham had been a Texas Ranger scout under Captain M. T. Johnson who was against secession, but Johnson was willing to accept a commission as an officer in the Confederate Army. "Tate" Johnson took his men to Richmond to receive his commission, but he was rejected after his opinions became known to Jeff Davis. The men in Johnson's Command were assigned to another. This may have been another reason Sam threw the fuss that nearly cost him his life. Texas Governor Sam Houston was also against secession and attempted to keep Texas in the Union, but was deposed from office and died in 1863, with his son enlisted in the Confederacy. Houston's last words were "Texas . . . Texas . . . Margaret." Margaret was his last wife.

**The Woman's War: Confederate Money Wallpaper**
Sarah Ann Roberson "stayed on her farm all during her husband's absence, and after his death continued to manage the (160 acre) farm as long as she lived. The women often met together to work on clothing to be sent to the soldier husbands or sons . . . Mrs. Roberson taught a twenty-year-old neighbor girl to read and write so she could write to her soldier brother."

"The war added to the already trying life of the early frontier days . . . Before the war a number of things could be bought at the Alvarado and Grandview stores, where they had been hauled in ox wagons from Houston and other points . . . but during the war nothing could be bought; everything had to be produced at home." On many of the farms the women had to do men's work. "During the war Sarah had three slaves; two old women and a young boy to do the hardest tasks such as the plowing of the fields, the chopping, and the picking of the cotton. The eldest daughter would do the spinning while the four young boys would pick out the cotton seeds and the mother would do the weaving . . . Every housewife had her own spinning wheel and loom, for each household had to supply not only the clothes and linens for the family needs, but had to make everything that the soldiers wore; Their homespun clothes, their socks, and even their blankets." At one point she sent $50 to Dallas to purchase cotton cards and enough calico to make a dress for her fourteen-year-old daughter, Ellen. They looked after the milk and butter and growing all their food. They killed and tanned their beef hides with black jack (oak) bark to make shoes for the children and the slaves. "Because of her frugality and enterprise when the war was over, she had enough Confederate money to paper the house!"

John Ellis, a slave who was born near Cleburne in 1852, recalled farm work from the slave's point of view:

*I've done all kinds of work which it takes to run a farm. My boss he had only fourteen slaves and what was called a small farm, compared with the big plantation. After our days work we would sit up at night and pick the seed out of the cotton so they could spin it into thread. Then we went out and got different kinds of bark and boiled it to get dye for the thread before it was spun into cloth. The children just had long shirts and slips made out of this homespun, and we made our shoes out of rawhide, and Lordy! they were so hard we would have to warm them by the fire and grease them with tallow to ever wear them at all.*

While the men were gone to war, for their protection the women of the Myers settlement would all go to one log house to work in each other's company. John Myers's wife, Elizabeth Campbell Myers, died while he was off at war, leaving two small children.

At intervals men from each regiment went on leave back home to pick up clothing and supplies produced by the families and bring them to the men in the war-front states.

Richard Beasley was a Kentuckian who had moved to Missouri. He enlisted in the Confederate Army. After coming home on leave he found his wife and family in a tent, with their home burned and livestock gone. He went after the Yankee plunderers and killed several before he was captured. Sentenced to be hung, he jumped the guard during the night before his hanging. After running many miles through an eight-inch snow in his underwear he arrived at his home so badly frostbitten that his legs were black up to his knees. He and his wife Prazda, with little preparation, headed west to Texas. Along the way

Burton Marchbanks, a private in the First Texas Partisan Rangers, received a neck wound during the Battle of Honey Springs in Indian Territory. He was superficially treated by a Federal physician and sent home. He lingered on for six months, bedfast, and died with pneumonia February 12, 1864, in Cleburne.

His wife of fourteen years, Mary Emiline Vance, had woven the material and sewn his uniform. At her husband's death, the grieving widow cleaned and folded the beloved frock coat, the shirt, trousers, gloves, and socks and carefully stored them in a trunk. Marchbanks' wonderfully preserved uniform is on display at the Layland Museum, as well as his portrait, discharge paper, and a letter from his commander. (Layland Museum, Cleburne, Texas)

she treated him by pouring buckets of water over his legs. Their mules gave out in Johnson County and they settled where they would later buy 100 acres of land. Not long after, he was arrested and taken to Waxahachie on charges of desertion from the Confederate army. When the officers he was brought before saw his legs and feet, they formally discharged him for physical disabilities.

Elbert G. Billingsley was one of the pioneer Billingsley boys who came to Texas in 1843. After the Civil War Elbert always carried a folded letter from his wife written on October 18, 1863:

*Elbert I want you to try to git a discharge and if you cannot git a discharge try to git a furlow and if the officers are so mean that they will not let you come home in no way I want you to give me leav to come and see you.*

1872 portrait of Col. Barzillai Jefferson Chambers (December 5, 1817–September 16, 1895). At the age of twenty Chambers joined the Kentucky volunteers in the Army of the Republic of Texas. He was commissioned a captain by his uncle, Gen. Thomas J. Chambers. Arriving too late for San Jacinto, he was honorably discharged after one year active campaigning in Texas.

Col. B. J. Chambers, the "Father of Cleburne," was a surveyor for Robertson Colony. Stephen F. Austin's third empresario grant in 1831 included the part of Johnson County that drained to the Brazos River. The question of authority for control of the district was unsettled. Chambers first surveyed in the Johnson County area as a Robertson Surveyor in 1841 and 1847. The Robertson Colony and later Robertson County eventually administered the land between the Trinity and Brazos Rivers.

He became a surveyor for the Robertson Land District in 1839. In 1841 on a survey expedition, he first came to the area which later became Johnson County. At Alvarado's future location, his group was spotted by a band of Indians who indicated they were friendly.

He came to live here in 1855 after acquiring considerable land in the vicinity. He left in 1859 and moved back to Johnson County in 1865 after the close of the War Between the States. He and Col. William F. Henderson offered to donate half the lots on a hundred acres of land to the county for site purposes. After the election resulted in favor of the present county seat, Colonel Chambers continued to donate lots to aid in the founding of schools as well as churches.

In 1876 he co-founded the Greenbacker organization which advocated the radical idea of the Federal Government printing paper money not backed or based on gold or silver. In 1880 he ran as their vice-presidential candidate. He also studied law and obtained a license to practice. He followed, at different times, stock raising, merchandising, banking, farming, and looking after his property interests. At one time he was the largest taxpayer in Johnson County. (Dr. Jack Burton)

*You may think me foolish for making this request but I tell you I want to see you once more and I no you canot live long if you stay thare. And if I git down sick again like I have been I will dispair of ever giting to see you again . . . I had a spell of sickness this summer and still have a huring in my back that I can hardly git about. My body has sufered a grait deal senc you left home and my mind has sufered more than my poor body . . . Dear Elbert I want you to write me a leter as soon as you git it and let me no whether you are ever coming home or not. O do try yore best to git to come home to stay this winter any how I will send you a pair of socks by Mr. Jobe I will write no more at this time only I remain yore true and affecionet wife until death. Emiline S. Billingsley to her dear companion Elbert G. Billingsley*

"She died before he got home . . . On the night she died, even though they were hundreds of miles apart, he dreamed she stood beside his bed, where he was ill in an army camp."

In 1863 the Confederate Congress compelled the funding of payments to bond holders with Confederate paper money instead of gold as promised. Also the Texas Constitution was changed on December 14, 1863, making it easier to convict Union sympathizers under the "Overt Act," giving new definitions of the crime. The penalty was death—few accused ever escaped.

*(T)here is a good many long faces in consequence of the Confederate tax. Pa says all the objection he has to the law it is not heavy enough as some men in this country have been gagging at the Confederate money, and he wants the tax heavy enough to make them smack their mouths to get it to pay their taxes.*—Elisa Jackson.

*Buchanan was the county seat, I think it was early in 1864 that Confederate money, which was of little value, became so abundant in the county treasury that the county court decided to distribute it, prorata, to the families of soldiers. This duty the court assigned to me, which I faithfully performed refusing to accept any compensation for the same. To give some idea of the worthlessness of Confederate money at that time, Some man on the Brazos . . . made twelve gallons of brandy from Mustang grapes, brought it to Buchanan on court day and retailed it for $100 a quart. $4,800 for twelve gallons of mustang brandy!*

*I saw Zilpha, a daughter of Uncle Joe Shaw, now the wife of George W. Stephens, give ten dollars in gold for ten yards of calico, such as now (1894) can be bought for five or ten cents a yard. But calico at the time was a rare and scarce article in Johnson County.*—J. G. Woodson.

Billingsley's $400 registered bond paid to the Confederate Treasury in Dallas, June 17, 1864. (JCA)

A Buchanan store journal showed the cost of cotton cards rose to $25 by the end of the war. Cow hides sold for 10 cents throughout the war while it cost $5 to have a cow killed and dressed in 1862. Quinine, a basic frontier medicine, was embargoed by the North during the war. In the South its price rose to $16 an ounce, its weight in gold. Deprivation of medicine brought great hardship on the populace.

## Protecting the Frontier

The Texas legislature declared the part of Johnson County west of the Brazos, "frontier." Frontier counties were to raise home guards to defend against the raiding Indians and possible Northern invasion. Companies originally designated as home guards were eventually mustered into regular Confederate service leaving the frontier unprotected.

*The militia meets the 6th of July (1863) at Buchanan for the purpose of organization, and when organized are disbanded until needed. The governor, I learn, has called for ten thousand men to be ready for service with a short warning.*—Elisa Jackson.

During and after the Civil War, the settled frontier ebbed back towards the settlements in Johnson County. Comanche and Kiowa raided all the counties to the west and even parts of Johnson.

## Civil War and the Indian Nation

On the frontier of Texas and in the Indian Territory, leaders of the Five Civilized Tribes attempted to keep their people out of "the White Man's War."

John Ross was a Cherokee chief, more Scots than Cherokee, and a slave owner. He reflected the opinion of his friend, Sam Houston, that the Indian Nations should stay neutral in the fray, but by 1862 he folded to political pressures. Cherokee and Creek Confederate units fought alongside Texas Partisans from Johnson, Dallas, Fannin, and Cooke Counties.

Confederate States of America $500 bond from the estate of Dorothy Kelly Richards, granddaughter of Colonel B. J. Chambers. This bond, along with others amounted to $1500. Note, only one coupon for $30 was ever clipped for redemption (lower right corner). (AC)

The Federal government made null and void treaties even with Loyalist Indians during Reconstruction. The Civil War was a nail in the coffin of tribal organization and land ownership, even for the Five Civilized Tribes.

José Maria and his Caddos had been residents of Johnson County for many years just prior to the war. In keeping with their 1846 treaty with the U.S., the tribe attempted to remain at peace and loyal to the

U.S. Government after the war began. Tragically at this critical time during the summer of 1862, José Maria (Aasch) died. He had been the primary chief among the Caddo tribes for twenty-seven years. Without his thoughtful leadership, his remnant people were attacked by the Kiowa and Comanche while fleeing from the Confederates. However, the Caddo survived the ordeal of the Civil War and remained intact as a tribe.

## The Soldier's Dilemma

*To: George W. Jackson,*

*I have come to the conclusion that this war will last a long time as I see no hopes of peace. You have been in the service a year yesterday, and I would not be deprived of the pleasure of my home and your company for no amount of money or property. One year ago tomorrow I left my own dear home which has been the source of so much enjoyment to me, and I wonder how long it will be before I can enjoy those endearments of home and your company again. Oh I fear it will be a long time . . . It makes my soul sick to compare those days to my present ones . . . Oh if I could only see you this evening . . . May the good Lord protect you through the dark hours and days that we may meet again soon is the prayer of your loving Elisa.*

Written for the use of Miss Susan Shropshire and her sister Parmalee E. Barnes.

Little Rock

*June 1st 1862*

*My Dear Nieces'*

*After my love and respects to you I will inform you that I received your kind favor both on the same sheet which afforded me great pleasure to hear from you. In Parmalee's letter she spoke of brother's death which the boys told me of when they came from home. The sad information gave me great pain to hear of the sad misfortune that befell the family, but God says all things for the best and death is a thing we all have to yield to not with standing it grieved my inmost soul to hear of the death of my beloved Brother. I was very much helped up when I was at your house and he told me that he was going to see his old vetrand father and I was so much helped up with the idea of Susan going to stay with her Aunt Matilda till I would get back home, which I fear now will be a long time for this consript law will force us all in service for three years. It grieves my heart to think that I have to leave my hearts delight. To think that I will have to stay away from her I dearly love for three years and especially when I can hear so often of the Indians are all around her but I will pray for her welfare and*

*preservation from the ruthless savage foe, but my Bible teaches me that God will provide.*

*I want you all to do the best you can now whilst this war lasts and if we are spared to get home I hope you will all move down to where I live and then we will all live in happiness together . . .* —Benjamin N. Shropshire. Lieutenant, 15th Texas Cavalry, Johnson's Brigade.

## Our Beloved Horses

As the war lengthened, local cavalry troops were dismounted from their "beloved horses," a circumstance which was greatly protested and resented. Uncle Charlie Gilmore was a hunter and trapper in the area now just southeast of Keene. "He always wore a suit of green just the color of the tall prairie grass which covered the prairies . . . (His) dearest possession was his horse, Starlight. When the war broke out many came to him to buy Starlight to ride to the front. Repetedly he refused to sell him: but finally when William Roberson had trouble finding a horse suitable for the long ride, Uncle Charlie offered him Starlight." William rode off to war and died in Louisiana of illness after enlisting in Childress's company of Stone's Brigade at Camp Henderson.

*July 4th 1862*

*Duvaull's bluff, Prairie County, Ark.*

*My Beloved Sister,*

*After three days and two nights march we arrived at this point on the White River to meet the enemy's gunboats and land forces. We reached this place yesterday evening, and today is the day we expected the fight would come off, the gun boats being some 10 miles below. We received news this morning that they commenced falling back as soon as we arrived. It was thought that they had fallen back to get reinforcements. If they have, the battle will come off in a few days. We are lying in readiness at a moments warning sis, that is the rumor. I know not whether it is reliable or not. We are not allowed to know anything about the movements. For what we know, we may be called into a battle this evening or tonight, for I think the prospect is good for a fight immediately. No man is allowed to leave camp, and when we go out to graze our horses the whole command goes together with our arms and ammunition. We have to sleep with our saddles under our heads and guns either in our arms or beside us. We have not got but one commissioned officer with us and that is Neal. Whit and Haley are both sick. I know not where Barnes is. Sis, We are nearly all wore out. During our march we got only two meals during the march, and six ears of corn for our beloved horses, but if we have a chance we will give them a good fight. They out number us but we can whale them out. Sis, when we want a change of diet from corn bread and poor Arkansas beef with our salt we take a quart of parched corn when we can get it for desert. We came through a prairie five miles from here where we go to graze. When we came to it, It seemed so much like Texas it cheered every Texan so much they all raised a shout, the prairie being some 6 or 8 miles in length and 4 miles width. We hollered while the Gen'l made us hush. We all feel like we was getting home once more. Write soon sis and often for Gods sake. I do not know whether you can read this or not for my pen is no account.*

—Written to sister Susan Shropshire staying near Grandview, Texas by James Shropshire a "Musician Private."

Green Shropshire had gone off to war along with his three sons, James, David, and John, and his brother Benjamin. Green and his sons . . . "enlisted in Company C, of the 12th Texas, the first regiment that left the county. Before the year was out Green Shropshire became ill, and died shortly after reaching home on a sick leave . . ." All three boys survived the war to come back home. David, who was twenty when he enlisted, became a prominent doctor. John, the youngest, "was wounded by a minié ball at Yellow Bayou, Louisiana, May 18, 1864, taken prisoner and carried to Helena, Arkansas, where he was placed in a hospital. Seven months later while he was on his way to prison Camp Douglas, John made his escape by the aid of a federal soldier who had become his friend, and went with his friend, N. V. McDowell, to his parents' home at O'dell, Illinois. Here John Shropshire fell in love with the young sister, Susan McDowell and was married to her. In the mean time John Shropshire's family thought that he had been killed and buried at Yellow Bayou, until after the cessation of hostilities, when a message could reach his parents." The couple moved back to farm here in 1871.

## Providing for War

Charles Barnard, friend of the Indians and most settlers, built a mill on the Paluxy River during the war. The local citizens asked him to place gun slots in the walls so they could fort up there during Indian raids. Charles acknowledged the need and provided slots in the thick rock walls—there were a growing number of attacks and deaths in the Brazos River Valley.

Charles, a native of Connecticut, owned slaves but had been reluctant to support this war. The county commissioners threatened to confiscate Barnard's mill for the use of the citizens to make needed food, clothing, and other

supplies. He made the mill available to the people and sold it soon after the war. He and his wife Juana moved back to Barnard's Trading House—their honeymoon home. During the war Charles sold a large portion of his land for Confederate paper money. His financial condition worsened as he and his wife grew older until they were forced to sell the old Trading House and acreage.

*Government is pressing beeves in this country, Government agents hire hands and go and gather a drove and then leaves the mark and brands at the clerks office in each county, (see road papers, page 80) and a man can prove his mark and brand and get a certificate that so many of his cattle was taken in a certain drove, and then take the certificate to Dr. Lightfoot, the agent of this district and (get) pay for his cattle 30 dollars a head is all the law allows. People generally don't grumble about the pressing of the cattle . . .* —Elisa Jackson.

J. P. Scurlock owned a general merchandise store in Grandview before the war. Scurlock, "a Confederate sympathizer" attempted to deliver a herd of beef cattle to a Confederate camp in Louisiana. He was captured and died in a federal prison.

### Orphan Boy Joseph McClure Goes to War and Finds a Mother:

*On Jan. 18, 1862 at Eagle Ford in Dallas County our 18th Texas Cavalry was organized under H. H. Darnell as Colonel. The Dallas city people there presented him with our Regimental Flag.*

*(David) Mitchell had one son Lafayette. He served in Co. A, 18th Texas Cavalry with me . . . Our first march was to Pike's Works in Indian Territory on the Blue River. While there we had many cases of sickness. I for one had the measels . . . I was given up to die, so nothing was done for me . . . they had my coffin made and set beside my bunk waiting for the last breath to leave. But a change came to my fever and Lafayette Mitchell . . . died and was buried in my box, and I am yet here telling the news . . . Afterward we were ordered to Brownsville, Arkansas and had several hot skirmishes with the Federal Cavalry around there and at Cotton Plant . . . Soon after I lost my horse the entire command was ordered to Little Rock, Ark. and all were dismounted and ordered to Arkansas Post for proper winter quarters.*

*After Gen. Grant and Sherman failed to capture Vicksburg they turned their ninety thousand army with their Iron Clad Fleets attention to us and came up the Arkansas River without any trouble to the post. They shot our guns and forts down, killed our artillery, horses, and surrounding area and fought with us for three days before we surrendered Jan. 11th, 1863. We were in our* works and I used three guns while the loading was done by others in the ditch . . . it got so hot I could not hold it in my hands at Arkansas Post. When our white flag went up my orderly sergent Ples Davis snatched our regimental colors from the staff and concealed it in his clothes carrying it all through prison and exchanged back April 6, 1863 at City Point, Virginia . . . After (prisoner) exchange our regimental army was transferred from Virginia to Tulahoma and Wartrace. After fighting there a consolidation was made when the 17th and 18th Texas Cavalry dismounted and were consolidated as one and placed in Dasher's (and Granbury's) Texas Brigade in Gen. Pat Cleburne's Division Army of Tennessee . . . While there Ples Davis brings out our Dallas flag and restaffs it and we fought near a hundred battles under it in the Chickamauga, Chatanooga, and Atlanta campaigns . . . I was in the front of eighteen hard fought battles. Us Texans were always lucky to get in the front it seemed . . . it fell a second time July 21, 1864 where I and my entire company was shot down the second time . . . When in that (Atlanta) battle on the morning . . . just a few moments before our Captain William Corn was killed, I received two wounds from a cross fire the enemy had on us. This ended my service and I lay in the hospital of wounded in Griffen, Georgia till I got a cripplers furlough for 30 days.

At that time Mrs. G. M. Garlick a noble woman of Senoria, Georgia called with her buggy and pleaded for a Texan that could not get home that she might take him home and care for him. I was the lucky boy and she proved to be a mother to me. She did not allow me to need or want for anything until July 15, 1865 when I started for Alvarado, Texas on two crutches. She gave me money, clothes and an extra lot of bandages for dressing my wounds. The railroads being destroyed in many places I had to walk quite a ways to get home. I landed in Alvarado on August 15, 1865 just a month making the trip. On the way I was scorned at many places.—Joseph McClure.

### Home at Last

[At] the battle of Prairie Grove. There the men fell thick and fast, leaving their brave wives at home to care for the little ones alone. I was in several close calls; was in places I believe that if my head had been on either shoulder it would have been shot off, for the heat of the bullets would burn my ears . . . At last when the war was all over I was glad to go home to meet my dear wife and (five) little ones at my cabin door all in good health. It was a happy day . . . I was down to bedrock . . . but thanks to God for having that much . . . what a sad thought to remember so many homes where no man came back to embrace his loved ones.—Abraham H. Onstott, 1912, first Sheriff of Johnson County.

The local veterans who returned after the war were proud that a number equal to the total eligible male population of the county had served. Of the 1,100 eligible men who served, including young teenage boys and older men, over 300 died. When you combine the dead with those injured who survived their wounds, the total number grows to the staggering amount of over 50 percent casualties to Johnson's County's male population.

## Camp Henderson Becomes Cleburne

During the Civil War and its aftermath, some of the worst Indian raids in Texas history took place. The formation of Hood and Somervell Counties was influenced by the wish of citizens to remain conveniently close to home during Reconstruction and the Indian Wars—it was a long way to Buchanan. Close to a third of the county's land was taken to form Hood (1866) and what would later be Somervell (1875) Counties. Johnson County's seat of government was moved closer to the center of the land that remained.

On March 23, 1867, the location of Camp Henderson was chosen for the new Johnson County seat. A name change was discussed at a picnic at the new location. The name selection's committee included veterans of the late war. Samuel G. Graham suggested to B. J. Chambers, the name of Cleburne. Cleburne being the valiant commander of the battalion that many had fought under. The Texans who served under Cleburne were so stirred by their memories that the vote was unanimous. Confederate President Jeff Davis ranked Cleburne's leadership, skill and conduct as a general behind only Robert E. Lee and Stonewall Jackson.

With no major springs, streams, or trees many citizens of Buchanan were relieved by the move to the centrally located Camp Henderson which abounded with these essential elements. After the vote to move, W. M. Wilhite was appointed "to watch and protect the timber on the donation for the town of Cleburne, to prevent any one from cutting the same." Many buildings in Buchanan, some say including the log jail, were moved as a "city on wheels" across the prairie to Camp Henderson. Other people stayed on to benefit from trade the Chisholm Trail brought as it followed the fort supply road down the main street of Buchanan. By the 1920s it was noted that only one business remained.

## Refugee Caravans

A different type of settler was arriving in Texas during and after the war; many came not only seeking opportunity but out of desperation. "The years from 1870 to 1876 witnessed a great immigration to Johnson County, from the southeastern states and to all this part of the Texas. And it is surprizing how soon the flocks and herds disappeared before the advance of the man, the plow and the hoe."

Many Southerners from war-torn states brought their slaves to Johnson County during the war in a futile effort to protect their human property from emancipation. The number of blacks living here doubled during the war. Joseph McClure said that "When I returned from the war this country was over run by refugee negroes brought here by the thousands, which changed this country almost into a solid cotton country, worked mostly by negroes."

Bill Bell had been sold away from his mother as a child. In the aftermath of the Civil War, a compassionate family let him hitch a ride to Texas in their wagon. The trip was very dangerous for black refugees. Along the way, there were some areas where, if blacks were found, they would be harassed, assaulted, or even killed. It was also becoming dangerous for blacks and whites to travel together. Young Bill was hidden down in the wagon for the long journey. On the trip there were several close calls, but they made it unhurt to Johnson County. After arriving here, Bill was overjoyed when, by chance, he was reunited with his mother. Bill went on to buy land and live out his life in the Nathan community.

Newspapers of the time commented on "Colored Immigrants," coming through from the old South, looking to "secure cheap lands, (to) form some sort of colony and engage in agricultural pursuits. They say that there will be a number of other families to follow them if they report favorably of the country . . . They were a very clever, orderly-looking set of people . . . to all appearance, an industrious class and have some money."

Many groups arrived in caravans during this time—Johnson County was a jumping off point for areas north, south, and west. Larger roads from the East played out here. Settlers would then break off and scatter their separate ways. One tragic family arrived on the Cleburne square in 1869—only the children were alive—the mother and father were found dead in the wagon.

## Reconstruction Courts and Vigilantes

There was a time on the advancing frontier when in each newly settled territory the law was yet to be recog-

Major-General Patrick Ronayne Cleburne was named by Jefferson Davis the "Stonewall Jackson of the West." Cleburne's leadership was described by Robert E. Lee as "a meteor shining from a clouded sky." At Missionary Ridge during the Battle of Lookout Mountain, Cleburne's regiments held out against the best that Sherman could throw at him. At the Battle of Franklin, Tennessee, Cleburne led his men into the fray after his horse was shot out from under him. With his cap raised and sword sweeping, Cleburne cried, "Follow me!" and moved his Texans and Arkansans toward retreating Union troops. No one alive after the battle saw him fall; his body was found on the battlefield six paces from the enemy line. More Confederate generals died in this battle than any other in the Civil War. With his military council protesting, General Hood sent his command into a furious battle where twelve of his generals became casualties on November 30, 1864, six of these died. Napoleon lost ten of his generals at Waterloo by comparison.

Pat Cleburne never traveled further than the Mississippi. Born in County Cork, Ireland, on St. Patrick's Day, March 17, 1828, Cleburne immigrated to America in 1849. He established a law practice in Helena, Arkansas. He is said to be the only Confederate general who had served as an enlisted man in the British army. Cleburne proposed the freeing of slaves in exchange for their enlistment and service in the Confederate Army. He led his division of the Army of the Tennessee against great odds in the battles of Shiloh, Perryville, Murfreesboro, Chickamauga, Missionary Ridge, Kenesaw Mountain, Peachtree Creek, Atlanta, Jonesboro, and Franklin. (Carter House Museum, Franklin, Tennessee)

Eula Ann (Nana) Bell Slaton was the daughter of Bill Bell, who was born in slavery and separated from his mother. Bill Bell came to Texas with a white family who hid him in a wagon to protect him from harm. After coming to Texas he and his mother were reunited by chance. Bell bought land in Nathan from his son-in-law, W. G. Slaton. Bill Bell would sit on his porch with a spy glass and a rifle across his lap. He could see anyone coming for miles. Eula was part Indian. (Charlee McNeil)

nized. John Billingsley and Joseph McClure both commented that in the early settlements there was, "very little law" and that "law wasn't needed." Many new arrivals had seen the law's uneven hand, some were fugitives and had little or no use for established law. Every town had at least one sharp-eyed, watchful citizen who did not welcome questions.

After establishing local government and courts in the 1850s, the rule of law was to ebb and flow. During the Civil War the local processes of civil and criminal justice became luxuries for which there was no time. People knew that under the U.S. Constitution, they themselves were the government. But the exact legal status of local elected officials was in question. Most were removed from office under Reconstruction.

Under Reconstruction measures, local courts were disbanded and disorganized. The District Court met only twice a year. For seven years, between mid-1866 and 1873, there were no regular elections held for offices. During the first session of court after the Civil War, the provisional government commissioned and appointed a man whose last name was Scott as judge, James Hiner, clerk, and Joseph Shaw, sheriff. On June 25, 1866, an election was held with J. R. McKinsey elected judge, James Hiner was clerk, and E. M. Heath, sheriff. Heath was removed April 19, 1869, because of his Confederate service. The next election for local offices was on

service. The next election for local offices was on December 2, 1873.

During the Civil War, the backlog of cases grew; many legal matters were continued on the docket for years. The laws and statutes of limitation had been suspended between January 28, 1861 and March 13, 1870. Many volunteers had rushed off to war, leaving hastily on borrowed horses. Good mounts were hard to find and those who had them were asked repeatedly to sell them. An oustanding horse could make a difference of life and death in battle. Some horses were taken by anxious recruits without the asking. Upon returning home they found themselves welcomed by the sheriff holding "capias"(warrant) papers on them. The verdicts of even minor local cases required provisional Texas Governor Davis to sign and seal appeals for reduction of sentence. This situation in the courts caused great frustration among the people.

With little or no money in the country, the courts and attorneys were accepting in payment whatever the people would offer. J. C. Terrell said, "I remember collecting a good fee in peltry, buffalo and other hides which our merchants had no trouble in exchanging for money." The courts were still accepting whiskey and other "stock in trade." Another liquid that was accepted as currency was quinine. Squire Terrell also took a fee in former CSA "French" quinine that was paid him by a Buchanan saloon keeper for legal defense. Druggist Samuel J. Darcy (see page 94, ill. top of page), a wounded veteran, helped Terrell sell it off at $16 an ounce.

Federal troops and carpetbaggers would, in the name of the United Sates, search out and confiscate Confederate supplies, equipment, or arms brought back to Johnson County by the men returning home. Sam Myers was forced to pay the Federals for a wagon that had been part of the CSA Trans-Mississippi Department. His only involvement had been to finance the purchase for a returning soldier. Abernathy says:

*After the war the patrolling Yankee soldiers brought hardship to the settlers; the Myers children called them "jayhawkers." One day Margaret Myers saw the dreaded "jayhawkers" coming, she crawled under the bed to hide. The searching soldiers spied her and yelled, 'Come out, you little devil.' Tremblingly with fear Margaret crawled out and got behind her mother.* Undoubtedly these soldiers were looking for items to confiscate or steal. Local folklore has it that Belle Starr's family lived along the Chisholm Trail in Johnson County. They were harrassed and eventually driven off by Yankee soldiers, however some say a direct descendant still lives here.

CLEBURNE CHRONICLE—January 16, 1869: *Eight to ten soldiers from Jacksboro came to the home of W. A. Robinson, a quiet, orderly citizen living three miles from town and proceeded to treat him in the most inhuman manner, abusing him more like savages, than civilized men. He was struck several times over the head with a pistol, inflicting a wound 2 1/2 inches long and as deep as the skull and several other contusions and punching him in different parts of the body with the muzzles of their pistols . . . When Mrs. Robinson begged for her husband, this inhuman officer answered her with curses. They then proceeded to search the house, as they said for arms. In jerking a quilt off the bed, they hurled Mrs. Robinson's sleeping babe in the middle of the floor. Finally they started carrying with them a new fine hat belonging to Mr. Robinson. When about 25 or 30 yards of the house, Mr. Robinson made his escape running down the side of his garden palings. One of the soldiers getting in between Mr. Robinson and the rest of his party, was mistaken for Robinson and fired 5 or 6 times, three of the shots taking effect, and mortally wounding him . . . We have since learned that the pretext for the arrest was that Robinson had killed a Mr. Billard, since the war in Buchanan in a personal encounter and that the authorities had refused to notice the matter because Billard was a Union man. But this is not the case. Billard was intensely Southern . . . The grand jury failed to find a true bill, upon the grounds that the act was committed in self-defense . . . Had he been even as guilty as was alleged, it would not have justified the treatment he received from his captors. In a military, as well as civil court, a man should be heard before he is Condemned.*

CLEBURNE CHRONICLE—July 24, 1869: *On Thursday last a squad of soldiers came to our town, with an order from the military authorities at Waco and took Johnson who was confined in our jail awaiting his trial for an assault with intent to kill, to Waco for safe keeping . . . Rumor says that the military have charges against him, and that he will not be brought back, but will be tried by military commission.*

CLEBURNE CHRONICLE—December 1869: *THE ELECTION—Passed off quietly, Although the groceries were all closed by military orders, liquor has been flowing pretty freely; but little drunkenness has been visable.—There has been a great indifference in regard to the election.*

Under Reconstruction most local residents were excluded from voting or holding office by the require-ment of an "iron-clad oath" swearing that they had not participated in the "Rebellion." Locally this was enforced from 1869 to 1873. During these dangerous times, the people occasionally took the law directly into their hands.

*. . . (T)he times were queer, peculiar and without precedent,* said Captain J. C. Terrell, a Fort Worth attorney, who regularly attended the court sessions of Johnson County. He described the days during and just after the Civil War: *We had a civil government in Texas, which existed only in name. The criminal law was much in the hands of vigilance committees . . . but I must say it was rarely abused. These vigilance Committees, (were) composed, as a rule, of the very best elderly men . . . In 1867, when a pocket pistol was the most important part of every Southern gentleman's attire . . . every man was a law unto himself . . . ordinary human life was held rather cheaply, lynch law, for aggravated offenses (and) for many reasons (was) necessarily and rightfully obtained. Justice did not travel with leaden feet, and taxes were nominal. Two crimes were never condoned—theft of horses and disturbances of religious worship, they were severely punished, without the benefit of clergy.*

## Gold Rush to Judgment

The circumstances of this peculiar period might help explain what happened to a young man named Tucker who stole a fortune in gold from Uncle Sammy Myers. Frances Abernathy tells the story:

*Colonel Myers was always ready to trust people until they proved themselves untrustworthy. He sold corn, wheat, and any needed provisions to the new settlers, refusing to take their notes and saying "If your word is not good, your note is worthless." In the fall of the year Colonel Myers would start the rounds to collect what his neighbors owed him. As there were no banks and no paper money was used in this part of the world at that time, he put the gold into shot sacks or stockings and hid them somewhere in the house. His older sons would freight products to market and bring gold back home.*

*Working for Colonel Myers shortly after the Civil War was a young man named Tucker whom he believed to be wholly trustworthy, but temptation came headlong upon the youth. He had fallen in love, and the girl of his fancy was moving away to quite another world. The young man needed some money so that he might accompany the object of his affections and guard her along the way. In a stocking in Mrs. Myers's trunk was a quantity of gold. The girl's mother was a widow, and if he could go along to protect them, he could surely win the affections of the daughter. So, quietly, earnestly, the young man told Colonel Myers that matters had come up to call him back to his home. He was paid off and took his departure a short time after the widow and her young daughter left.*

Tucker's rash actions in pursuing and courting the widow's daughter would soon have him pursued and courted by vigilantes.

*In a few days after moving he came back on the sly and at night carried three large trunks out of Col. Sam Myers house in the summer time while Myers and his wife were sleeping on the south porch in front of an open door. Tucker walked between them carrying the trunks out into the orchard. He broke them open and took about $700. He was gone for several days when uncle David Myers says to his wife that it could have been done by Cal Tucker as he had just been working there and knew how everything was. So Dave and Thomas J. Myers went horse back to Dallas and near there they happened to call on Mr. Tom Pollard and he had just a few days before sold Tucker a wagon and seven yoke of oxen for cash in gold . . . The next day the three men went on and caught Cal Tucker. He gave up at once, with his revolver in his hand, to the older sons of Sammy Myers. The wagon that he had bought with the stolen gold, the pistol, a violin, and $75 in gold were found with him.* After spending the evening in camp playing the fiddle they started for Johnson County the next morning. *On the way back Tucker escaped only to be recaptured. Upon taking the thief to what would be later College Hill, his capturers began to question their handing out punishment without a formal trial.*

Tucker heard them argue as he stood nervously teetering on the wagon bed, a hangman's loop stretched snug around his neck from a tree limb. He plead for his life as the discussion ensued. Suddenly, however, "Judge Lynch" overruled the objections and handed down his verdict. The order was that the verdict should be carried out immediately. The "gavel" came down, landing squarely on the back of the horse harnessed to the wagon. The reins whipped the horse off to a run leaving young Tucker "suspended."

The Myers boys' price for "justice" had been the taking of Tucker's life by an unlawful hanging of the guilty. In an ironic and curious twist of fate, the Myers would later pay a price for "justice," but this time the price would be the lawful hanging of the innocent.

## Vigilante Law and Disorder

In post-Civil War Texas there was a mistrust of the law. The rebellious Southern states suffered revenge and retaliation during Reconstruction. Northern oppression was personified in Federal troops wearing blue uniforms. Appointed Reconstruction government officials would hand out unjust punishment or fail to act at all. On the frontier, local officers of the law and courts were at times intimidated by powerful and notorious outlaw groups. Vigilante groups and posses formed to hand out needed reprisals and to protect communities from chaos.

As the Southern troops surrendered after the war, Ben Bickerstaff and his gang were among those who continued the war as a personal matter.

Both grudging and revengeful, they violently resisted Reconstruction efforts. Ben's short and deadly career came to an end in 1869 after terrorizing one particular town in Johnson County. The results in Alvarado for Ben and his gang were deadly.

Federals controlled Texas under military rule and stationed garrisons where needed. Post-war Texas was full of hard feelings and division. Ben served in the Eleventh Texas Cavalry, CSA. Legend has it that after the war he killed a hired black man who was beating a horse with a singletree. Ben was associated with the "Cullen M. Baker School of Bad Men" and had a large following in East Texas. At one time the Federals believed two or three hundred cooperated with him. His group had killed and tormented blacks and harassed carpetbaggers and skalawags in East Texas. Ben's outlaw gang overwhelmed Federal soldiers from Pilot Point led by Lieutenant James H. Sands of the Sixth Cavalry sent to subdue him at Sulphur Springs. A wagon train of Federal supplies was attacked in the spring of 1867. The mules were taken, the wagons drawn close together and the harness placed upon them; they were soon a smoking ruin. The gang surrounded a Federal troop and held them "holed up," for several days threatening to "fire the town." After that fiasco the Federals beefed up the military in East Texas, placed a reward of $1000 on Ben's head, and made it dangerous for Ben and his gang to remain. They scattered to the Texas frontier where there were fewer troops and they knew a few Confederate veterans. By the time Ben arrived in Johnson County, it is said he had become a regular outlaw, robbing and stealing at will, even from those loyal to the South.

## Ben Bickerstaff in Johnson County

While in Johnson County, Ben and his gang were accused of killing, raping, and running off former slaves from the Kennard Plantation; and shutting down the county courts and threatening the judge. Ben and his gang, partner Josiah Thompson, an Alvarado merchant and Major W. H. Cathey, Johnson County's tax assessor and collector, a sympathizer and possible accomplice in the robbery of the Johnson County tax funds, set up an ambush in Hill County.

Bickerstaff robbed Johnson County sheriff and deputy tax collector, and former Confederate Major E. M. Heath of $2,800 in county funds on the way to the State Treasury in Austin. During the holdup, one bullet whistled right by Sheriff Heath's head. Heath's pair of pearl-handled pistols were taken from him by the robbers. Major Cathey, traveling with Heath, was forced to ride off with the group. When Cathey showed up later, he claimed he had been robbed of $1000. Cathey was suspected of being involved and helping to plan the job with Ben.

## Alvarado Ambuscade

After Ben's associate Cullen Baker was killed, Ben headed off with his group of roving malcontents. Ben camped in hiding on Chambers Creek south of Alvarado and Cleburne. Alvarado, then the largest and most developed part of Johnson County, provided good pickings. The influential Alvarado Baptist Association had organized the Alvarado Institute and later the Cleburne Institute schools. Earlier they persuaded the Texas Legislature to pass a special act prohibiting liquor sales in Alvarado in the 1860s. However, many citizens and businesses continued to sell liquor under the counter in violation of the state law. Upon arrival in Alvarado, Ben Bickerstaff and Josiah Thompson openly defied the town by opening up a saloon. The Reverend Mr. Powell was a leader among those who challenged and forced Ben Bickerstaff and Josiah Thompson to close their door. Personal feuds developed between Ben and several local people. One night one of the contenders was shot through the window of his home. Ben forced the court to disband before handing out warrants. These circumstances led to the shootout in Alvarado.

The two outlaws threatened to burn the town, saying they would come back the next day at five o'clock. As they came into town, people ran to their homes and businesses. Ben took them for cowards and yelled, "Rats, to your holes!"

Around five o'clock the first shots came from Powell's store, then a hail of bullets and buckshot rained down on the outlaws as they dismounted on the southeast corner of the Alvarado square. Thompson was shot through the heart in the first volley. One of Ben's shots went down the gun barrel of Ben's chief opponent, the Reverend Mr. Powell, knocking the gun from his hand. When the smoke cleared Ben was said to have been shot between twenty-six and forty-four times. Ben lingered before death for some minutes, claiming he was a loyal Southerner and had been betrayed by the town. He asked that his gun and belongings be given to his wife and cleared her of any wrong doing.

The locals gathered around the dying outlaw. The doctor who had been called was attending Ben as best he could, but informed Ben he was going to die then and there. There was nothing that he could do except relieve some pain. The doctor told Ben it might help him in the great beyond and might help the doctor with the town's people if he would tell him which of the local people were involved. Ben motioned the doctor to come closer.

Ben asked: "Doctor, can you keep a secret?"

The Doctor replied: "Yes, Ben."

Then Ben whispered his last words: "Well, Doctor, so can I."

Ben Bickerstaff fell over limp and dead.

Major Cathey was arrested. Ben and Josiah were left on the square overnight. The next day there was an inquest and photographs were taken of the dead outlaws and sold as souvenirs. One of the boys in the crowd had witnessed Ben's dying moments and described the scene and conversation to nine-year-old T. U. Taylor who visited the site of the Alvarado shootout a month later.

The two outlaws were buried in the northwest corner of the Balch Cemetery. They are said to be buried facing west—opposite the direction of Christians whom some bury facing east towards the second coming of Christ. Major Cathey was later released for lack of evidence. General J. J. Reynolds, the Federal Magistrate in charge of the five military districts in Texas, paid the $1,000 dollar reward offered for Ben on August 27, 1868, to the townspeople. The vigilantes of Alvarado decided to donate the reward to a county school fund. The vigilantes, who shot the outlaws down, were so proud that they advertised their formerly secret group's meeting five days later.

CLEBURNE CHRONICLE, Sat. April 10, 1869:

*The citizens of Alvarado and vicinity have organized an association for the putting down of lawlessness. They hold a meeting today at 2 o'clock and desire as many of the citizens of Johnson County to attend as possible.*

News traveled all over Federally controlled Texas of the bloody ambush the townspeople pulled on the threatening desperados. The price for "taking on" Alvarado was sent out strong and clear. The 1869

Bickerstaff Shootout on the Alvarado town square stands as a remarkable and outrageous event in Johnson County history.

## Indian Raids—During and After the Civil War.

During the Civil War there was a depopulation of many of the counties to the west of Johnson. Families fled back to the relative safety of Johnson County and the Cross Timbers. Many Indian tribes took sides raiding for the Union or Confederacy. After the loss of their Texas reservations and hunting grounds, the friendly tribes were no longer a buffer for the white settlers—the raids became more deadly.

John Myers served the Confederacy in Company H, Twenty-first Texas Cavalry under Colonel Bass. His first wife, Elizabeth Campbell Myers, died during his absence, leaving two small children. In the meantime, a number of families moved to Johnson County to escape Indian raids to the west. In one raid near Mineral Wells nearly all the people for miles around were scalped. George Truitt's family survived and quickly retreated to the the safety of the Myers's community during 1865. Among them was step-daughter Margaret Moyer who, only a few years earlier at the age of fifteen, drove one of her grandfather's big covered wagons with Percheron horses all the way from Illinois to Parker County, Texas. John Myers fell in love with the lovely, spirited, fearless girl and soon they were married. He built her a story-and-a-half double log house which still survives.

Just after the war, Reconstruction-era attorney Terrell said, "The Indians gave some trouble then, and killed a man on the Clear Fork (of Trinity River), between Weatherford and Fort Worth; hence the attorneys went from Fort Worth in an body."

Pivotal events in the Indian Wars occurred just to the west and northwest of Johnson County. The wilder Comanche and Kiowa took full advantage of the weakened protection on the frontier. Running battles took place along the Brazos River valley on the western edge of our county. To add terror to their raids and aid in their escape, it was the practice after a raid to murder anyone encountered on the retreat.

For ten years after the Civil War the Indians' leaders and their raids were headliners in local newspapers. Indeed the last of the war chiefs became political figures in both the white and red world. Locally, Santanta, the famous Kiowa Chief, is the subject of articles in the CLEBURNE CHRONICLE of the early 1870s, recognized as a force to contend with. As weekly articles covered the ghastly details of Indian raids and murders in counties immediately to the west, editors commented on government policy.

CLEBURNE CHRONICLE, Sept. 21, 1872: *Grant's Quaker Indian policy has come to grief. He might as well have sent out an equal number of crows to 'caw caw' the Indians into civilization, as those of his broad brimmed friends.*

CLEBURNE CHRONICLE, July 17, 1874: *The Indians have left the reservation, and the excitement on the frontier is intense. The Indians in great numbers are on the war path.*

CLEBURNE CHRONICLE, July 25, 1874: *Indian Chiefs Santanta, Big Tree, and Lone Wolf are in collusion against the whites, and serious trouble may be expected.*

CLEBURNE CHRONICLE, September 19, 1874: *The Indian war is assuming some proportions. If the government would send a few thousand of its troops to our frontier, instead of scattering them through the Southern States to uphold villainy, it would have the appearance more of a republic than it does. It boots but little if the redskins raid our sparsely settled frontier counties, kill, scalp and plunder, . . . What does the powers that be take us for?*

Kiowa Chief Santanta, like other American Indians, loved to gamble. Horse racing was a favorite game to him. Santanta raced at Barnard's Trading Post at times and once came back and stole a prize race horse from Charles Barnard that he could not acquire through trade or winnings. If a warrior could steal or kill in some valiant manner he could count "coup," each of which could be displayed as eagle feathers in their war bonnets. Warfare, cunning, and deception were a way of life, making them worthy of honor in their warrior society.

Barnard's Mill was completed in 1864 at what would become Glen Rose. Charles Barnard allowed settlers to use the mill as a fort during the dangerous periods of the "Comanche Moon"; the full moon was the time the Comanches preferred to raid.

A common misconception is that the Comanche rode bareback. In reality they copied and rode Spanish type saddles fashioned of rawhide over wood frames. They rode as one with the horse, and are thought by many to have been the finest horsemen in history. Their community became a warrior society—the path to greatness came by counting "coup" on enemies through acts of bravery, and achievement. The warrior would bestow on the rest of the tribe the fruits of war—thus gaining influence in the tribe.

When Texas was a nation (1836–1845) and later during the Civil War (1861–1865), the Comanches were quick to notice and take advantage of opportunities presented by the separate political powers. The Comanches could raid in Texas and make peace with the Americans. They would steal and pillage, yet camp without fear just over the border in the Indian Territory and Kansas. There they could trade in stolen goods and captives. Some Texans did not honor borders and crossed over, chasing them long distances to retrieve loved ones and livestock. Comanches greatly resented raids deep in their stronghold of west Oklahoma and the panhandle of Texas where they felt secure. They especially could not understand how the Texans could kill their prized horses. Stealing them held much more honor in the eyes of the Comanche. They hated the Texas buffalo hunters who left carcasses to rot. The Texans became their most hated foes.

Near the end of the Indian Wars, the chiefs were informed by the Indian Agent and the military guard in Indian Territory, that they must stop raiding the settlements in Texas. One chief slyly remarked, "If the Great Father [the President] did not want his young braves to raid in Texas, then he must move Texas far away, where they could not find it."

Some estimates of the number of North Texas settlers killed or captured by Indian raids during the Civil War and Reconstruction are higher than four hundred men, women, and children.

The pioneers who settled along the Brazos moved onto a favorite raiding route south into Texas and Mexico. Comanche Peak was an ancient bivouac and re-supply point, there was constant danger during the raiding seasons of the Comanche and their allies, the Kiowa. Many farming families and ranchers paid with their lives and their property.

The Indian's raids were becoming intolerable, and with the Texas Rangers decommissioned during Reconstruction, the Federal soldiers were all that officially stood between the Indians and the settlers.

In 1871 President Grant ordered General William Tecumseh Sherman to find out if the Indian raids were indeed as bad as claimed in North Texas. The Federals suspected the Texans were exaggerating. Then Santanta fatefully sealed his own doom by giving General Sherman a close call near Fort Belknap in Palo Pinto County.

General Sherman arrived in Galveston by ship and followed the Old Fort Supply road to Fort Richardson in North Texas. Sherman riding in an ambulance with a small escort of fifteen cavalrymen passed under the

Pre-war Indian fighter and Texas Ranger Riley Dennis "Den" Richardson was with Sul Ross and the group of Rangers who recaptured Cynthia Ann Parker. He came back from the Cicil War to find "not a board or stone left standing of the comfortable house" his family owned in Jack County. Federal soldiers dismantled the structures and used the materials to build portions of the buildings at Fort Richardson. Naming the fort after the family was small compensation for the loss of their home and lands. After attempting to reclaim the family's ranch and cattle, he sold their mark and brand to a gambler for nine hundred dollars and came to the Fairview community in Johnson County where his parents and siblings had moved during the dangerous war years.

Beyond the ornamentation, frontiersmen wore fringe to create larger, indefinite targets to miss. Fringe also would drain water from leather clothing through capillary action. (Mollie Gallup Bradbury Mimms)

"Sioux Indians in Ambush Preparing to Attack Settlers," by W. M. Cary, (HARPER'S WEEKLY, May 2, 1868 AC)

watchful eyes of Santanta and over 100 Kiowa and Comanche in a canyon along the fort road without seeing one warrior.

A tribal medicine man dreamed the night before that he was not to attack the group coming through the next day but instead to attack those coming through the day after. A group of twelve teamsters were attacked instead. One of the captured teamsters was tied by his arms and legs then stretched spread-eagle between two wagons, gutted and roasted to death. Five fortunate teamsters of the Warren wagon train escaped. Sherman had been skeptical of the horror stories the Texans kept emphatically telling him, until he interviewed one of the wounded teamsters. Afterwards Sherman summed up his conclusions to President Grant: *"The more I see of these Indians, the more I am convinced that they will all have to be killed . . . The more that we kill this year, the less we will have to kill next year."*—Gen. W. T. Sherman, 1872. This "Salt Creek Massacre" episode strengthened the Federal military with orders to pursue and push the raiding tribes back into Indian Territory.

With Sherman's new insights it appeared a change might come. CLEBURNE CHRONICLE, June 23 (n.d.): *We publish Gen. Sherman's letter in this paper, from which it will be seen that he is very far from endorsing Gen.*

*Grant's peace policy. We publish his utterances as we think it will afford our frontier inhabitants some assurances that they are to have some protection, here after, more worthy of the name than any they have had heretofore.*

Shortly Santanta and the others were back in Indian Territory. They were asked point-blank by the Indian Peace Commissioner if they had been involved in the killing of the teamsters. Santanta with pride insisted, "He that says, I did not do it—lies." Santanta, Satank, and Big Tree, were taken prisoner. As they were being taken back to Texas for trial, Satank stabbed and killed the teamster who was driving the wagon, with a mysteriously concealed knife. Guards shot the handcuffed chief as he ran from the wagon. He died on this, his final escapade.

All of the Comanche Tribes could not be brought together under one treaty of peace. The various tribes were like small townships, which traveled around over the land following the migratory buffalo and raiding for any wealth they could acquire. Their traditional culture took them over the prairies of several western states. At Medicine Lodge around 1870 some of the Southern

The defiant Kiowa chief Santanta proudly resisted white domination. In 1871 his warriors destroyed the Warren wagon train at Salt Creek and killed seven teamsters hauling supplies between the frontier forts northwest of Johnson County. After boastfully admitting responsibility, Federal troops captured him and returned him to Texas for trial and incarceration. He was paroled from prison only to ruthlessly continue his deadly raids. Imprisoned once more, he died after jumping or being thrown from the second-story window of a prison hospital. (National Anthropological Archives, Smithsonian Institution #1380-A))

Quanah Parker and two of his eight wives, Pi uuh (left) and So hnee (right). Quanah was the last of the Comanche War Chiefs to bring his tribe into the Oklahoma reservations. He was the son of famous Comanche Chief Peta Nacona and his wife, Cynthia Ann Parker, a white woman who had been taken captive at the age of nine. Twice in her sad life, twenty-four years apart, Cynthia was forcibly removed from her family and taken on a trail that passed by Comanche Peak. This photograph was taken after removal from Texas to Indian Territory on June 2, 1875. The destruction of the Comanche's horses, their winter provisions, and the buffalo forced them onto the reservation. The Comanche were slow to adapt to the white man's ways and religion. At the turn-of-the-century, Quanah was asked by President Theodore Roosevelt why he did not rid himself of his eight wives and keep only one. Quanah solemnly replied to Roosevelt, "You tell them which one I keep." After considering the task, President Roosevelt departed, still in possession of his scalp. (Donna Davidson, Silver Horse Gallery Collection, Cleburne, Texas)

Comanches entered into a peace in which they agreed to discontinue their ancient lifestyle. Quanah Parker and his tribe rode off early before the closing ceremonies and left a message that, "The Kwahadi tribe of Comanches are warriors and are not afraid; the soldiers could come and fight them."

It took ten years for U.S. Troops, many of them black "Buffalo" soldiers of the Ninth and Tenth, to chase the Comanche down. This followed the near total annihilation of thirteen million buffalo and complete destruction of their horses. Quanah Parker became the last Comanche War Chief to resist white domination. He rose to leadership after he showed great courage during the June 27, 1874, fight at Adobe Walls in the Panhandle of Texas. On June 2, 1875, Quanah brought his Kwahadi band on foot to the reservation. Like all perplexed peacetime generals, Quanah, chief of a warrior society, had no more war to fight.

These mighty horsemen ended up in southern Oklahoma. They had for two hundred years driven back the formidable Apache tribes, the Spanish and Mexicans, and on another side, stood off the Texans, and the American invasion of the land that they controlled. In historic terms, they ruled the plains of Texas for a longer period of time than both Texas and the U.S. combined have been in control of it—not a bad record for a "wild and primitive" people.

Kiowa Guards raided alongside their Comanche allies in western Johnson County. Still defiant, these "Reservation Police" stand on their government assigned reservation land in southwest Indian Territory. They would stop trail drivers on the Western Cattle Trail where it crossed the Red River. A fee in cattle was demanded for crossing reservation land. If refused, the Kiowa would stampede the cattle. (From an original Irwin Smith print, Donna Davidson, Silver Horse Gallery Collection, Cleburne, Texas)

Unidentified Indian and commissioner shaking hands. Over the years the alliances changed with new personalities and events. Indian agents and policies changed regularly with elections. Rations and gifts often did not arrive in time to help peaceful chiefs keep tribal members from going back to the way of life they had known. Some tribes stayed within the smaller assigned areas, others continued to attempt to follow the buffalo's seasonal treks and their traditional raiding and trade routes. In the end 99 percent of the treaties made between the U.S. and Indian nations were broken or disregarded. (AC)

Rations were divided among Native Americans after their removal from Texas. With their way of life permanently changed they were now dependant on the federal government. (From an original Irwin Smith print, Donna Davidson, Silver Horse Gallery Collection, Cleburne, Texas)

Buffalo soldier. Drawn by F. Remington. (AC)

## Cowboys, Cattle and the Chisholm Trail

The need and opportunity to convert the plentiful Texas cattle into hard currency existed long before the famous cattle trailing days just after the Civil War. Before the war the Shawnee Trail brought cowboys up the east side of the Cross Timbers through Alvarado. It went up to Dallas along Preston Road and took Texas cattle to mid-western and eastern states.

Joseph McClure told a story of cowboys and Alvarado whiskey: *The ordinary western store of the day ranked whiskey as part of the groceries. My Uncle D. D. Myers rented the store and sold whiskey and other groceries in Alvarado . . . we sold no less than a quart of whiskey at a time. While I was working there in Uncle D.D.'s store before the war, about 20 regular Texas cowboys dropped in one evening late in 1860 . . . our bottled goods were all kept on the shelves. These boys formed a line one after the other and rode in at the north door and turned south fronting on the shelves. With six-shooters in hand they shot at the bottles and when they went out the other door kept it up until all the bottles were all shot down. Then they rode back to camp without saying a word. They were drunk as they had drunk five or six quarts of whiskey. The next morning they came back and asked what damages they owed and Uncle Dave told them so they never said a word handing him the money and asked for each an extra quart. It pleased me to see their backs as they left . . .*

The cattle trailing era only lasted about two decades, but those twenty years are in many ways the most memorable in our nation's history. The legend of the cowboy materialized, which for many has come to fill our national need for a "heroic past." The distinctiveness of the cowboy was recognized in the towns along the trail. The "cow-boy" became "a legend in his own time" and was glorified in the dime novels and newspapers of the 1870s to 1890s. Many young men captivated by hero worship showered on the cowboy in periodicals of the day, left home and went west.

Numerous cowboys were born, reared, worked and lived out their lives in Johnson County. Some local young men joined up with the herds going north and were never seen again. Many remained in the western plains states with the cattle they brought. "The cowboys got about forty dollars per month and the trip to Abilene or Dodge netted each cowboy about one hundred dollars." (T. U. Taylor)

"In from the Night Herd," HARPER'S WEEKLY cover. Drawn by F. Remington. (AC)

### "I See, by Your Outfit, That You Are a Cowboy . . ."

Editor Graves printed a tribute to the "cow-boys" in the August 9, 1873 CLEBURNE CHRONICLE at the very time these tough young men were coming through town:

*CATTLE HERDING. The Dashing Centaurs of the Texas plain—Material for a matchless Cavalry*

*The "cow-boys" of Texas are a peculiar breed. They are as distinct in their habits and characteristics from the remainder of even the Texas population as if they belonged to another race. The Lipan (Apache) or Comanche are not more unlike the civilized white man than is this nomadic herdsman to the Texan who dwells in the city or cultivates the plains . . . these men who sleep, eat and live on horseback, never leave their "bunches" of cattle except to chase the Mexican or Indian marauder and know or care for nothing but their avocation.*

The real cowboy, "Charlie Bodie on Tracy bucking," circa 1900. Swan Land & Cattle Co.—49 Ranch, Chugwater, Wyoming, (Print from glass negative. AC)

*Nor is cattle-herding an easy life. Think of driving the wild, fierce brutes from the Rio Grande to Kansas, compelled to watch them day and night. If they stampede, as they often do, the cow-boy must ride after or before them, and the dangerous race most frequently occurs during dark nights, through drenching storms, over yawning barrancas, and in the midst of tangled thickets that fearfully test the strength of the leather fenders on his arms and cowskin leggings which protect his lower limbs . . .*

*Ten thousand of these incipient soldiers roam over western Texas, all sons of frontiersmen and inured from infancy to hardship and danger . . . A few lessons in subordination and they would become invincible . . . A cavalry commander with such troops might attempt anything for he would have a corps rapid as the horsemen of Kaled, resistless as the hords of Genghis.*

The people of Cleburne and Johnson County observed these cowboys first hand and did business with them everyday.

## Up the Chisholm Trail

Herd after herd of longhorns were pushed north by the tireless cowboys. Millions of cattle made their way along the Nolan River Valley two to three miles west of Cleburne. The long, strung-out herds typically numbered from 2,000 to 5,000 cattle. Occasionally there were only a few hundred steers in a herd. However, according to the Caps family of "Nolands River," (Rio Vista) there was one memorable herd that came from Mexico on the way to Indian Territory. It extended from their ranch to Cleburne, a distance of about ten miles, and was estimated in the tens of thousands. Another outstanding herd took two days to pass by. The drovers worked hard to keep their herds separate and keep a distance between them. But on occasion a stampede would hopelessly mix two herds which would then force them to travel together or take days of sorting them out. It is believed that between six and twelve million head went north over the trail from 1866 to 1884. These numbers amount to the largest forced migration of animal life in recorded history.

The mythical cowboy, "A Bucking Bronco," drawn by F. Remington. "Remember old Midnight, the big black horse of Bob Gatewood's that nobody could ride? He went to the rodeo, fairs, shows. Well, a fellow from West Texas come down here and put up $25 he could ride him. He borrowed a saddle. They went down to Gorman Park. He asked the people to pass the hat. A big crowd gathered around. He got on Midnight. Rode him around and around all over the park. He rode Midnight down, he give out. He got off of him, got back on him and Midnight would not buck. Bob Gatewood made a plow horse out of him. That was the end of Midnight. The rider's name was Grover Jones from Mundy, Texas." (I REMEMBER, by Faye Burton, circa 1900. AC)

The stamping hooves cut a path roughly one hundred yards wide, which was beaten into a fine powered dust, barren of vegetation. Off to each side there were smaller, parallel cattle trails, weaving in and out of the grass, similar to trails in a cow pasture today. The dust raised by the tramping cattle clouded the sky for miles, coating everything in its path with a fine powder. The herds traveled about ten to twelve miles a day in a grazing, browsing walk; often cattle had to fatten on the drive.

Lawyer J. C. Terrell remembered seeing the cattle buyers in towns along the trail. *Just after the Civil War, when the country was full of cattle, then in great demand, the hotel . . . was full of cattle buyers from the*

Richard "Dick" Smith Sewell (1851-1947), his wife Polona (Kennard) Sewell and family, came to Texas at the invitation of the Kennards to educate the freed slaves who lived at Nathan. Dick, at one time the richest black man in Johnson County, lived to be 96 years old. As a young man, he took part in cattle drives from Morgan in Bosque County to Wichita, Kansas.

Sewell told his children about the drovers along the trail coming on a small family of Indians of a man, woman and children. As the lead cowboys approached them, the patriarch of the little tribe greeted the cowmen with an overture of "Howdy-Doody — Howdy-Doody." The trail boss of the outfit rode up yelling, "Damn your Howdy-Doody," pulled his gun and shot them all dead. "A good Indian is a dead Indian" policy was applied universally by some. (Gracie Norwood)

*North, with lots of money. Strangers to us they were and to each other, waiting for the grass to rise. They were an uncommunicative set and all dressed with the regulation six-shooter.* In the days before bank drafts, the cattlemen coming down the trail and buyers from the North often carried large sums of gold in their saddle bags or upon their persons. There were also many supply wagons and teams hauling goods to market and coming back with full treasure boxes. Needless to say they all went well armed, because Indian raiding parties, outlaws, and renegades from as far away as Mexico were known to use the Chisholm cattle trail regularly.

The old cattle trail also provided a convenient route and gave cover for the activities of outlaws. Walter Prescott Webb wrote: *Many a criminal found occupation and even protection in the cow camps, and it is said that some outfits preferred men who were on the dodge, because they stuck closer to business, avoided the towns, and were always ready to fight their way out of a difficulty.*

De Cordova Trading Post. Jacob DeCordova and Richard Kimball (a New York lawyer) established the village called Kimball in 1853 or 1854. It was at a point on the Brazos where the only good crossing for miles up or down the river was to be found. Most of the east-west and north-south travel, was funneled through the new town, and at this place the old Chisholm Trail crossed the stream. Each year tens of thousands of cattle were driven up this old trail to northern markets. The location of Kimball made it a convenient stopping place for ranchers and the cowboys who drove these herds on the trail. (Layland Museum, Cleburne, Texas)

## Origins of the Trail

The 1849 Fort Supply Road (map, page 30) originally carried many of the "forty-niners" south to San Antonio and then west to El Paso on a southern course to the California gold fields. This path skirted the homeland of the Comanche Indians who roamed North and West Texas. Emigrants and fortune seekers made their way along these trails to California and back.

In 1851 another branch of the road which paralleled the Brazos, following the divide on its northeast side, was staked out. This gave a second connecting link to supply the growing chain of frontier forts: Fort Worth, Fort Graham, and Fort Gates stood on the edge of settlement from about 1848 to 1853. This 1851 trail forked heading north, one road leading to Fort Worth and the other to Fort Belknap. While marking these military wagon roads, trees were blazed, stakes were driven, creek beds were cut down and wagon ruts were made. The eastern line of forts were abandoned by 1852–53. However the roads were still used by the military to supply forts further west during Reconstruction and the Indian Wars.

Today local historians speculate about the exact location of the trails, but little remains to show where they actually were. One spot on the 1851 military supply road is clearly marked on an 1853 Peter's Colony map, placing it "four and one-half miles east of the tip of De Cordova's Bend on the Brazos at a point eight and one-half miles due west of Cleburne."

The Chisholm Trail followed portions of the old fort supply roads through Johnson County. The old trails were used until the coming of the railroads when ranch and farm owners cut across the old roads

The roots of Charles Goodnight's cattle empire reach deep into Johnson County. In 1856 Goodnight bought fifty head of blooded cattle from the Jessie Cameron Ranch on Camp Creek, now the Freeland Community. Goodnight let the cattle graze on Camp Creek during that summer and camped under a huge "Burr Oak" tree. The tree is still standing and is known as the "Goodnight Oak." Local author Viola Block tells of measuring its fourteen-foot circumference in 1970. Goodnight spent some time in Johnson County helping Sam White, who moved his family from Hunt County in 1856, build a large log cabin on the Brazos. The next year, 1857, he drove four hundred choice head out to Palo Pinto County and founded his ranch. After the Civil War, Goodnight carved a cattle kingdom out of the stronghold of the Comanches, the walls of Palo Duro Canyon in the Texas Panhandle. While the U.S. Army struggled to defeat the Comanche and Kiowa, Charley Goodnight and Oliver Loving lived an uneasy life among them and drove their herds to the Kansas railheads. Goodnight's partner, Loving, is quoted in Andy Adams's LOG OF A COWBOY as "Oliver Loving, the first man who drove a herd north used to say, 'Don't go lookin' for trouble and don't cross a river 'til you get to it.'" (Courtesy of the Western History Collection, University of Oklahoma Library)

Unidentified cowboy of Spanish heritage. George Saunders, president of the Old Time Cattledrivers of Texas said that of the 35,000 cowboys who worked the trails between 1866-96, one-third of them were African-American or Mexican. (AC)

## Stampede!!!

The herds would stampede at the slightest provocation: a clap of thunder or lightning, a gunshot, a wild animal, rustlers; even a strong "blue norther" could start a herd on the run. Charlie Russell said a longhorn stampede was "one jump to their feet and running, and the next jump to hell." The Sterling Caps family who farmed near Nolands River (Rio Vista) saw the herds of longhorn cattle stampede. They recalled that the noise made by the clattering and clash of the horns, rose above the rumble of the pounding hooves. At least one stampeding herd took cowboys careening with them as they thundered off the high cliffs around the Kimball Bend above the Brazos River. The same cliffs probably had been used by Native American hunters to stampede herds of buffalo to their death. At other high points along the cattle trail are buffalo wallows, still visible over a century after the great buffalo herds disappeared from Texas. Cattle had forever taken the place of the bison on the plains of Texas and America.

"Stampede," CENTURY MAGAZINE, drawn by F. Remington. (AC)

with wire fences and eventually the last traces were finally plowed under. T. U. Taylor is a much respected Chisholm Trail authority who as a young man visited the cowboys at their night camps from 1866–1872. Taylor said the camps were two miles west of Cleburne's square during 1870–1872 (in the area of modern Nolan River Road). Most cattle drivers reported the main trail ran along the Nolan River at a point due west of Cleburne. Camps of the trail drivers were also reported to be on the west side of the Nolan. The path of the trail was pushed further to the west over the years by settlers and fences. The written memoirs of old time trail drivers mention Cleburne and Buchanan as memorable towns and supply points on the old Chisholm Trail and list them along with San Antonio, Waco, Kimball, and Fort Worth on the Texas part of the trail.

## A Trail Diary

Joe Evans, an old trail driver of Johnson County, reminisced in the 1893 CLEBURNE DAILY ENTERPRISE, of his days trailing cattle:

*I was born in a cow camp and raised in a tent.* Some herds were driven as far as New York City. *Ben Barnes drove about 1400 head to California in 1869 and lost $10,000 in the venture. Dry weather, failing crops, and no grass necessitated the feeding of cattle on the sage brush in the mountains, and accordingly the* (value) *of the cattle fell. One night while Ben was sleeping near his cattle in the mountains, a band of Indians stole his horse, leaving him to herd the cattle* (the rest of the way) *on foot.*

Crossing rivers was the most dangerous part of the drive. Dr. U. D. Ezell described how some cowboys did it. *If the herd was driven leisurly down to the river, the lead-cows would plant their forefeet firmly into the soft earth, and refuse to budge; and thus the whole herd would be held up. In order to prevent these leaders from balking at the water's edge, we would start the herd running, four or five hundred yards from the stream. So, when the lead-cows reached the stream they were swept into the water by the oncoming herd. The other cattle would follow their leaders into the water; and the whole herd, sometimes consisting of several thousand animals, would crowd into the stream. The real work of pointing the cattle across the river now began. When they reached the main current of the river the lead-cows might become crazed with fear and begin to mill about in circles, drifting down the stream, all the while. As an entire herd could be lost this way it was essential that something be done immediately. The experienced pointer was ready when this happened, and he acted quickly and effciently. He would swim into the torrent, face one of the lead cows toward the opposite bank and then force her head down under the water for a moment. After this dunking, the old cow would come up with a snort, and make top speed for the shore; and generally, the other cattle would follow this leader out of the flood stream.*

George C. Duffield in the spring of 1866 kept a day-to-day account on his trip up the Old Fort Supply trail through Johnson County and on to his ranch in Iowa. Duffield's diary remains one of the few authentic, daily accounts of trailing cattle. The following entries cover Johnson County:

*May, 1866*

*10th Crossed Bosque at Meridian & travelled to Brazos River and find it very high 14 miles Pleasant Day*

*11th Beautiful warm day lay in camp waiting on R(iver) Rode 3 miles to Kimballville & back veiwd river & Killed Beefe*

*12th Lay around camp visited River & went Bathing*

*13th Big Thunder Storm last night Stampede lost 100 Beeves hunted all day found 50 all tired Every thing discouraging*

*14th Concluded to cross Brazos swam our cattle & Horses & built Raft & Rafted our provisions & blankets &c over Swam River with rope & then hauled wagon over lost Most of our Kitchen furniture such as camp Kittles Coffee Pots Cups Plates Canteens &c &c*

*15th Back at River bringing up wagon hunting Oxen & other lost property Rain poured down for one Hour It does nothing but rain got all our traps together that was not lost & thought we were ready for off dark rainy night cattle all left us & in morning not one Beef to be seen*

*16th Hunt Beeves is the word-all hands discouraged & are determined to go 200 Beeves out and nothing to eat*

*17th No Breakfast pack and off is the order all Hands gave the Brazos one good harty dam[n] & started for Buchanan traveled 10 miles & camped found 50 beeves (nothing to eat)*

*18th Everything gloomy four best hands left us got to Buchanan at noon & to Rock creek in Johnson Co distance 14*

After the war the Midwest and central plains were where the cattle would often bring a good profit. In 1867 Joseph G. McCoy built cattle pens at the railhead of the Kansas Pacific Railroad in Abilene. He surveyed a line across Kansas to Jesse Chisholm's trail in Indian Territory and connected to the Old Fort Supply trail in Texas. This completed what was to become the Chisholm Trail from Texas to the Kansas railhead where trains took the cattle to the Chicago packing houses and the East. This trail became the "interstate highway" of all old cattle trails.

T. U. Taylor, as a boy of six to twelve years old, was a young observant witness to what occurred on the old Chisholm Trail. His father died in Parker County, so he and his mother moved here for work and safety. Taylor lived in Cleburne from 1866–1872, and he often visited the cowboys who camped just west of town. Up and down the trail for forty miles he hunted for stray horses and cattle. He hung around the night camps and listened to the cowboys sing in their camp and on horseback to calm the cattle. His "greatest fascination" was the night herding where the cattle were driven to a nearby knoll or draw:

*The cattle were all laying down and the few "night herders" were riding around their long watch humming or singing some old song that had a slow beat. There was never any jazz or jig music. I have heard many of the old songs on the stretch between Nolan River and Mary's Creek. The old hymns were the favorites with their long, drawn out meter. Many is the time I have heard such old songs as: "How Firm a Foundation" . . . One of the more frequently sung songs . . . was . . . a song that seemed to catch on and nearly everyone on and off the trail was boasting the "Yellow Rose of Texas Beats the Belles of Tennessee."*

*I have heard one lone rider around the sleeping herd break into "Oh Susannah don't you cry for me," but it was a long drawn out dirgeful prayer.*

*On some occasions it fell to the lot of an old fiddler to ride night herd, and a few of them had recourse to his fiddle, and the rider would make the strings sing out a song to some long drawn out howl. I recall that one rider was adept in the song: "Over There," and the way he could make those old strings plead to the listener on a dry night . . .*

*"The Drunkard's Hiccoughs" was a favorite around the night herd. It is often called "Rye Whiskey."*

Trail driver W. L. Evans said that at its beginning Cleburne was "a wide place in the cattle trail." T. U. Taylor "saw many cowboys in Cleburne" and recalled one instance in particular:

*While the herds were slowly winding their way up the Nolan River the head boss would often permit some of the cowboys to come to Cleburne. They all rode good horses and were unanimous in wanting to roll ten-pins. There were two or three ten-pin alleys in Cleburne, one on the west side, and one on the south side of the square. The one on the west side was run by Doc Shaw in the rear part of his saloon. It was great sport to make up a contest of about a dozen rollers and let the loser pay for the drinks of the crowd.*

*It was a rare thing when money was bet on the game, but it was either rolled for the fees or the drinks.*

*On one occasion I saw a cowboy considerably under the influence of liquor, challenge the whole of Cleburne as a dancer, the contest to be staged on the track of the alley.*

*His challenge was accepted and about six entered the contest and all started at once on certain sections of the alley. It was an elimination dance, with such steps as the double shuffle, the back step, the hoe down and a few others that I have forgotten. The contest raged for an hour*

*and finally a local gambler was left against the cowboy, and then they bet the enormous stakes of two dollars and fifty cents apiece. They danced twenty minutes longer and the local gambler was declared the winner.*

*One other peculiar thing I noticed in Cleburne was that the gamblers and saloon keepers rarely drank. The gambler had to keep a cool head.*

Racing horses was another trail pastime. Drovers on the Chisholm Trail always had a favorite mount they wished to pit against Johnson County horses. Occasionally if the horse could not be bought or won, it disappeared.

CLEBURNE CHRONICLE, June 7, 1873: *Several horses disappeared in a rather mysterious way from town and vicinity one night last week. Some suspicious characters disappeared about the same time.*

Several local families, including James Hagler on Haley's Branch and Ben Williamson near Bono, built respectable stock ranches from the newborn calves and yearlings that were left behind on the trail to die. "The cattle drovers would bed the cattle down for the night and next day drove the cattle off leaving a lot of young calves behind . . . they would raise the calves and that way built up a big herd of cattle." "Marks and Brands" on local livestock were regularly printed in the newspaper and ranchers registered their brands at the county clerk's office. Estray sales day in Cleburne was a big event and always brought a huge crowd to town. Horse swappers and auctioneers made things lively.

Round-up. Four cattle drovers on horses in the midst of penned cattle in Alvarado, Texas. (Layland Museum, Cleburne, Texas)

A Johnson County round-up with the cowboys gathered by the chuckwagon. Before barbed wire closed the open range, each spring would bring the round-up of cattle and the branding of calves. (AC)

Branding the calves. Local cattlemen worked together at a gathering point to pair up the mother cows and new calves. They branded them like their mothers. One of the cowboys is wearing high button shoes instead of boots. (AC)

CLEBURNE BULLETIN, March 2, 1881: *Monday was estray sales day, it formed no exception to such sales days in the past. The town was full of country people, attracted hither to invest in scrub stock. Nothing but small pox, or yellow fever in epidemic shape, would keep the people away on estray sales days.*

About 1870 the auctioneer was 220-pound George Stevens. He would stand on the top step of the courthouse on the west side of the square holding the animal by a rope about ten feet long. When he was selling a cowpony he would always extol the virtues of being "gifted with extraordinary gaits, gentle as a lamb, sound as a dollar, was not bone spavined, knock-kneed, nor hide bound, did not have fistula nor the sore back." Many ponies sold for as little as fifteen dollars. He would sell cows, horses, oxen, and mules, but he never sold a saddle for "A Texan would cling to his saddle as if it were part of his anatomy."

Dr. U. D. Ezell grew up along the trail near Kimball and worked as a cowboy during his youth in the 1870s: *As has been said, some of these herds were very large. I recall that one such herd was strung out down the old Chisholm Trail from the crossing at Kimball clear back to the town of Morgan a distance of ten to twelve miles. As such vast herds were driven through the country, it was difficult to keep other cattle, along the way, from joining them. Ranchers would sometimes hire me to help cut out these off brands. Usually the herd would be driven some distance from the river before any attempt was made to cut these strays out. I often went as far as Cleburne for this purpose. Camp would be made for a*

Remuda of horses and wagons at the extreme end of the Texas cattle trails near the Laramie Plains of Wyoming. Each cowboy had a string of horses of from three to five mounts which he rode in rotation. The remuda was the herd of horses watched over by a young wrangler and the cook. The horses trailed along with the chuckwagon and tent wagons. At night they were held by a rope corral or tied to a rope strung from a wagon to a tree. The tent wagon might also serve to carry the newborn calves. Some Texas trails reached all the way to the portion of Wyoming shown in this picture, part of Wyoming originally claimed by the nation Texas. ("49 wagons & horses," Swan Land & Cattle Co., 49 Ranch, Chugwater, Wyoming AC)

"Road Papers" filed in Johnson County. These registered papers of purchase, simple "bills of sale," could prove ownership on a herd. This group was purchased and registered in Johnson County then driven out on the trail in 1863 during the Civil War. They may have been on their way to feed Southern troops. (JCA.)

Below: "Dispute over a brand," drawn by F. Remington. Many steers were newly branded for the drive north, but others were altered by rustlers. Some cows were covered with brands all over their hides. Most had both a brand and an ear crop or cut. One of the few ways to determine without doubt whether a brand had been altered was to look on the underside of the hide and observe the scar of the original brand. This of course would require the cow to be dead. If caught trailing a herd and you had not registered your brand, couldn't produce a bill of sale, or even if your papers looked questionable, the sheriff would take you back to town for a visit. (AC)

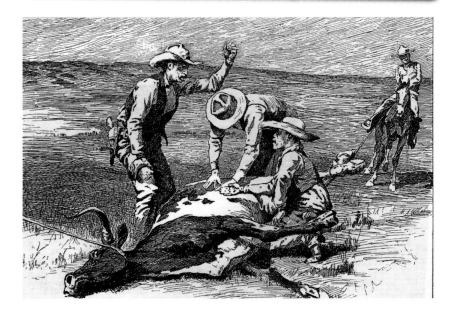

O. P. "Perry" Arnold, Johnson County Sheriff. June 31, 1873, CLEBURNE CHRONICLE: Sometime this week a fellow who claims to be a "drover" made his advent into this county with a herd of cattle, . . . Sheriff Arnold had received information that this man's herd had in it some stock that didn't possess the road brand which the law requires to be placed upon stock traveling through this state, . . . Arnold started in pursuit of the parties and succeeded in overtaking them somewhere near the Tarrant County line. Arnold very politely requested of Walters, who claimed to be the owner of the herd, permission to look through his herd, also serving upon him papers which he had placed in his hands. Mr. Arnold was at first abruptly refused permission to look through the herd, and Walters at once commanded his men to allow no one to go in among the cattle, but after thinking over the matter concluded that he had better grant the request. Mr. Arnold, on looking through the herd, found several cattle-without the necessary brand, and informed Walters that he would have to take him back to town. Walters's next expedient was to try a game of bluff on the sheriff, . . . He rushed furiously off to his wagon and returned with his hand in his pocket and menacingly informed Mr. Arnold that he or no other man could carry him back to Cleburne. Nothing daunted by these threats, Mr. Arnold walked up to him, laid his hand upon his arm, demanded to know if he was armed. When the fellow found that the officer would not bluff he said that he was not armed, and was arrested and brought back to town. Mr. Arnold informs us that their conduct and actions taken as a whole justify a suspicion that the entire herd is traveling not exactly on the square. (Dr. Jack Burton)

*few days while the cowboys busied themselves cutting out these strays and grouping them according to the brands they bore. I soon came to know every brand in Hill, Bosque, and Johnson counties; and I could quickly tell to whom each brand belonged. Sometimes there would be cattle of several brands, that had joined a herd as it passed through the country, plus a few old family milk cows that had felt a sudden urge to roam. After these strays had been cut out and grouped, their owners must be notified as to where they might be found; or, as often happened, the owner of the main herd would have his own men drive those strays back to their homes.*

Some unscrupulous ranchers were involved in "mavericking." They drove off and separated the calves from the mother cows on the open range and branded them with their own brands. Johnson County record books show a large number of felony cases filed involving the "unlawful driving of cattle," "theft" of various types of livestock, and breaking the "stray" laws which governed the ownership and herding of livestock on the open range. "By 1869 the old practice of 'taking cattle' was fast playing out." However, rustling was never completely stopped or controlled. The job of inspecting cattle was so important that for many years there was an elected position in county government.

CLEBURNE CHRONICLE Nov. 27, 1873: *We are authorized to announce the name of Jno. Stephens as a candidate for cattle and hide inspector.*

The route of the Chisholm Trail was pushed further and further west by settlement and wire. The wire fences eventually cut it off during the mid-1880s. If the cattleman wanted to drive a herd north he had to go on the Western Trail or the Goodnight-Loving Trail connecting to the Colorado Trail. However, the Chisholm was the trail that carried the largest number of cattle.

The railroads pulled into Fort Worth in 1876, Whitney in 1879, and into Johnson County in 1879. Slowly the traffic on the dusty cattle trails was being siphoned off by the railroads who shipped the cattle north by rail. The "golden age" of the cowboy was disappearing into the past.

Well before 1890 the open range was closed and the Chisholm Trail and the drives north would live on only in the memories of the aging cowboys. Among the lasting effects which the cattle drives brought to the nation was a permanent change in the American diet—the preference for the main course of a meal shifted from ham to beef—and where the buffalo had roamed, cattle and ranches now filled the void and established the western ranching economies.

"Business Men and Houses of Cleburne, Texas" (Dr. Jack Burton)

Opposite Page: Scenes from an 1872 Portrait of Cleburne. The photographic collage contains the individual portraits of eighty-five people of whom eighty-three are listed. It shows the 1868–1869 courthouse which was torn down in 1882. There are street scenes and views of the various business houses of the town. Over a century ago, in 1895, the photograph was called "One of the most cherished souvenirs." In 1917 again it was brought to the attention of the public in the following newspaper article. "Judging from the number of people in the picture it contains practically all the adult male population of Cleburne at that time. There is but one brick building shown, and it seems to be the one on the north side of the square now occupied by R. M. Speer. It was then occupied by T. D. Lorance, druggist and physician. George Mulkey had a store here at that time. C. Yeager ran a meat market, and the picture shows his small wooden building. Among the business houses were two or three saloons. In the center of the picture is the courthouse, a two-story building of brick, with a small wooden fence enclosing it. There are trees in the streets of Cleburne and old plows and other machinery litter in the front of a blacksmith shop owned by A. Day. The Chronicle office stands along on Wardville Street, just back of where the Leyhe Piano Company is now domiciled. The paper at that time was owned by W. H. Graves, and his picture and the picture of his son, Lester, then a small lad, are among the number. These are the only ones we know to be alive (in 1917). Here is the list of those in the picture: 1. John Guffey 2. Ance Whitten 3. Jack Clark 4. John B. Wright 5. Rev. Nash 6. _____ Bennett 7. J. F. Stroop 8. Orville Menefee 9. J. A. Willingham 10. W. Robinson 11. S. B. Allen 12. W. F. Heard 13. W. E. Gates 14. _____ Ponder 15. Edward Heyder 16. J. C. Mabry 17. William Graves 18. Lester Graves 19. Sam Keating 20. N. H. Cook 21. B. J. Chambers 22. T. D. Lorance 23. Dr. Jim Kerr 24. Dr. J. R. Keating 25. Dr. Andrew Young 26. Dr. M. S. Kahle 27. Unknown Musician 28. B. L. Durham 29. A. Day 30. A. M. Brumley 31. Henry Donohoo 32. T. A. Mohler 33. Milton Berry 34. Rev. R. E. Warren 35. Rev. J. R. Clark 36. _____ Elston 37. Unknown tailor 38. Joe Rushing 39. Jack Davis 40. M. A. Oatis 41. _____ Wyatt 42. Green Maxey 43. Father Brannan 44. Major E. M. Heath 45. O. P. Arnold 46. Jesse Berry 47. B. Hartsough 48. Sol Lockett, Jr. 49. Chester Heath 50. Judge H. W. Barclay 51. L. B. Davis 52. Captain Hendricks 53. D. T. Bledsoe 54. C. Y. Kouns 55. J. W. Brown 56. Josh Billingsley 57. Monroe Wren 58. John Haley 59. J. W. Mitchell 60. Dr. Hayden 61. Mr. Wright 62. Captain J. N. English 63. C. Vosburg 64. Tom Boykin 65. George Mulkey 66. T. Lawrence 67. Mr. Wright, brother of the Mr. Wright above noted 68. V. Gray 69. B. P. Leach 70. L. D. McMillan 71. Milt McConnell 72. _____ Parish 73. George Legg 74. Joe Tatum 75. L. Q. Roby 76. Solomon Lockett 77. C. Yeager 78. Willie Scurlock 79. John Shaffer 80. George Harle 81. Volney Robinson 82. John Guepel 83. Major Sparks." (AC)

"Cheap Cash Courthouse," circa 1872. In May 1867 the Buchanan Courthouse and jail were moved to Cleburne. They were placed on the south end of the east side of the courthouse square. The wooden courthouse was described as a one-room building with seats arranged in a semicircle and a raised platform in the center. The two-story jail, visible in the background on the left, was made of logs. After being brought to Cleburne it was rebuilt with both windows and doors fitted with iron. Prisoners were taken up into the second story and made to go down to the ground on a ladder which was moved as soon as they landed. The first term of County Court opened in the new county seat of Cleburne July 1, 1867. (Dr. Jack Burton)

The 1868 Johnson County Courthouse in Cleburne was a two-story, brick building enclosed by a four-plank fence. The courthouse had a hall running east and west, and one joining it on the south. The halls, having no doors, were open at all times and had dirt floors. The rooms off the halls could be locked. "When the more progressive citizens wanted to cut down the trees around the courthouse (where men tied their horses) the less progressive people objected vigorously. The controversy got so strong between the two groups, that serious troubles threatened. Six-shooters were carried by many men, and excitement ran high. Finally, the anti-tree fraction won, and the trees were cut down." Senior History Papers, Donald Sells, 1912. (Dr. Jack Burton)

These are scenes in the frontier village that greeted the cowboys and settlers in the early 1870's. (1st Row) "N. H. Cook" and "Polk, Ponder and Allen" stand on the southwest corner of the courthouse square in Cleburne. (2nd Row) West side of the Cleburne courthouse square, "Cleburne House" is the two story structure to the far right. (3rd Row) CLEBURNE CHRONICLE, December 20, 1868, "The gentlemanly proprietor of Cleburne's Star Saloon, suggests that folk drop in to sample a little for the stomach's sake, and other infirmities." The Star Saloon is the log building at the center standing next to the City Saloon on the north corner of the west side of the square.

(4th Row) Mulkey's and Mabry's stores were at the west end of the south side of the square, while "City Drug Store" and "Brooke and Nash" were on the east side of the square. (5th Row) The "Tin Shop" was on the east side of the 100 of block South Main. (Portions of Dr. Jack Burton's photographic collage)

The CLEBURNE CHRONICLE office, circa 1872, 115 E. Wardville Street, where many of Johnson County's old west stories were reported and printed. Tree stumps still obstructed the public square and right of ways. Major Jack Davis transported the equipment by oxcart and set up the old George Washington hand press. He began publishing the CLEBURNE CHRONICLE in 1868. The inset is J. W. Graves and his son, Lester. Graves purchased the paper, sold it to F. W. Wells, and bought it back again in 1874. A. C. Scurlock bought the Chronicle in 1878 and published it for twenty-five years. Although damaged three times by fire, in 1868, 1880, and 1890, it did not miss printing an issue. (Dr. Jack Burton)

Mr. Bennett was an early-day Cleburne boot maker, circa 1872. Notice he has a boot stretched on a lap last with a thong held taut by his foot. The boots he is working on are square toed and square topped. A local boot customer of that day was quoted in the CLEBURNE CHRONICLE as saying, "They fitted us up the other day, and we are constantly expecting to become engaged to be married, for if those boots do not get us a wife, we shall have no confidence in the effect of gear, hereafter," June 7, 1873. (Dr. Jack Burton)

Dempwolfe Grocery Store interior, circa 1888. Mr. Dempwolfe came to Cleburne in 1866 and was one of the first merchants here. In 1889 a merchant was quoted as saying, "Boys, when you are selling a bill of goods on credit, and a fire breaks out, charge the goods and then put out the fire." Such was the prudent merchant of the day. (Dr. Jack Burton)

In 1897 Ferdinand "Ferd" Stoffers moved to Cleburne and worked for T. R. James & Son Wholesale Leather Company. His brother Hugo moved to Cleburne in 1898. Ferd Stoffers went into business May 5, 1908. He owned the F. Stoffers Saddle & Harness Business which was located on the west of the square in the J. J. Wofford Building. Hugo and Edward Stoffers worked for him. (Layland Museum, Cleburne, Texas)

## Hot Pistols and Fast Horses

Editor Graves ran this ad in the CLEBURNE CHRONICLE:

*Caddo Grove*
*Johnson Co., Tex.*
*March 15, 1874*
*Mr. Editor: Dear Sir:*

*Believing you to be a progressive man desiring the improvment of north Texas stock, &c., I hope you will publish the following:*

*THE CADDO TURF AND JOLLY CLUB, meets every Saturday evening in a big lane one-quarter mile north of Caddo. Terms of admission: the applicant shall certify and prove that he has intentionally been on a big drunk three times in his life; that his respect for ladies will not prevent him from "cussing" in good sailor style, in their hearing. That he bids defiance to parental rule and never rides a horse in a walk.*

*The advantage of membership are as follows: If you are a coward we will give you a lot of backing and you may with impunity cuss out whomsoever you please.*

*No one is allowed to bet more than $2 nor less than 10cts, on a horse race, unless he gets it up himself: then he can bet pocket knives, or quirts, or lariets.*

*Respectfully,*
*Bill Ruster,*
*Sec'y*

The "Caddo Turf and Jolly Club" article suggesting that the racing competition could improve local equestrian bloodlines may have proved correct.

Alvarado street scene outside of saloons. (Layland Museum, Cleburne, Texas)

Richard Haley settled the Haley Branch in 1852. A year later, his brother, Captain Tom Haley, built a race track along the Nolan River and began breeding racing horses. After Tom Haley's death from Civil War wounds, his two sons continued the racing tradition. John Haley owned and ran a famous horse named Rondo, a foundation sire of the American Quarter Horse Association. Charles Barnard also loved horseracing and his brother-in-law, Juan Cavasos brought some blooded Spanish horses from Mexico when he came.

Others in Johnson County worked to develop improved horse flesh. Soon after Moses Barnes arrived in 1856, he went to Mexico and purchased 100 Spanish brood mares to cross with his blooded horses and began his horse ranch.

In later years some famous horses were known to have come from Johnson County. A July 29, 1902, newspaper headline read: "Sallie McMillin who held the Dallas track record dies in Cleburne last Friday." Col. S. E. Moss and later Charles Furguson owned Sallie McMillin, "She will be remembered by race horse men and admirers of fast horse flesh as the 4-year-old who in 1894 took the Dallas fair track record by going around the three-quarter mile elipse in 1.14, a figure which stands today unbeaten in the state and is only two seconds below the world's record. Sallie McMillin was the fastest 4-year-old ever known in Texas and . . . was cared for at the Cleburne Jockey Club track stables where her death occurred."

"The horse was the supreme animal in Texas after the war and it was the ambition of every Southern boy to own a fast pony, a good six-shooter and a good saddle." Cowboys loved to gamble "and nearly all herds had with them a certain pony or fast horse and they were always ready for a horse race with the local talent." "It was always a 'quarter mile' or any short distance that fit the ground. It was a whipping race from start to finish, and it was always for small amounts, maybe for a saddle or a six-shooter, generally five dollars was the take." Real money was hard come by.

### Sam Bass in Johnson County

Uncle A. D. Hadley told of Sam Bass running his sorrel mare Jenny at the Caddo Grove race track on several occasions. Jenny, "The Denton Mare," was a remarkably fast horse and was rarely beaten. Sam bought the mare and was taking her south along the Chisholm Trail to the tracks he had become familiar with during his trail driving days. It is also reported that Sam Bass camped out nearby at a spring on the edge of the cross timbers. Also rumored was that while Sam visited the Harrells at Covington he made plans to harass the bank in Cleburne.

The electric excitement of the horse racing sport and gambling surrounding "The Caddo Turf and Jolly Club" races made an ideal destination for Sam Bass after his most successful train holdup. Sam and the gang struck gold when holding up the train at Big Spring, Nebraska, on September 18, 1877. With his $10,000 share of $60,000 Sam could afford to raise the stakes. However the trail left behind by the newly-minted $20 gold pieces was an ever present problem. Losing several of his men on the way from Nebraska to Texas, Bass immediately began to recruit local talent, and among those stepping forward was Fleming Doggett. Bass initiated his new members with the robbery of the Fort Worth to Cleburne stage between today's Burleson and Joshua around December 20, 1877. The heist produced a paltry $11.25; and one of the outlaws lost his life and was buried in an unmarked grave in northern Johnson County, perhaps in the Doggett Cemetery. After several of the stage holdups proved disappointing, Bass and longtime members of his gang went back to robbing trains, a more lucrative venture. Youngsters Fleming Doggett and Goodman Franklin stayed close to home, continuing to waylay stages "because they wanted to be like Sam Bass." They continued to prey on stages and travelers near the family's farm where the jurisdictions of Johnson, Tarrant, and Parker Counties met. This area was called "Robbers Hollow" in the newspapers of the day and for several years was a dangerous place through which to travel. In October 1878 they had robbed three west bound stages in less than a week. Early in November, they stopped the Fort Worth-Yuma coach and a freighter, John Ross, shot Franklin's horse

Sam Bass and his outlaw gang returned to the refuge of Texas in November, 1877, after netting $60,000 in twenty-dollar gold pieces in a train robbery at Big Spring, Nebraska, on September 18, 1877. When the Pinkerton detectives and the law enforcement hounds got too close after his robbery escapades in the North, Bass ran for the excitement of Johnson County because of his love for horse racing. Two years earlier he brought his little sorrel mare, Jenny, for the racing festivities at Caddo Grove and Cleburne. (Texas State Library and Archives)

from under him. Ross's rifle cracked again as Franklin vaulted behind the saddle of Fleming Doggett. Doggett was struck by Ross's second shot and Franklin, assuming he was dead, shoved him from the horse and rode away.

Doggett was not yet dead. He dragged himself to the banks of Dutch Creek where his brother, Thomas Doggett, and Bill Hunter found him dead, his pockets turned wrong-side-out, two registered mail bags nearby, and his limp hand in Dutch Creek. Fleming Doggett had outlived his mentor, Sam Bass, by four months.

In 1878 Sam and his gang rode south on the Chisholm Trail through Johnson County. As they entered Bosque County near Morgan the eight men

Richard Doggett was the father of Fleming F. Doggett. Fleming was a one-time associate of Sam Bass's Texas gang. Fleming Doggett died in November 1878, as he attempted to rob the Fort Worth-Yuma stage. (Gary Meador)

The stagecoach stop at Station Branch, southwest of Godley and a few miles south of the area where many hold-ups occurred in Johnson County. The building had been a small troop station on the Military Road and in this photo it is occupied by the Stephen Clements Terry family. Some reports say it was built in 1876. In 1998 the walls are still standing on Station Branch Creek. (Layland Museum, Cleburne, Texas)

rode up to the Nichols ranch and made camp outside the fence to fix a meal. Fifteen-year-old Ed Nichols was inside the fenced melon patch and greeted the group of men that were "well-dressed, well-armed and all had good horses." They asked if his mother could make them a couple of dozen biscuits. He brought them biscuits, eggs and a watermelon. They cooked and ate their food. As they prepared to leave, Ed tells what happened. *"A real nice-looking man walked over to the*

fence . . . and said, *'You're a pretty fine boy. You don't know me and I don't know you, but you'll hear of me later on.' 'What's your name?'* asked Ed. *'Sam Bass, I'm a train robber and I'll have to die with my boots on. Bud, that's a bad shape for a man to be in. But I'm going to ride a good horse and have plenty while I live. I hope you'll never be like me . . .'* He walked back to the others . . . Each man threw me a silver dollar, waved and rode away. They were about the best looking outfit I ever saw."

Sam and his dashing men rode on towards Waco and stopped by the Ranch Saloon where he paid for a round of drinks with the last of the three thousand 1877 gold "double eagles" from the train heist. Sam was considering robbing a Waco bank, but observed the vigilance of the Waco lawmen. Sam and colleagues, Seaborn Barnes and Frank Jackson, went looking for an easier job to pull. They rode into Round Rock in Williamson County on Friday, July 19, 1878, intending to rob the bank the next day. As they entered a dry goods store, they attracted the attention of two deputy sheriffs, Grimes and Moore, who were forewarned of Bass's arrival.

When the lawmen asked if they were armed, all three outlaws drew their weapons and began shooting. Deputy Grimes died instantly. Outlaw Barnes collapsed and died as he attempted to mount his horse for a getaway. Bass rode out of town, gutshot with a portion of his right hand shot away. He and Jackson escaped into the countryside, pursued by a covey of Texas Rangers and all hands in town that owned a gun.

Deputy Sheriff Tucker and Constable Lane of Round Rock led a detachment of "eight or ten Texas Rangers." The next morning, they found Bass sitting exhausted under a tree. He surrendered peacefully and died on a cot in the Round Rock Hotel two days later, July 21, his twenty-seventh birthday.

Wells Fargo receipt from the Cleburne office. (AC)

## W. H. Johnson & Co.,
# U. S. MAIL AND STAGE LINES.

---

### ARRIVAL AND DEPARTURE OF STAGES.
#### CLEBURNE, TEXAS, 1879-80.
Leaves Cleburne at 7 a.m. daily.
Arrives at Fort Worth at 2 p.m. daily.
Leaves Fort Worth at 7 a.m. double daily.
Arrives at Weatherford at 1 p.m. double daily.

☞ The best of Drivers and Teams on the route. Every courtesy will be extended to Passengers.

Advertisement from BYRD'S DIRECTORY. (Layland Museum, Cleburne, Texas)

The Pollock family. The older girl standing in the back was Audie Bass. It is thought by some members of the Pollock clan that relatives in Johnson County gave Sam Bass welcome. Female members of the Pollock family from George's Creek are known to have had the maiden name Bass. Some Bass families are still living near there. Propriety kept some older female family members from revealing the relationship. (Ron and Susie Pollock)

## Hot Time in the Old Town . . .

CLEBURNE CHRONICLE, December 27, 1869:

*Thieves about. On Friday night the 24th, a valuable horse was stolen from Mr. Jas. Williams, 1/4 mile north of town, a buggy from Mr. Cox, and Mr. John Brumley's house was broken open and robbed of $18 specie. On the previous night Mr. Jack Davis, Esq., was robbed of bridle, blanket, and a first rate saddle. Our citizens feel assured that the thieves belong to an organized band, and that the scoundrels live among us. Let our people keep a sharp lookout. We have a suggestion to make: Our county jail is not in a condition to hold the scoundrels, should they be caught.*

CLEBURNE CHRONICLE, August 28, 1869:

*Deputy Sheriff Harrison attempted to arrest two young gents from the country, who were running their horses through town, yelling like two Comanche Indians. One of them had too much mean whiskey on board to ride steady and tumbled off in the street. If the fall had broken his neck he would behave himself the next time he comes to town.*

CLEBURNE CHRONICLE, September 13, 1869:

*The young men of the county are wearing too many six-shooters, jingling Mexican spurs, broad brimmed hats with snakes coiled around them, and practicing too freely at gin mills . . . If parents do not wish the happiness of their declining years dimmed and clouded by having a son convicted of theft or hung for murder, they will see to it that their boys are kept away from low-doggeries [saloons], gambling and outraging the peace and morals of society.*

The town was full of cowboys and strangers, many of whom were young ex-Confederate soldiers. H. W. Barclay explained:

*I am sorry to say I did not always conduct myself in a gentlemanly manner. After a four-year war it was not expected we could settle down all of a sudden . . . Those men were not mean or vicious, but seemed to take advantage of the free and easy way things were moving along, enjoying the situation, and would do you a kindness at any time. About now I was elected Justice of the Peace, when every morning Perry Arnold would have a crowd of them rounded up and I would have a regular matinee. The fines imposed were always light, always paid, and they never got mad at me. I knew to go the extent of the law would only enrage them and also believed they would leave off after a while, which they did, the most of them becoming good citizens.*

N. L. Poole years later recalled:

*I found Cleburne a frontier village with only a few stores here. The cow boy of the early day was largely in the ascendancy in population . . .*

Phil Allin said:

*Those were happy days though not withstanding the fact that in many instances the gay and festive cow boy would come to our village, stop at the tavern long enough to fill his hide with valley tan, shoot up the town and make life a burden to its inhabitants.*

William James said,

*Now and then a crowd from the forks of the creek or off the cow trail would come in, tank up on whisky and shoot up the town, but they meant no harm. They were just giving vent to their feelings, and meeting with them* when sober if in trouble or distress, their purses or themselves were at your service.

In the early 1870s another justice of the peace was Squire Hicks. While a case was in progress he moved his jaws chewing his wad of tobacco. When he was ready to announce his decision he would spit into a pine box full of sand and say, "Ten and ten" or "Ten or ten." This standard fine interpreted as ten days in jail with the second *ten* being how many dollars was to be paid. If he suspected that someone was lying he would call attention to the witness that he was under oath.

CLEBURNE CHRONICLE, February 17, 1872:

*The jail door that is being made is of ponderous proportions, made of solid iron, and when completed, with the casing, will weigh about twelve hundred pounds. Messrs. Whitten & Day are doing the work, and it is a compliment to their superior workmanship.*

CLEBURNE CHRONICLE, June 4, 1872:

*Four prisoners escaped from the Cleburne jail tonight by removing a log: How often will we have to announce the escape of prisoners from our jail.*

CLEBURNE CHRONICLE, August 9, 1873:

*Three miles east of Cleburne, vigilantes shot a boy for horse stealing, then dropped the body down a well. The good name of Johnson County is likely to suffer from the acts of bad characters within its borders.*

CLEBURNE CHRONICLE, November 1873:

*A band of suspicious characters are now in this part of the state. Where they came from is not known, but they showed up in Fort Worth last week . . . a strong patrol guard was kept up of nights lest they should attempt to burn the town, that they might have good opportunities for plunder. On Saturday night the Post Office was set on fire, but was discovered . . . Five of the suspicious fellows left Fort Worth in the direction of Cleburne, and it may be proper for our citizens to be on the alert.*

CLEBURNE CHRONICLE, March 20, 1874:

*Horse thieves struck near Alvarado last night, but apparently got lost during the night and were discovered by Sheriff Arnold's posse asking directions to Waxahachie.*

Young T. U. Taylor observed that in Johnson County "The lowest form of creeping thing was a horse thief." "To steal" [a man's horse] "was to steal something more than cash . . . When caught it called for the rope without a trial and without jury unless the sheriff caught him first."

## A Mere Killing

CLEBURNE CHRONICLE, June 8, 1872:

*The board of alderman of the town of Cleburne passed an ordinance this week making it a misdemeanor to ride a horse on the sidewalks.*

In January 1873, a "Do-Nothing" slate of candidates including Mayor B. P. Leach and Alderman Major Sparks of the Cleburne House did away with the previous administration's ordinances and issued milder ones of their own.

CLEBURNE CHRONICLE, March 30, 1873:

*Cleburne has been in an uproar for some nights in the vicinity of the square. Around midnight there have been hideous yells, low ribaldry and obscene songs and blackguard bandying and bullyings and almost continuous discharges of fire-arms . . . disturbing the sleep and shocking the ears of the decent portion of our population.*

CLEBURNE CHRONICLE, November 1873:

*A SHOOTING GALLERY ON THE SQUARE*

*If one were to judge from the frequent report of pistols . . . to be heard almost hourly in this town, we would conclude that a shooting gallery would be well patronized here. If some enterprising person would take advantage of the proclivity that some seem to have around about here to keep continually discharging firearms within, not only the limit of the city, but right in the heart of the town, we think they would do well. Have we no ordinance for the suppression of this dangerous practice? If so, we think that its rigid enforcement is "loudly" called for . . . Those chaps, vandals, will "smell the patching" one of these fine evenings. (Editor, CLEBURNE CHRONICLE.)*

Dr. U. D. Ezell's observations of the cowboys at play at Kimball and Cleburne explain what was happening in the trail towns: *Often the drivers camped with their herds just outside of town, then they would frequent the stores and saloons there. Upon arriving in Kimball, the cowboys were often tired, lonesome, and dry from the long days spent in the saddle. And it was the patronage of the cowhands that enabled Kimball to support four saloons. Most of those who patronized these places were courteous and peaceful when not molested. Yet there was a keen rivalry between cowboys working for different outfits; and this chivalry sometimes led to free for all fights when the boys were drinking heavily. These brawls seldom resulted in anything more serious than a few bloody noses or a few blackened eyes. It sometimes happened too, that a group of young fellows would get tanked up* on liquor and decide to take over the town. Pistols would bark and bullets would whine as they were fired into the trunks of the large live oak trees that grew near the town square. When they tired of this sport, the boys would go from one business house to another, ordering the owners to close up their places of business. If a merchant refused to comply with this order, a pistol shot through the floor or the ceiling of his store would, generally, convince him that it was best to humor the drunks by complying with their demands. It would be surprising to know how many pounds of lead are still embedded in the trunks of those old live oak trees that stand near old Kimball. The numerous trees on the square of Cleburne were also the target of the gunplay of the cowboys.

*There were a few brawls of a more serious nature than those mentioned above. The later were caused by someone getting too much 'pizen water,' or by the appearance of a would-be bad man . . . It must be understood, however, that there was made a clear distinction between a murder and a mere killing. If one's victim were armed and given an opportunity to defend himself before he was killed, then this was a killing, and society did not undertake to punish one for this. On the other hand, if one shot an opponent who was unarmed, or killed him from ambush, then this was murder, and society did punish one for murder.*

On occasion, it was not the cowboys who were responsible for these disturbances, W. L. Evans recollected seeing hometown boy Quincy Wren as he "paraded the little village" looking for trouble.

The CLEBURNE CHRONICLE, April 4, 1872, reads: *A difficultly occurred in our town, on Monday night last, between Quincy Wren and Jim G. Thomas, in which the latter was shot through the leg. Wren surrendered himself to the sheriff and gave bond for his appearance. The wound is a serious one, but it is thought his leg will not have to be amputated.*

All that year the newspaper was filled with letters to the editor and editorials alternately urging the council to do something or nothing. The reports and statements reflected the delicate problem that law officers faced in keeping the peace—a fine line between restricting trade and allowing total anarchy. When they didn't act, vigilante groups would form. When they did, they were accused of hurting business and relieved of duty.

### Progress and Do-Nothings

CLEBURNE CHRONICLE, March 14, 1874:

*Mr. Editor, I was glad to find in your last weeks issue, a few punches at our do-nothing Town Council, and*

hope you will continue to goad them, until they are aroused to a proper sense of the demands of the situation. The policy enunciated in the platform, on which they were elected, and which they have so persistently carried out, thus far—has in the minds of our citizens, like Grant's do-nothing Indian policy, failed of accomplishing any good; and action is now imperitively demanded.

A do-nothing Alderman replied to criticism of their policies in the CHRONICLE:

*Maj. Sparks, says that though he was run and elected Alderman on the "do-nothing" ticket, without his knowledge or consent, yet he is not in favor of "going back" on the people. He says he was elected to do <u>nothing</u>, and insists that he is well qualified to fill that office as any man living.*

CLEBURNE CHRONICLE, June 11, 1874:

*The prevalence of crime and the inauguration of mob-law should arouse every good citizen to the importance of changing this terrible state of things.*

A "Clean-up" slate of reform "Progress" candidates ran for city office. The "do-nothing" incumbents must have been asleep or overconfident for at the city election on November 3, 1874, the progress candidates M. M. Clack for mayor and James Aiken for marshal, won by a few votes. There was to be stricter enforcement of fines for cussing, for being seen with disreputable women, and for the shooting off of guns. There was also the ability to tax any type of fight: men, cocks, dogs, bears, bulls, and other animals. There was talk of a hog law.

In 1866, before there was a town, Camp Henderson was just a wide place in the cattle trail. Some of the merchants such as N. H. Cook had specifically moved here to get the trail driver's business. They realized immediately that if these actions were enforced it would curb business and prove too restrictive for the good of the town's merchants. If Cleburne became known as intolerant—trail drivers would go elsewhere. Trail bosses could not afford to lose time or their cowboys to a stay in jail. They didn't like paying off their men's fines, or the bother of breaking them out of jail. If the word spread up and down the cattle trail the "big spenders," and the lovers of thrills and excitement would be gone.

During the peak years of the Chisholm Trail the cowboys were very good business for the town's merchants. The main attractions in Cleburne besides supplies were whiskey, gambling, ten pins, music, dancing, and women. A number of local saloons, provisions stores,

Major Sparks, a do-nothing alderman and owner of the Cleburne House. (Dr. Jack Burton)

and trading posts did well selling to the trail drivers. The display ads in the CHRONICLE of that time show that besides the saloons, almost every drug and supply store also sold alcohol in some form. As the number of ordinances increased it took its toll on businesses of all types.

In 1874 shortly after the vote for stricter measures:

. . . *a long petition numerously signed by leading citizens,* [called for and voted] *the disestablishment of city government in Cleburne . . . Among other things it was alleged that municipal government had outlived its usefulness.*

Cleburne, the county seat, would have no town council and no marshal.

Night camps of the traildrivers were on the hills on both sides of the Nolan just to the west of Cleburne. Word of the intolerant, strict ordinances got around, some of it spread by competing merchants in Kimball and Buchanan. Quickly word was put out on the trail that the settlement was wide open and the cowboys were more than welcome. Trailbosses were reassured by the presentation of cigars. "Medicinal Whiskey," a necessary part of a camp outfit, was given as an inducement to do business and let the cowboys come into town for doctoring, provisions, "wet groceries" and amusements of the "she-type." For nearly two more years the cowboy's evening entertainments went unre-

Tattooed lady. In her day she was considered "outlandish." In early days, it was not considered safe for a proper lady to walk on the west side of the Square. At the turn of the century, there continued to be cases filed against madams keeping "disorderly houses" in Cleburne. In 1915 any male person over fourteen years of age who knowingly rode in a vehicle or walked on the street with a woman who had a bad reputation could be considered guilty of a misdemeanor and could be fined $5 to $100. (AC)

stricted as the rowdy boys came to town to "see the elephant," "buck the tiger" and "paint the town red."

**Daylight Robbery of Two Banks**

Dr. T. D. Lorance operated a bank with his large store, on the northwest corner of the square. Next door, J. W. Brown and Col. B. J. Chambers bought out the Hollingsworth's Bank, the first bank in Cleburne in 1869. On April 21, 1875, two men made one visit to Chambers and Brown's bank and two visits to T. D. Lorance's bank on the pretense of changing a gold piece for currency. Then the two men tied their horses about 100 yards down from the banks and went back to the Chambers and Brown Bank. One man presented a $10 gold piece at the desk while the other man quickly pushed by to get

M. Phegley and A. F. Murphy of Phegley & Murphy located in Cleburne in 1887. Murphy preserved the trunk with the photographic collage of female entertainers pasted to the inside lid of the trunk. (Layland Museum, Cleburne, Texas)

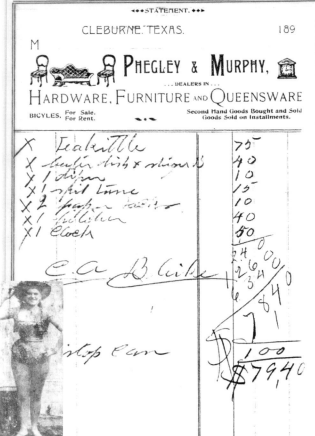

"Cowboy Pin-ups." These Dance Hall girls and entertainers of the old west era were found pasted inside the lid of a trunk belonging to Mr. Murphy of the Phegley and Murphy's secondhand store. The photographs were so daring that Mr. Murphy kept them as souvenirs of the old days. Later the impressive ladies were passed along to his son Pat. Some of these frontier entertainers made respectable attempts at Shakespere, theatre, and acrobatics. Others were not much more than well-advertised ladies of the evening. (AC)

Samuel J. Darcy's Drug Store in the middle of the east side of the public square in Cleburne 1872–73. In the frontier period, each drug store on the square had a resident doctor who would office and see patients at the store during the day. Dr. William A. Heard was at Darcy's and "Particular attention (was) given to Surgical operations, and treatment of diseases of the eye." Note: the heavy shutters used to close up the windows of the stores at night when the cowboys shot up the town. (Dr. Jack Burton)

Right: T. U. Taylor said that in the 1870s, "There were many suspicious characters coming through the county. A man could brand himself as a dude or as an objectionable citizen in many ways. There were three ways that were absolutely certain to queer the public and rank the individual as a foreigner. One of these ways was to wear a silk hat, the second, use the broad 'a' and say 'eyether' and 'neyether,' and the third way was to part your hair in the middle." (AC)

in range of the safe door and drew his pistol. Benjamin Hartsough, the cashier pulled his gun and ordered the men to "Get out of here! Get out of here!" As Ben came around the counter, his gun misfired. One of the robbers shot at Hartsough but missed. Hartsough rushed towards the men, but stumbled and fell against them as they all pushed out the door into the street. Hartsough fell to the ground as one of the men told the other to kill him. The cashier was shot in the face. The ball entered his upper lip, came out by his windpipe and lodged against his collar bone. In spite of the wound he continued to fire away. The shootout attracted other citizens, causing the robbers to flee, shooting their way out of town. During their escape they lost one of their horses. The county sheriff sent a deputy after them locating them in southern Collin County. Evading capture there, they were never to be heard from again.

### Rip-Roaring Human Beings

The tide of opinion ebbed and flowed with events such as these. In October 1875 another vote was taken, eighty-one voted and city government remained nonexistent in Cleburne. Even the county

T. D. Lorance Bank and Chambers and Brown Bank where in 1875 an attempted robbery of two banks was foiled. The location is the west end of the north side of Cleburne Courthouse square. (From Mohler's "Business Men and Houses" photographic collage, circa 1872, Dr. Jack Burton)

The cashier at Brown and Chambers Bank named Benjamin Hartsough was shot in the face during the attempted robbery of two banks in 1875. (Dr. Jack Burton)

sheriff seemed unwanted because the Johnson County Commissioners would not furnish him with an office in the courthouse. So Sheriff Arnold built an office at his own expense on the lawn of the Courthouse where he conducted business. After the newspapers praised the sheriff, the commissioners court, not to be circumvented, ordered the sheriff's office torn down and the gate in the fence closed.

After two years of experiencing the exciting life of a:

*wide open town . . . the rehabilitation of city government was a lively subject for discussion in the spring of 1876. Cleburne was agitated from centre to circumference, but with no casualties worth mentioning.*

The big herds were just outside of town; the cowboys were still on the move driving north and returning south. Many immigrants and refugees were headed west. "Gunmen rode into saloons to get their drinks and rode out again unmolested." Drunken cowboys, teamsters, buffalo hunters, and gamblers attempted to enter private residences. A bullet smashed into the home of Mrs. Featherstone embedding itself in a wall and barely missing her. The fun of shooting up the town began to wear on the nerves of the toughest and the most liberal of cit-

izens. Another vote was made on July 14, 1876, to "reestablish on a modest scale" corporate government in Cleburne for the "repression of rip-roaring human beings." It passed and Judge J. M. Odell was elected mayor; W. F. George, secretary; W. H. Brown, marshal.

## Hung by Trial and Error— The Samuel H. Myers Jr. Story

Ironically, when Johnson County held the first of five legal public hangings it would take the life of innocent young Samuel H. Myers, Jr. Sam was the younger half-brother of Thomas and David who had lynched Cal Tucker about ten years earlier for stealing $700 of their father's gold.

Uncle Sammy Myers died in 1874. He was the first permanent settler in eastern Johnson County and located his land grant of three thousand acres about three miles north of Alvarado. Uncle Sammy had been married three times and through the years he had given each of his children a good start in life with 160 acres, a mule, and until the war, a slave. Sam Myers' will was filed and three administrators were appointed: Mary Ann Myers, Bill Hunter, and Thomas J. Myers. Mary Ann (Hunter) Myers was his third and surviving wife. Mary and Bill were brother and sister. Bill was married to Helen, Uncle Sammy's oldest daughter by his first wife, Patsy Wallace Myers. Thomas was also a son by Uncle Sammy's first wife.

Mary Ann Myers was directed to give various amounts of land and money to each of the children at age eighteen. She was to have the use of the rest of the property during her "natural life" or until she remarried. After Uncle Sammy's death, she married John A. Hester on January 4, 1877, but did not distribute as instructed. Some children of the first two wives were angry. Many in the family saw her influenced by her brother Bill Hunter who assisted her in gathering up all the property, loans, and notes.

On the evening of February 21, 1877, while sitting at the dining table with her family, Mary Ann was shot in the head by a bullet that came crashing through the window of her home. The wound to her head was six inches deep and three inches wide and her husband and children were splattered with her blood and brain tissue. No one saw the killer, but tracks led away through a field, near to a crossroad and then to the home of stepson-in-law James Bowden. Threatening statements had been made by Bowden but in the ensuing uproar other sons of Uncle Sammy were also suspected. Bowden was arrested that night at his home. A month went by but Bowden would not talk. His jailers tried to lubricate Bowden's tongue with whiskey. After he found that his wife had deserted him, Bowden saved up a quart of the whiskey and gulped it down all at once, but his suicide attempt failed. One night a raucous crowd in hoods broke Bowden out of jail—not to free him—but to put a noose around his neck. The mob and jailers, including then Deputy John C. Brown, were still hoping to make Bowden talk. This time they tried a rope.

WACO DAILY EXAMINER, April 20, 1877:

*This week a mob took a prisoner out of the Johnson County jail and prepared to string him up, attempting to elicit a confession: Such a proceeding has never been heard of before, and Johnson County should be able to have a better state of affairs.*

The rope trick worked. Bowden with a noose around his neck agreed that there was another person involved, and that if he had just a little more time, he would make a statement. After three weeks, the sheriff obtained the name of Samuel H. Myers, Jr., as the one who pulled the trigger—Bowden claimed to have only assisted Sam in the shooting. Sam was a son of the second wife of Uncle Sammy Myers. Sam Myers, Jr., protested that he was innocent and was having dinner with a group of at least five people at the time of the murder. Sam's brother Thomas J. Myers was also arrested as he stepped forward to confirm the alibi that he was with Sam at the dinner table. Thomas was bailed out, and was pursued by armed vigilantes who rode about the county intimidating anyone who supported the Myers boys. There

Samuel H. Myers, Jr. (1858–1880), son of early settler Samuel Houston Myers, was dispatched from this life by hanging in November 1880. Many now believe Sam Jr. was innocent—framed as the result of a conspiracy. His life was taken to atone for the murder of his father's third wife, Mary Ann Myers Hester, who was shot in the head while sitting with her family at the supper table. (Mary Dugan)

were several others at the table the evening of the murder. Some of the others were not related to the family but believed that if they provided an alibi they would also be arrested. They fled the county and could not be found to subpoena as witnesses even after several years of effort.

The muddy boot tracks that led away from the murder scene near the crossroad and on to Bowden's house led to Bowden's arrest that very night. Later Sam's boots were studied and "expert" testimony confirmed that Sam's boots made the tracks, they had a distinct crack at the edge of the sole on the same foot that matched the tracks in the mud—no mistake. "Den" Richardson, well-known local Texas Ranger, scout, and Indian fighter testified for the prosecution before the Grand Jury.

The community one by one lined up on one side or the other as witnesses. The tragedy that escalated out of this fatal family feud ruptured the extensive Myers family and the community as a whole. The testimony of Helen Myers Hunter changed during the trial.

Sam Myers protested that he was innocent for three years, through more than one trial. Sam escaped from jail and got 250 yards only to be cornered and recaptured by a crowd of people. Deputy John C. Brown was elected sheriff in the meantime. At a critical moment in Sam's final trial, a witness was unable to come and testify because she was in labor with child. She was the only other person left who would testify to have been at the table with Sam, Thomas, and the others. On appeal her essential testimony was disregarded as being partial to Sam and all appeals were dismissed. The final sentencing was that Sam should be hung March 19, 1880. At his sentencing Sam said:

*Bowden will confess, ere long, the truth. It may be too late to benefit me, but it will be a lesson to those whose hands are dyed red in the innocent blood of Sam Myers. They will wish, when they are brought before the Judge of Judges . . . that their hands had been washed clean.*

The day came for the hanging and from the gallows Sam said:

*I do believe, as I have ever done, that James M. Bowden, the self accused culprit, is the bloody assassin of that woman . . . the populace wanted a sensation in Johnson County, and no mean subject would furnish the proper material. They must have a sacrifice of some well known and highly respected family. They have selected your humble servant as their victim.*

Sam went on to say that Bowden must have been:

*. . . thinking that the influence that I could wield through my friends would be the means of extricating himself from this unpardonable, merciless, murder. And the manner of his confession, wrung from him in the dead of night, with a rope around his neck, under the leadership of your high sheriff, John C. Brown, should ever blot his (Brown's) name from the roll of honorable and law abiding citizens. He stands before you now and dares not deny it.*

Sam accused the district attorney of being among those who forced Bowden to confess at the end of a rope. Sam also accused Bill Hunter of bribing numerous witnesses with Sam's own father's money and circulating a petition asking the governor not to stay the execution.

*I have never dispared for a moment that whenever Bowden hangs, as he should be, he will be likely to tell the truth . . . many of you will then look upon the hanging of Sam Myers in a different light . . . I bid all of you, friends and foes alike, farewell! May the God of mercy guard you through life and I myself through the realms of the great unknown beyond the grave.*

Sam was then hung by the neck by Sheriff Brown in front of a crowd of between six to eight thousand spellbound citizens. Sam's half brother, Thomas J. Myers, who provided Sam's alibi of being at home at the supper table, was also convicted and sentenced to hang. However, the verdict was eventually overturned on appeal—there had only been eleven jurors who decided his guilt. In a change of venue and appeal in Hood County he was eventually pronounced "not guilty" and

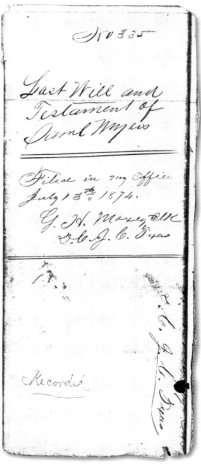

The will filed July 13, 1874, of Samuel H. Myers, Sr. Its legacy was a family feud which caused the murder of his last wife, the hanging of his namesake son, and the rupturing of his large family. (JCA)

released. James M. Bowden, who had confessed to being an accomplice, was convicted after a change of venue to Somervell County and was sent to Huntsville for life in 1882. After having serving fifteen years in jail for his supposed complicity, Bowden at age forty-six became very ill. He was pardoned by Governor Culberson in July of 1897 so he could go home to die. Bowden confessed repeatedly on his deathbed to visitors and family members that he was indeed the murderer. He had used Sam's boots to walk to the murder scene, shot Mary Ann Myers, and put the boots back on the porch.

The true scope of the tragedy that had befallen the Myers Family was revealed—not only had a wife and mother, Mary Ann Myers Hester, been treacherously murdered, but also an innocent son had been implicated and "legally" murdered as well. During the difficulty many of the Myers descendants scattered from the county. When the word of Bowden's deathbed confessions started getting around the thought was so terrible, some refused to believe it saying the Myers were making it up. However, the general feeling among the Myers and some Hunter family descendants is that Sam Myers, Jr. was an innocent man. J. Hunter Pearson, a grandson of Bill Hunter and Helen Myers Hunter, informed the author he was sure that Sam Myers, Jr. was innocent. One Hunter descendant believes Sam Myers was guilty.

The law could make mistakes and lawmen did not always act lawfully.

Waco Daily Examiner, August 16, 1876:

*A posse from Johnson County last week went to Comanche County. They were to arrest a man who had fled after insulting the daughter of one of the deputies. Returning through Bosque County the posse took him to Johnson County's cliffs above Kimball Bend and cut the tendons in his legs so he couldn't escape. They then pro-*

Hanging of John Wilkins in 1896. (Dr. Jack Burton)

*ceeded to torture him to death "in a manner more horrible than anything we have ever heard of." His body was left hanging from a cliff above the Brazos River. Upon returning back home, they claimed that he had escaped and gotten away. But the posse themselves were arrested on the 14th, betrayed by the possession of the victim's horse and gear.*

### Jesse James and the Angels

Lillian does not sound like a place which might be the hideout of the most famous outlaws in the old west. Nor would one quickly associate the name Angel with Jesse and Frank James. Maybe these are some of the reasons, aside from tight lips, the secret was kept for over a hundred years.

For many years the ladies of the Angel family insisted that the story be kept a secret. Now the stigma of being related is long past, and one of the last of the aged grandchildren of the family volunteered to talk. So the secret is out, though a century late, that Jesse and Frank James hid out in Johnson County.

The newspapers carried stories of rough and dangerous looking characters coming through Johnson County in those days after the Civil War. They might have been referring to members of the Jesse James Gang, also known as the James-Younger Gang. Frank and Jesse

Frank and Jesse James sent letters postmarked from Fort Worth and other points in Texas to the newspapers and dime novelists. For over two decades the Pinkertons pursued the James Gang. The James boys often came to Texas when hiding out. They had a sister whom they visited in Grayson County. In Johnson County the local Angel family legends held that the James boys hid in the barn behind their home near present day Lillian. The maiden name of the matriarch of the Angel family was James. The Angels kept the family relationship a secret until one descendant chose to reveal the story in his last years. The Missourian James boys posed as cowboys and cattle buyers along the Chisholm Trail and in their letters claimed to be involved in buying and driving small herds of "beeves." They would have blended well into the fabric of frontier Johnson County. (Courtesy of the Denver Public Library, Western History Department)

James were open about their trips to Texas. They fled to Texas to hide out during cooling off periods from their heated Missouri activities.

### Longhaired Jim

Jim Courtright was lightning fast with a gun. Jim was an army scout with James Butler. "Wild Bill" Hickock was also an army scout and they seemed to have developed other similarities. Courtright and "Wild Bill" were similar in the fact that both were purported to have been the fastest guns in the West. They both stood over six feet tall, and occasionally wore shoulder length hair. Their matched pair of pistols were holstered butt forward, although occasionally both pistols were stuck into a colorful Mexican sash at the waist. Courtright and Hickock both enjoyed gambling and performed in Wild West Shows.

T. I. "Longhaired Jim" Courtright, Ft. Worth's most famous gunman, was involved in a gunfight in Cleburne in 1882 and was a Johnson County sheriff's deputy in 1886. (Fort Worth Public Library)

As a shootist, Jim was billed alongside Annie Oakley. After gun wadding injured Courtright and the show left him behind, he drifted into Ft. Worth. The wide-open cattle town needed a marshal and he was elected to serve in 1876. Just as in Cleburne, Ft. Worth's bosses didn't want to put a damper on the freewheeling and free spending types. "The merchants felt he should keep blood from flowing but not the liquor." In 1879 Jim Courtright resigned his marshal's job in Ft. Worth after he felt he was prevented from doing his job.

For the next few years he ran his own detective agency and worked as a regulator (hired gun) offering "protection" for a cut of the action. It was during this period that Jim showed up in Cleburne. The WACO EXAMINER on May 23, 1882, reported this story. Jim was checking out the "business climate" of the new railroad stop on the Santa Fe. Courtright was waiting on a train, so to kill some time, he stepped into a restaurant on the Courthouse square to get a "cup of coffee." A fellow named Davis insulted Jim, so Courtright proceeded to pistol whip the man. The gun went off catching Davis's clothes on fire. Courtright was arrested and released on bail in time to catch his train back to Ft. Worth. Davis was lucky. Perhaps Marshal Brown let Courtright off

because of the obvious kindness he showed in not killing Davis. With Courtright's reputation, it would have been considered great restraint to have only pistol whipped the man.

Jim had been indicted in New Mexico for two of the seven killings he was involved with while regulating there in 1879. However, by 1883 he was a well-liked deputy in Ft. Worth. Jim was finally acquitted of the murders in New Mexico for a lack of evidence after several narrow escapes.

In 1887 Jim was back running his "T. I. Courtright Detective Agency" when he was killed in Fort Worth's most famous shootout. Luke Short was in the company of Bat Masterson. Jim was thought to be running his protection racket again and was said to be shaking Luke down for a cut. Jim lost his life outside the White Elephant Saloon where Luke was a dealer. During a conversation Luke made a move Jim didn't like; Jim pulled his gun. They were standing so close, that as Jim's hammer came down to strike the firing pin, Luke's watch chain caught under Jim's hammer, preventing the gun's discharge. Luke wasted no time, drew his .45 Colt and emptied it. Jim died with three bullets in him, one through the heart. His funeral was said to have been the largest in Ft. Worth up to that time, with carriages lined up for six blocks.

### The Wild Bunch,
### Tom Horn and Matt Rash

The Wild Bunch is considered by many to be the first interstate crime syndicate that operated in America. At Cassidy Point in Brown's Park, Utah, on August 18, 1896, two hundred outlaws gathered from various rustling operations. The outlaws had been drawn to the freedom and opportunities presented by the open plains. Butch Cassidy proposed they form the Train Robbers Syndicate, later known as the Wild Bunch.

A squabble arose between Cassidy and Kid Curry over leadership. A contest was proposed by Cassidy. He and Curry would each lead a gang for a year; at a meeting at the end of the year, the most financially successful gang leader would assume leadership of the entire group. Cassidy won.

In 1883 Matt Rash of Cleburne moved to the Brown's Hole area, where Utah, Wyoming, and Colorado borders meet. Rash claimed he was a nephew of Davy Crockett, the martyred Alamo hero.

Living in Brown's Hole, Rash was a cow puncher described by those around him as "a likable, friendly young man." He worked as a hand for the Middlesex

ROBT. A. PINKERTON Manager.
EASTERN DIVISION, NEW YORK.

WM. A. PINKERTON, Manager.
WESTERN DIVISION, CHICAGO, ILL'S.

PINKERTON'S NATIONAL DETECTIVE AGENCY
"FOUNDED BY ALLAN PINKERTON, 1850"
"WE NEVER SLEEP."
GEO. D. BANGS, Gen'l Supt. NEW YORK.

This Pinkerton National Detective Agency letterhead from a wanted poster was sent to Johnson County in the late 1800s. (JCA)

"Robert Frentrance James in buggy near Forrest Hill." The father of Mary Jane James Angel, is believed by at least one elderly Angel descendant to have been closely related to the famous James boys. (A. T. "Hoot" and Mary Grace Angel)

This picture was made at the home of Eli "Doc" Angel. The farm has been in the family for 110 years. Left to right, back row: Eli "Doc" Albert Angel; in his lap, his son Frank Angel; Nora Appleton Angel, wife; Mary Jane James Angel; Eli Ward Angel; Charlie Prater holding his son; Julie Angel Prater, wife; Mary Frances Angel Mothershed; Sis and Ellen Angel with girl in chair (unidentified). Front row: Jim Angel; two Mothershed brothers; Chestley Mothershed and Finis Mothershed (Mary Frances Mothershed's brothers), circa 1895, Lillian, Texas. The Angel family was large, but that did not keep them from taking in orphaned children such as the Mothershed boys. This compassion may have been why their door was open to other relatives like Frank and Jesse James whose father had died in California. (Ralph Angel)

outfit, Tim Kinney and the Two-Bar Ranch on the Little Snake River. They fired him and he stole seven hundred head of Kinney cattle to start his own ranch on Cold Spring Mountain. Rash became associated with the cattle rustling by the Wild Bunch around the Hole-in-the-Wall hideout in Central Wyoming. He became a major rustler along the "Outlaw Trail" region and was a target for extermination by ranchers with larger holdings.

Tom Horn, former scout for the U.S. Army during the Indian Wars, persuaded Geronimo to surrender to General Crook in 1886. Horn lived with an Apache band, spoke their language, and learned braiding and roping as well as Apache tactics and strategy. Horn was in Teddy Roosevelt's Rough Riders during the Spanish-American War.

Horn was hired by the ranchers' association to discover who was involved with the Wild Bunch. This association, which purchased vast areas of land and key watering rights, did not wish to be officially involved; so they turned down the proposition of paying $500 per outlaw killed. They left it instead to individual ranch owners to contract with Horn and get the murders accomplished. Horn, one of the most mysterious and controversial figures in Western history, was connected

to Alex Swan of the T-Bar Ranch and the Swan Land & Cattle Company. Swan built an empire as one of the largest land and cattle owners.

Horn's method of operation was to work as a ranch hand for small ranches. Through observation he would confirm the rustling activities and then quit, knowing the habits of the ranch owner. Horn had been working for Matt Rash for a spell and then quit the job. Soon after, Matt Rash was found dead at his cabin door July 10, 1900, by Felix Meyers and Uncle Billy Rife. His horse, tethered outside, had been shot as well. Matt had last been seen alive July 7, riding back to his ranch after a July 4 celebration in a town nearby. He had been shot

three times with a rifle. He was buried July 13 near his cabin on Summit Springs.

Matt had been courting Ann Bassett on a neighboring ranch "and the depth of that attachment was not realized 'til his death." Ann filed a will in which she was named beneficiary of Matt's estate. In August, Matt's father came from Cleburne, Texas, with Attorney Bledsoe, to claim Matt's estate.

On the day appointed, all interested parties started for Hahn's Peak, the seat of Routt County, Colorado, where the killing occurred. Ann relinquished her claim to the estate for $300 and returned home. "At the time of the compromise Ann Bassett charged Tom Horn, who was present, with Matt Rash's murder."

When the elder Rash and his lawyer returned from the county seat, they stayed at Bassett's ranch. A few

In September of 1900 Butch Cassidy, the Sundance Kid, and Bill Carver robbed the bank in Winnemucca, Nevada. After escaping to Fort Worth, Texas they met some of the rest of the Wild Bunch and celebrated. All duded up in the latest fashions, they stopped by Swartz's studio and posed for this now famous picture. The photographer was so proud of the picture he placed a copy in his window display. A passing lawman recognized one of the outlaws from an old wanted poster. Butch sent a copy of the picture with a note to the bank thanking them for their "contribution." The Wild Bunch's gloating and their recently escalating number of train robberies made the Pinkerton's more determined than ever to break up the gang. Within a year many of the members of the gang were dead or had fled the country. Standing left to right: Bill Carver, and Harvey Logan (Kid Curry); seated left to right: The Sundance Kid (Harvey Longabaugh), the Tall Texan (Ben Kilpatrick), and Butch Cassidy (Robert LeRoy Parker). (AC)

weeks later, Matt's cattle were sold and his father returned to Texas with his son's body for burial at home.

A number of bounties were paid to Horn before he was caught and charged with a similar murder in an area controlled by the small ranchers. Tom Horn was convicted and died by hanging.

### The "High Five" Black Jack Gang of the "Wild Bunch"

Johnson County's other connection with the infamous Wild Bunch centers on the opposition of a wife to her husband's irregular lifestyle. Brothers Tom and Sam Ketchum maintained a "ranch" in Snake Valley, through which they moved stolen horses and cattle. They ran the southern stretch of the "Outlaw Trail" of the Wild Bunch that ran all the way to Mexico. They also participated in train robberies.

After robbing a train with part of the gang near Cimmaron, New Mexico, on July 11, 1899, Sam Ketchum was wounded in a shootout with a posse. He was captured and died from his wounds thirteen days later in the Territorial Prison in Santa Fe.

Sam's wife, Louisa, had left this uneasy existence and taken their three-year-old son, William Berry Ketchum, back to the safety of Cleburne, Texas, where she lived for several years and married John LeCompt. She died in 1943 in Hall County, Texas. Young William B. grew to adulthood in Cleburne and married Mattie Hines. They lived most of their married life with their four children in Lubbock, where he died in 1954.

Tom "Black Jack" Ketchum, who had separated from his brother, attempted a robbery of a Colorado & Southern train near Folsom, Arizona, August 16, 1899. His brother had made the same attempt at nearly the same spot a month earlier. Tom took a blast from Conductor Frank Harrington's shotgun that blew away a portion of his right arm. He fell from the train, and it proceeded to its destination. On a return trip two days later, Ketchum was found wounded and unconscious beside the track. He was taken into custody and his arm was amputated at the New Mexico Territorial Penitentiary. A trial in 1900 yielded a verdict of death by hanging. The authorities at Clayton, New Mexico, where the hanging was to occur, had never hung a prisoner. They miscalculated his weight, the rope was too long resulting in a long drop from the platform of the gallows. Black Jack was decapitated by the noose.

After Sam and Tom Ketchum's deaths, the remaining members of the Ketchum gang, Bill Carver, Kid Curry, plus George and Ben Kilpatrick, joined Butch Cassidy and his associates in the Wild Bunch. Members of this group posed for the famous photograph of the Wild Bunch taken in Fort Worth at Swartz Studio in 1900.

### The Cowboy's Lament

Slowly the old Wild West changed and drifted into history. Locals who had lived through the time such as W. L. Evans reminisced in 1908: "But things have changed. The day of the pistol toter and the desperado have gone to return no more to Texas." Phil Allin lamented: "Those were also the days of the stage robber, but they are gone, and civilization has driven away the fishes, most of the birds, the prairie chickens, the deer, the antelope and the wolves that were then abundant . . ." William James observed, "But this sort who served their day and generation are all gone, and with progress and enlightenment we have another sort, wanting perhaps in all the elements that constitute the real man as they . . ." the raucous, young boys of the wild frontier.

## Saloons, Breweries, and Prohibition

The town of Alvarado was not an incorporated city with a town council until 1878. After the Civil War and until the 1890s, Alvarado was the largest city in the county with a population which grew from about two thousand in 1870 to seven thousand in 1886. Prohibition had been a hot topic for local businessmen and residents from the founding of both Alvarado (1853) and New Town (1881). After 1881, New Town, a Missouri Pacific Railroad Addition located one mile south of the square near the tracks and the railroad shops, circumvented the state law. This brought relief to the many railroaders and the rowdy crowd who enjoyed taking a nip. In 1882 the two towns combined, instituted ordinances, and went officially wet. The "socializing" at the saloons led to increased disturbances, and for some a violent end.

CLEBURNE CHRONICLE, March 11, 1872:

*How to use whiskey without injury: Pour a glass half full of the best rye whiskey, sweeten it with sugar, grate in a little nutmeg, let it stand for five minutes; then add a few drops of Jamaica ginger . . . then pour it into a slop pail . . .*

### Cleburne Brew, Palace Saloon

**"Double Deed of Death"**—From 1875 to 1878 a brewery was operated by John Guffee and Mike Dixon. In 1878 the partners disagreed about who should get the final nickel as they were dividing up their proceeds in front of Durham & Mabry's Drug Store on the courthouse square. Guffee pulled a knife and held Dixon with one hand demanding that Dixon take back something he had

Top: Byrd's 1879–1880 Directory. (Layland Museum, Cleburne, Texas.)

Bottom: "When I was just a boy, one day as I went into a saloon on the north side of the square (Cleburne), about one-third of the way, Tom Boynkin, the proprietor, held a highly colored decanter to his lips, took a copious draught, set it back on the shelf in front of the huge mirror, wiped his lips and turned and looked at me, the only eye-witness. Then he exclaimed, 'Buddy, never let a drop of that cursed stuff go down your throat!' " T. U. Taylor (Unidentified bartender, AC)

Eli Wiggins (1824–1899), shown holding a Bible, was married to Elizabeth Johns. Eli was a "Traveling Preacher." Many religious leaders became involved in the fight against whiskey and alcohol. Rallies for and against prohibition raged in Johnson County townships in the 1880s. These efforts culminated in local option votes that would alternately put prohibition into effect and then remove it. This created an unstable business environment for the saloon keepers until national prohibition settled the matter in 1919. (AC)

said. Dixon tried to break loose and as he was falling, pulled his six-shooter and shot Guffee through the abdomen hitting his spine. Lige Guffee, John's brother, was standing nearby and, seeing his brother shot, raised his Winchester rifle and shot Dixon in the back. Lige ran to the brewery in the 400 block of North Main where he fortified his position, holding a crowd at bay until about midnight. He would only surrender to the sheriff who took him under guard to the jail.

Both wounded men died soon after the shooting resolving the matter. It was not reported which dead man ended up with the nickel.

This was typical of the past ten years, the Western frontier village of Cleburne found payday night with cowboys brawling at the saloons on the west side of the square. The cowboys spent a large part of their pay on drink and then rode about the town shouting and shooting their pistols—"painting the town red." The stores stayed open until 8:30 or 9 o'clock on these profitable Saturday nights and the owners "had to deal constantly in various ways with ruffians of all types."

The Saturday evening Mike Dixon and his brewery partner were killed, the town's families huddled behind locked doors and secured window shutters. Menacing noise and sounds of gunfire echoed while families waited anxiously for the safe arrival of husbands and fathers. Campbell Dickson's frightened wife, Lucy and their four children watched for him to return from his C.

"Cleburne is especially noted for it's fine hotels and genial landlords. Among the best in the city is the Exchange, run by Henry Gerstenkorn, and the headquarters for all the railroad men. Gerstenkorn knows how to treat his guest, and his table is supplied with every relish and delicacy to be found on the market." (CLEBURNE MORNING REVIEW, 1891)

Top: Henry Gerstenkorn, his wife Francis Daniel, and their children Henry and Beeler, owners of the Exchange Hotel and saloon. (AC)

Bottom: Henry Gerstenkorn's children pose with their goat cart in the park. Beeler is seated on the goat cart which has promotional signs for Anhauser-Busch "Buck" Lager Beer. Anti-prohibition forces were strong in Cleburne around the turn of the century and held rallies just as the prohibition groups did. The frequent local-option votes were always close and were often reversed at the next election. This caused the saloon owners to go on the road, or to change their signs and become druggists, or malt liquor and patent medicine dealers overnight. (AC)

Scene of a baptizing at Boothe Hole on Village Creek, circa early 1900s, with a local pastor, Reverend McDonald and visiting evangelist, Dr. J. Frank Norris. Norris was pastor of First Baptist Church, Fort Worth, and later a factor in an era of great foment in Baptist life in the South of the 1920s and 1930s. His firebrand reporting and editorializing on social issues of prohibition and gambling in THE BAPTIST STANDARD and his criticism of mission organizations and educational institutions led to conflict with Southern Baptist Convention leaders such as Dr. George W. Truett, pastor of First Baptist, Dallas. As a child, Dr. Norris had witnessed the shooting death of his father on the front porch of their home by a local bootlegger. The theological controversy finally resulted in a schism out of which came the independent Baptist movement in the South. (Layland Museum, Cleburne, Texas)

Phoebe Whitham came to Texas in a wagon train in 1849. The wagon train was attacked by Indians where she lost her second husband, and her medicine box was destroyed. Phoebe was an early pioneer medicine woman. She married Rev. Otis Whitham before the wagon train arrived in Cleburne. They lived a mile past Buffalo Creek. The Indians watered at her springs, and from them she learned the healing secrets of herbs. She worked with Dr. Marshall, one of the county's pharmacists. Patients called on her services to deliver babies and care for the sick. Henry Briden, an early settler, took a daughter of the medicine woman as his third wife. (Opal Seals)

"Harvest was quite an event in those days," recalls H. W. Collier, Sr. "My first recollection of grain harvest was seeing horse drawn reapers." The teams were strung out with three at the wheel and two at the lead. A boy would ride one of the rear animals and drive the lead team. One man rode the binder to see that the machine dropped the bundle as near as possible to those dropped previously. A cradle would carry six bundles of grain. It took two men as shockers to keep up with the binder and the shocks were stacked so that the grain part of the plants was on top. (AC)

(AC)

Dickson Hardware store. As the clock ticked long past his usual time of coming home Lucy thought, "What a place to bring up her children!" Suddenly, there was a rapid knock on the bolted door—one of the preachers of the town announced himself and was ushered in. Looking somewhat puzzled—he hesitated, asked if this was the "Dixon" home, and then proceeded to inform the horrified wife and frightened children of the shooting death of their missing husband and father, "Mr. Dixon." Upon hearing it, Lucy screamed and almost fainted.

Before long a delayed "Cam" Dickson stepped through the door to behold the tragic scene of his terrified, near hysterical wife and sobbing children. The "resurrected" Mr. Dickson was shocked and indignant to learn of the horrible blunder the preacher made confusing names and his misguided attempt to console the wrong "Dixon" family.

The Smith House was built in 1887. Pictured from left to right are Lowell N. Smith, Sr., Wesley Merrimon Smith, Alice Menefee Smith, Esther Smith Sowell, and Maggie Van Zandt. John Wesley Smith purchased the Captain Thomas Haley land from his heirs in 1887. The house was built of pine and poplar with square nails. The original part of the house was built with high ceilings. Each room had two windows per wall, providing much light. Opening the front and back doors at either end of the hall provided air circulation. The house has adapted to change with each generation. The house has been lived in continuously by four generations of the Smith Family, beginning with John Wesley Smith and Ann Cooper Smith, their children: Callie, W. Merrimon, George and "Josie"; W. Merrimon Smith and Alice Menefee Smith, their children: Lowell, Sr. and Esther; Lowell N. Smith, Sr. and Gladys Brown Smith, their children: Barbara Jean and Lowell, Jr.; Lowell, Jr. and his wife, Shirley, are the current owners. Smith Ranch was recognized in 1987 by the State of Texas in the Family Land Heritage Program "for a century or more of continuous ownership and operation as a family agricultural enterprise." (Mr. & Mrs. Lowell Smith, Jr.)

James and Elizabeth Renfro built their two-story plantation style home in Lillian. They moved their family in November 1879. The family farmed the land and ran four hundred head of horses. The Renfro brand was a "68," signifying the year they first settled on their homesite. Their son, George Jefferson Renfro, married Lillian June Brewer on July 31, 1890, and they continued to make the Renfro Plantation their home. George and Lillian had eleven children, seven of which were born in the home. As "The Father of Lillian," he gave right-of-way for the railway across his land and donated the depot lot in 1902. In 1905 he donated land for the Lillian Missionary Baptist Church. The town itself is named for his wife. When he sold the townsite to J. W. Cunningham, they decided the name "Lillian" appropriate, as it was both their wives' name. (Lyman Cronkrite, Lillian, Texas)

### Grangers, Greenbacks, and Farmers, and Fences

CLEBURNE CHRONICLE, August 9, 1873: *WHAT IS A GRANGE?, A grange is an organization of farmers formed to educate and unite all those interested in agriculture in a community.*

The full name of the organization was the National Grange of the Patrons of Animal Husbandry. It was a social institution, making a grand brotherhood and sisterhood which cared for the unfortunate, comforted the sick and distressed, was a husband to the widow and a father to the orphan. It sought to make every neighborhood a good, kind community. It informed its members of the best time to sell and how to acquire the best price for their products. At the age of eighteen a man could join for five dollars and at sixteen a woman could join for two dollars; dues were ten cents per meeting. The Grange officers wore costumes and ceremonial regalia.

Grange Hall was a community that once existed to the west of today's Rio Vista around the meeting hall of the Nolands River Grange in southern Johnson County. The seal of the grange gives the name of the community as: Nolands River, Texas, and their charter date: June 24, 1874. In 1884, at great expense, this grange accepted the responsibility of caring for the family of E. E. Capps that was ravished by disease. Caleb, Albert, Idea, and Augustus were taken first. Soon after, Willie and John Capps were also under the care of the Grange.

The Grange paid for Idea's coffin and burial as well as a coffin for Nannie Capps (possibly her mother). For over a year the local Grange paid for the children's clothes, food, board, tuition, medicine, doctor bills and some "ready made clothes." Eventually two of the children were sent to Hico, Texas. Each small expense down to thread, handkerchiefs and "mending boots" was carefully noted in the account book along with the regular expenses of the Grange.

In the 1870s the Grange became a vital influence in the rural communities of Johnson County. Each grange typically erected a two-story meeting hall which served the rural community as a town hall. A grange hall built in Cleburne by the Nolands River Grange served as the meeting hall for the Cleburne Town Council for a time.

The Grange held trials, kept notes on the testimony, and arbitrated disagreements that arose between members. A quarrel between James Cooper and E. E. Capps left several dogs poisoned and a yearling calf shot. The Grange held a trial and charges were brought against James Cooper. The verdict was not included with the rest of the testimony. During 1885 the Nolands River Grange provided the services of a jack donkey to breed mules for Grange members. Careful notes were kept on each farmer's mares and how many times they were brought in for stud service.

### "Cleburne Demands"

B. J. Chambers became an original thinker on the frontier of Texas. On the border of civilization, a national leader in a movement for radical monetary reform emerged. Chambers was one who developed and proposed new basic ideas which grew into the "greenbacker" or paper money movement. The Chambers and Brown Bank purchased the assets of the first bank in the county, Hollingsworth and Sons, which began in 1869. The ledgers of this bank have columns for gold, silver, notes, and trade goods. They reveal the great difficulty converting and trading in the mixed commodities, and the inadaquacy of the system for the needs of trade. The Panic of 1873 and the pains of the "Reconstruction" period made it evident to Chambers that the monopolistically controlled metals were insufficient for a strong diverse economy.

Bank notes were scarce in the West. Besides, they were looked upon as Yankee money. The only units of money most people came in contact with were the two-bit piece and the twenty dollar gold piece. In the early 1870s Chambers and Dr. Andrew Young, "in their shirt sleeves, discussed affairs of state and national government" in front of the doctor's office on the southwest corner of the public square in Cleburne. The words "gold," "greenback," and "specie" were often heard among quotes of the leading writers of the day.

Well before 1876, Chambers concluded the government should provide the medium of exchange for the nation. He thought it should be an irredeemable paper money issued directly by the government in sufficient quantities to meet the demands and wants of the people. He was opposed to all metallic money which could be manipulated by mining companies or owners of bullion. He believed the money should be "a cheap and convenient material such as paper." He was opposed to giving the power to print paper currency to incorporated banks or states, then also a part of the system. He felt this gave the power to control the financial destiny of the people over to a small group of powerful people.

Chambers was among the first in the entire nation to develop and advocate these theories of money. By 1876 Chambers closed out his bank and ran for the state legislature specifically to advance his theories. In 1880 he ran for vice-president of the United States on the National Greenback ticket.

Chambers's idea of printing U.S. currency not backed by metal reserves was a very radical proposal. The now accepted economic theories to provide a healthy and strong economy for business and citizens were many years off. Nineteenth-century United States was not ready for Chambers's proposal, but his idea eventually became the United States' dollar, a basic respected financial tool throughout the world. Our country would have to go through a number of financial panics and depressions before the nation would find the wisdom in his proposals. Chambers died in 1895, the Federal Reserve system was established in 1913, gold reserves backed U.S. currency until 1933. Silver reserves backed the dollar until 1965, when the U.S. created and printed currency close to what Chambers wanted—almost one hundred years after he came up with the idea.

CLEBURNE CHRONICLE, March, 1881: *The Cave of Gloom is the newest name for greenbackism.*

At the Lee Grange in Lee's Academy Community a plank of demands adopted in March 1886 included matters of common interest to farmers and working citizens. These controversial principles, including the "greenback" proposal, were adopted as resolutions of the Farmers Alliance in August 1886, in Cleburne. They became part of the platform of the Populist Party in 1886 and the People's Party in 1890. Over the next century most of the ideas expressed in the "Cleburne Demands" became state or national law.

**Fence-Cutting Feuds**

In Texas before 1880, the fences along the trails were wood-rail corrals near ranch houses. In a few places small tracts were enclosed with a living hedge of woven bois d'arc trees trained into a thorny wall. These fences kept farm animals in and often were used only for horses at night. The cattle roamed and grazed during the day on the free grass of the open range.

In 1880, as the trains arrived in Johnson County, Campbell Dickson was advertising that he had shipped barbed wire to the railhead and freighted by wagon "a car load, 20,000 lbs. or more . . . in any quantity desired" into Johnson County. By 1882, Dickson was selling 120,000 pounds of barbed wire in a ninety-day period. Dickson's ad ran:

"Riding the Line of the Wire Fence," drawn by F. Remington. (AC)

In 1878 Campbell Dickson (1836–1911) bought out a hardware firm from William Hill and changed the name to C. Dickson Hardware. About 1900 the firm dropped farm implements and put in a stock of furniture and rugs, along with their lines of hardware, stoves, and house furnishings. With the help of Campbell Dickson, the Santa Fe Railroad came to Cleburne in 1881. He also helped establish the city water works, sewage plant, Carnegie Library, country club, and Cleburne Ice Company. In 1897 the first National Bank was in trouble; he took over as president and saved the bank. (Layland Museum, Cleburne, Texas)

After the trains arrived, cattle ranching changed. R. E. "Bob" Gatewood would round up a train load of cattle for shipment to Chicago from these pens. Cattle shipping was a big business. The Gatewood home still stands two miles south of Cleburne; it was quite a mansion. (Layland Museum, Cleburne, Texas)

A blooded bull and its proud owner, one of the Gillespie family. Jackson Bradley, the brother-in-law of Uncle Sammy Myers, was the first to drive a herd of blooded cattle into Johnson County in 1852. His son Samuel Bradley became one of the best informed livestock men of the county. C. W. Mertz, who came to Johnson County about 1880, developed a herd of red shorthorns named the Ruby Herd. The Mertz herd won awards and was famous in the 1880s and 1890s at the Texas State Fair and in the Texas Panhandle. Charles Goodnight had a preference for good bloodlines in cattle and bought a starter herd in 1856 from cattle driven here from the old South. (AC)

Susan Jane Gill Filgo (1836–1912) married George White Filgo (1825–1892) on December 27, 1854, in Pontotoc County, Mississippi. George served as a First Sargeant in Co. I, First Regiment, Mississippi Partisan Rangers (later Seventh Regiment, Mississippi Cavalry) from 1863 to 1865. After the Civil War, with a baby due in a few months, they made the long move to Texas. They worked for the Carruth Brothers in Dallas County, later buying 390 acres in Johnson County on Nolan River near Buchanan. On April 28, 1877, George registered his mark and brand, which read: "Mark crop and under bit of each ear. Brand 'GF' on the right hip of cattle and on the left shoulder of horses." George became a well-respected member of his community and made cattle ranching a lifestyle, but his health was complicated after a fall from his horse. George died February 11, 1892. Susan filed for a Confederate widow's pension on July 25, 1899, and lived at 723 West Chambers until her death in 1912. They are buried in the old Cleburne Cemetery. (Patricia Smith Boatright Collection)

Cowboy Roper reading love letters from Nell Hague. Richard Bratton Roper was foreman of a sixteen-hundred-acre ranch near Klondyke. On Saturday nights he would come into Cleburne and was in a band that played at the Courthouse Square. He met a girl named Nellie Murrel Hague. It was love at first sight, and he vowed that he would remain in Cleburne to woo and marry Nell. They were married on June 30, 1909, in Cleburne at Nell's family home at 401 West Chambers. As a wedding present, Richard Roper's father presented them with a drugstore located on the east side of the Courthouse Square. Later they sold the drugstore and Roper became yard master at the Santa Fe Railroad Company. Mr. Roper owned the first movie theater in Cleburne called The Yale Theatre. (Travis and Vivian Morris)

The Alvarado City Hall, built 1878, was designed to house a market and a calaboose (jail) on the first floor and a town hall on the second floor. Sometimes people, wagons, and horses were so thick around City Hall one could not ride a horse around the square. On market day almost anything could be bought or traded here. There was a well with a bucket just west of City Hall, and later a trough was built around it where the animals could drink. In 1885 the Fire Department operated on the first floor of the City Hall. The tower on top of the building made a perfect place to spot fires. (Lyman Cronkrite)

*The Glidden Barb Wire has been pronounced throughout the great prairie states of the Northwest, to be superior to any fencing wire manufactured in the United States.*

Just after the Civil War, Cam Dickson in Iowa had his blacksmith make some barbed wire of his own design to help hold his stock in. He didn't apply for a patent until some time had passed. By then someone somewhere else had received the valuable patent in their name in Texas. Cam still profited from the invention of barbed wire by selling huge quantities. In 1880 C. W. Mertz, Dickson's next door neighbor, became the first

Johnson County rancher to fence his land, the 2,800-acre Ruby Ranch. Sometimes his fence would be cut between every post, but as fast as it was cut it was repaired. Mertz pleaded with the local people not to cut down any cedar trees in the brakes and gullies of his ranch because he needed the trees for fence posts.

Barbed wire was welcomed by grangers and large ranch owners to protect their crops and livestock. Wire fences allowed the farmers and ranchers to enclose their entire land claim with a very durable and strong fence. The cattle drovers saw more and more of these obstacles erected about 1880. The old-time cowboys knew this was their last stand.

The military routes had not taken land grants into consideration when they were marked off. The Chisholm Trail and other old roads went right across the boundary lines of ranches. Now the roads were being forced around the fenced properties. Small ranchers and property owners were being surrounded. This situation initiated fence-cutting feuds which lasted over five years. People had been accustomed to crossing the range in the most direct route they wished from their

Cleburne was the center for local cotton buying by 1879, when 3,500 bales were sold in the Cleburne market. Colonel W. C. Smith was most prominent among the cotton merchants. During harvest fifty wagons a day congregated around the courthouse to await their turn to unload. In 1898 Market Square was established and wagons drawn by tow horses or mules assembled in that more spacious area. In the fields, whole families would turn out to gather the precious commodity as quickly as possible. In December 1905, the Southern Cotton Association of Johnson County organized and planned for a massive warehouse to be built. The Farmers Cotton Oil Company of Cleburne was running full tilt as manufacturers of cotton seed products. (Gay and Helen Hopper)

Light two-horse wagons assemble with proud camaraderie one bright autumn morning on the square in Alvarado, Texas, circa 1879. Such peak years encouraged farmers to believe that cotton would always be king. There was competition among cotton farmers to gin the first bale of cotton in the county for the season. A premium price was paid for this initial bale, and it was displayed with great prestige by the merchant who bought it. A news article in the CLEBURNE ENTERPRISE of June 30, 1904, features a Professor Orton of Galveston examining cotton specimens from a Johnson County field and pronouncing the insects to be the true Mexican pest, the dreaded boll weevil. The beast had arrived. At one time Alvarado had the largest cotton processing plant in the world. (Bennett Printing, Cleburne, Texas)

This gathering is thought to be part of a Juneteenth (June 19) Celebration at Nathan about 1905. W. G. Slaton stands near the center in a vest. To his left is his wife Eula Ann "Nana" Slaton. To his right, the man with his foot up on the porch, is H. E. Snipes who later worked for the offices of the Cleburne Santa Fe shops. The guitarists may be from the Thompson, Delk, and Thomas families. The middle musician holds a two string bass fiddle handcrafted from a shipping box. On the left, two of the group "strike" a pose as batter and pitcher. (AC)

homes and farms to their destination. Now they were suddenly stopped in their tracks with a dead end road at a wire fence. They would cut their way through and travel on. Growing resentment caused those who needed the open range to organize into bands who worked at night cutting many miles of fence. This new type of crime—fence-cutting—was declared a felony and a penitentiary offense and is still on the books today. At one point the Johnson County Sheriff swore in a posse to guard the fences of a large non-resident ranch west of town. *The new deputies armed themselves, and their sweethearts prepared lunches for their refreshment that night. As the posse forded a creek west of town, they were captured by a masked band who divided the posse into*

*fence-cutting squads and worked them all night.* On January 14, 1884, fence-cutters destroyed the new barbed wire fences of Norman Miller, Wash Luce, J. W. Capps, and the Shaw and Henderson Ranch eight miles south of Cleburne. The Texas Rangers were called into many counties to infiltrate the organized fence-cutting bands and stop the problem.

Eventually, the ranchers were required by law to put in a gate every three miles. The fence-cutting wars peaked in Johnson County during 1880–1885, but were still going on during June of 1887 when a half mile of fence on J. W. Terrell's ranch ten miles south of Cleburne was cut. That same month P. W. Gray had a quarter mile cut by persons working out of Whitney who were attempting to keep a trail open to the north. Locally "at least one family had their house and barns burned by stockmen, who did not want anyone moving in and fencing off grazing land."

A fence-cutter defended his actions in 1883, saying:

*Big stockmen buy all the land around on all sides, his cattle graze on our land and ours on his. When he makes his "rounding," our cattle are driven off to some distant point . . . and branded. No sir, no man has the*

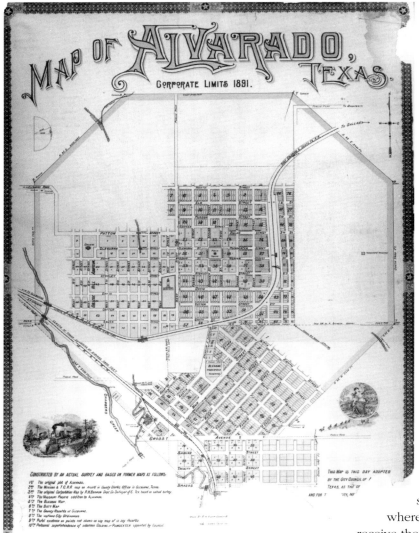

Map of Alvarado, Texas, circa 1891. (Linda Neely)

*right to fence you up or enclose the grass and water. He didn't plant the grass or have anything to do with making it grow. Neither did he create the springs and rivers. God made them free, and before those land-sharks and cattle kings put fences around them they were free.*

Dr. Andrew Young of Cleburne also defended the fence-cutters in 1884 saying:

*. . . the brave old Texan went to the front with their families and drove back the Indians . . . When danger disappeared the capitalists flocked in, and the land was sold in large bodies, or given to rich corporations, the country fenced. The old Indian fighters find themselves surrounded by wire fence . . . We ask punishment for unlawful fencing as well as unlawful cutting.*

On March 27, 1886, an election was held in precinct six to determine what constituted a "lawful fence (of) three barbed wires . . ." As fences went up, old disagreements over boundary lines intensified. Previously, trees or rocks had been marked, but there were few continuous standing barriers. Now the tracts of land were enclosed permanently. As late as 1907, John Force was shot and killed by Jim Franks on Camp Creek, over an old fence line dispute.

One pioneer noted the plight of the early day cowman and his family, *With his cattle upon a thousand hills, living easy and seemingly paying no attention, caring nothing for the prospective value of the land upon which grew his grass, the stockman, with few exceptions, lost his chance, and with his cattle lost his wealth. The children of many of these are now about as poor people as we have. As a general thing the cattle man is a whole souled, generous fellow and prodigal with his money.*

### A Farming Community

Nathan was the largest primarily black community in the county. It was located in the area of Parker and Friendship. Many of the families were land owners, shortly after the Civil War, which was unusual. Former slaves and emigrants had created a place where they could educate their children and receive the blessings that come from working your own land with your own hands.

Groups would gather for social events on Sunday and holidays at the Nathan Post Office or at homes such as the Slaton's. For a barbeque, a long, deep trough was dug in the ground the night before. A wood lining was placed in the bottom, and the fire was set to burning. A cow, pig, or other game would be quartered and placed on the embers, then more wood and then earth would cover the top, with holes on each end. People would play baseball, eat barbeque, improvise music and join in song and dance. The usual favorites at the get togethers were the old spirituals. Later in the day the musicians might turn to the popular songs and the blues. These diversions from hard daily work were memorable times.

After the trains came through, on Junteenth (June 19) people from Cleburne would ride down on the "Boll Weevil" (the Trinity and Brazos Valley Railroad) for the

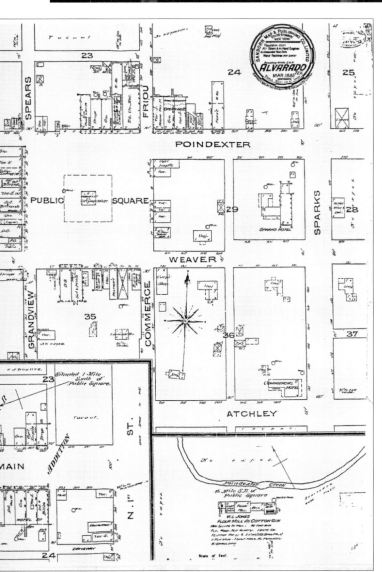

Above: Thought to be the cotton grading room at Denton, Bell & Company, cotton dealers, established at 114-1/2 East Chambers in Cleburne when cotton was king. At right is Howard Smith, eldest son of "Doc" George C. Smith a cotton buyer and classer with the company. Second from the right is Howard's cousin, Lyman Filgo. Lyman Filgo eventually took control of his father's business, the Snow White Laundry, and lived the rest of his life in Cleburne. Howard Smith remained a cotton buyer in El Paso until his death in 1967. (Patricia Smith Boatright Collection).

Left: Sanborn Map of Alvarado, Texas, circa 1885. (Layland Museum, Cleburn, Texas)

day. The railroad cars they were riding in were labeled, "FOR WHITES," and "FOR NEGROES," under the "Jim Crow" laws of the day. These signs were reversible and were just flipped over as needed. The same railroad coach was used by both blacks and whites—but not at the same time.

William G. "Grandpa Billy" Slaton and Richard Smith "Dick" Sewell were two of the teachers at Nathan School. Dick Sewell brought his children from his farm in Rio Vista to Nathan School even though he paid school taxes back in Rio Vista district. Bill Bell was one of the prosperous farmers of Nathan. Some of the others living in the area were the Thompsons (Will, James and Dee), the Fullers, the Goodwins, the Delks, and the Thomases.

These surveyors photographed in Johnson County worked for the T.&B.V. Railroad Co. which came into the county from the south through Parker to Cleburne in 1903. Pictured are P. C. Tucker (rodman), Boshany (levelman), Nichols J. Lane, Ely Chige, Durby, Jr. (front flag), Jess (Cook), Blanchard (bear chain), C. Blanchard (rear flag), Chili Chamman, Hog Peden (teamster). (Center for American History, University of Texas, Austin)

EARLY ATTEMPTS TO BRING A RAILROAD into Johnson County took place in the 1870s and included the Houston & Texas Central Railroad and the Dallas, Cleburne, and Rio Grande. Late in 1876 the first concerted local effort to secure a rail connection was mounted. On November 12, 1877, citizens meeting at the courthouse named a committee of five to report on the railroad matter: B. J. Chambers, E. M. Heath, S. B. Allen, Dr. T. D. Lorance, and W. Poindexter. They passed a resolution proposing an agreement with the Dallas, Cleburne and Rio Grande Narrow Gauge Railroad Company (D.C.&R.G. Railroad) to build a road to Cleburne through Alvarado. When the needed $25,000 per county could not be raised, a joint stock company was formed in 1879 to take subscriptions to raise local money. The narrow gage railroad was built in 1880, but inadequate roadbase under the tracks caused them to twist and give way. Frequent derailing of trains on the muddy blackland prairie forced passengers to return to Dallas on rented horses, buggies, and wagons. Freight and cattle shipments could not get through. Other standard gage railroads were being planned and were soon to be built.

CLEBURNE BULLETIN, March 2, 1881:

*The route of the G.C.&S.F. railway through Johnson County will be deeply interesting to the tourist from the fact that, the road passes through a most beautiful and picturesque country. From the moment the trains enter Johnson it will be amid peaks and timber and prairies and valley, with farms and farm houses dotting the country over, reminding one of the incomparable Mohawk Valley of New York State.*

CLEBURNE BULLETIN, March, 1881:

*Wagons loaded with railroad working implements, and with the railroaders wives and children, are constantly passing through our town, going for the G.C.&S.F. railway work and to the Missouri, Pacific at Alvarado and Grand View.*

*Chicago, Texas & Mexican Central is looming up again and Chief Engineer, George C. Waite says he has sent all the estimates to headquarters looking to the construction of the first fifty miles. We believe there is something in this business after all . . .*

*The Chicago, Texas & Mexican R.R. representatives were in Alvarado to secure depot grounds, and our informant thinks Major Sparks has arranged with the company to place the depot building on his property southeast of the Sparks House, almost in the business portion of the town. Col. Waite stated that he had obtained the right of way as far as Alvarado with no*

3

1879 TO 1896

# STEAM ENGINES AND STEEL RAILS

G.C.&S.F. Engine Number 38, a 4-4-0 with tall smoke stack, is the style of engine that pulled Santa Fe trains into Johnson County in 1881. This locomotive shown in the Cross Timbers is transporting flatcars. Flatcars such as these carried train passengers into Cleburne in the fall of 1881. Passenger cars did not begin service until January 1, 1882. Woodstoves arrived by boxcar on the early trains into Alvarado in 1880. (Layland Museum, Cleburne, Texas)

The home of Campbell Dickson, 719 North Anglin St., with the home of C. W. Mertz, 723 North Anglin St., (built 1892–93) in the background. Dickson's home was built in 1880 and is of the Gothic Revival influence. "Cam" designed the home to withstand storms with the windows protruding from the gables. It had a cellar and the trim was cut out on a jigsaw by Tracy the oldest son of Campbell and Lucy Ellen Tracy Dickson. In 1881, family members and neighbors watched the first Santa Fe trains pull into Cleburne from the second story porch of this home. Frances Dickson Abernathy said, "It was a big event in a little village." (Cleburne Public Library)

1884 G.C.&S.F. Railroad Bill of lading for a buggy. (AC)

Right: W. A. Whitman was the second man hired on the G.C.&S.F. Railroad at Cleburne. With a seniority date of November 6, 1888, he followed E. M. Mirick who had been hired July 10, 1888. Both were experienced conductors. The first Cleburne brakeman was D. W. O'Brien, hired May 2, 1889, and promoted to conductor May 2, 1890. (AC)

Below: G.C.&S.F. Railroad Ticket from the 1890s. Santa Fe passenger tickets were punched by Conductor Whitman with the punch he holds in his hand. The ticket punch made a distinctive shaped hole, such as a heart or cloverleaf. The other conductors up and down the line knew by the shape who had punched the ticket and therefore could audit the passengers' use of the ticket. (AC)

Conductor collecting tickets, Cleburne, circa 1890s. (AC)

William J. and Mellie Powell Flenniken, 1899. Mr. Flenniken was a Santa Fe Railroad conductor. His reports were criticized for being too lengthy and detailed. Flenniken developed a shorter report for his supervisors, writing, "Off again, on again, gone again—Flenniken." His report then became synonymous on the Santa Fe for short, efficient reports. (Anna Faye Etter)

Interior of sleeping car. This lady is in the water closet with a marble top sink and brass coat hooks. (AC)

Track workers, T&BV freight yards and section house. These stood where the Pavilion stands in present-day Hulen Park in Cleburne. (AC)

*trouble and at but a trifling cost . . . The engineers, tie men, right-of-way men, managers and contractors of the Missouri-Pacific were there.*

In 1882 the C.T.&M.C. Railroad rebuilt the D.C.&R.G. Narrow Gage Railroad into Cleburne as a standard gage with an improved roadbase. On August 1, 1882, the C.T.&M.C. became the Dallas branch of the G.C.&S.F. Railroad.

Alvarado was the first Johnson County city to receive train service and the citizens were deservedly proud. A depot was built by August 12, 1881. G. W. Cottar received a car load of woodstoves as the first freight which arrived on the first train into Alvarado during 1881. The first bale of cotton shipped out by rail from Alvarado was sent by J. J. Ramsey to Tuck Boaz of Fort Worth. Alvarado became a division point on the Missouri Pacific with a roundhouse and headquarters for trainmen in 1884.

Shipping the cattle north became a desirable option as the trains came into towns along the Chisholm Trail. The number of cattle making the long drive north

Right: Santa Fe Passenger Train No. 68 derailed near Highway 67 at Lockett Branch, April 17, 1908. The train was pulled by engine No. 248 with Alma C. Long, engineer, and Ed Alsup, fireman. The conductor was Fred Hallet. As the train left Keene at 9 p.m., the rain storm broke loose and inundated the whole county. Just east of the bridge over Lockett Branch the track gave way, and the engine went into the creek. Long and Alsup lost their lives. (Layland Museum, Cleburne, Texas)

began to dwindle. The drovers instead drove the cattle to pens along the tracks. In Cleburne the cattle pens were beside the west side of the Santa Fe tracks south of the depot area.

It was customary to pack the cattle in tight to prevent them from lying down and being trampled to death. The cattle cars were open pens in the 1870s, just above the walls:

*. . . could be seen a forest of wide-spreading horns, swaying as the cars rounded the curves . . . It was not uncommon to see sandwiched among the swaying horns, a half-buffalo, half-Texas steer, noticeable by its short horns and humped, heavy shoulders, the product of his wild ancestors.*

Before the railroads came, the villages and towns grew up where there was water, along trails, at crossroads, near timber, by rich prairies, or for protection situated on elevated hills and secluded river valleys. Now the citizens of Caddo Grove, Marystown, Grange Hall, and Grand View had to choose whether to stay put or move to the rails.

"It was a big event in a little village." It was bad news for J. J. Gallagher who ran the U.S. Mail and Stage Line which left Cleburne every morning at 7 a.m. through Fort Worth arriving in Decatur the next day. The railroads cut new straight courses through Johnson County. The rails divided farms from pastures and people from water.

Railroads cut across Johnson County bringing improved building materials and products from all over the nation. The county was being built up new and in

The Hotel Burleson was built by D. J. Murphy in the late 1880s. Soldiers from Barron Field visited the hotel as late as 1918. (Frank Norwood)

1895 the boomers said, "But with the coming of the railroad in 1881, the shanties gave way to blocks of brick business houses, and the huts, to pretty cottages and palatial homes."

Texas county courthouses of that time not only served as the legal nucleus of the county but symbolized the strength, wealth, and ambition of the county. The 1882–1883 courthouse was designed by Wesley Clark Dodson (1828–1914) a prolific courthouse architect of the nineteenth century. He also designated similar courthouses in Hood, Hill, and Parker Counties. First class materials included ornamental features of the Second Empire style. At the dedication ceremony, Parson Henry Renfro of Burleson spoke. For the first time a bell connected with the clock in the courthouse tower tolled out the hours. Stories circulated that parents awakened by the bell were finding their children sneaking back home in the middle of the night.

By 1881 when the railroads bisected Johnson County, the Indian wars were over and the map of Johnson County changed forever. The town names and locations, roads, and economies shifted. American civilization with all its benefits and problems arrived at the door of the depot.

The M.K.T. Railroad established a shop in Alvarado. In 1886 a strike by railroaders brought violence to Texas and to the center of Alvarado. In 1886 the Knights of Labor rail strike spread to Texas. Alvarado's railroad shop was the site of a major clash between strikers and railroad officials. Jim Courtright (page 99), former Fort Worth Marshal, was appointed a Deputy Sheriff of Johnson County as well as acting Deputy U.S. Marshal, in an attempt to get a train from Ft. Worth into Alvarado to relieve the situation and run the blockade. The Attorney General of Texas was on the train. Coming out of Ft. Worth a siding switch was thrown by strikers to ambush Jim and the five officers on the engine. Three of the officers were wounded, one fatally. They never made it to Alvarado. Much of the resentment felt towards the railroad by the populace fell on Courtright during this tense time. Jim would never again run for public office because of this incident. The governor sent two companies of Rangers to quell the situation.

Rev. Henry C. Renfro (1831–1885) entered Baylor University in 1853 to study for the ministry. At the university he met Dr. Rufus C. Burleson, the president of Baylor. Dr. Burleson became both teacher and lifelong friend. Rev. Renfro moved to Johnson County in 1858 and established the Bethesda Baptist Church in 1860. He married Mary "Mollie" Ray, November 24, 1859. He entered the Confederate Army with the Twenty-first Texas Infantry Regiment (Griffin's Battalion). After receiving support from Dr. Burleson, the chaplain in Colonel J. W. Speight's regiment, Rev. Renfro served as chaplain in Louisiana for the remainder of the conflict.

Left: This Johnson County Courthouse was built in Cleburne at a cost of $44,685. Wesley Clark Dodson was the architect and Lee Slaughter of Waco the contractor. The courthouse was completed October 1883. Parson Henry Renfro was selected as the principal speaker for the dedication in November. After an elaborate masonic ceremony in which the cornerstone was laid, the parson "made a short and happy speech, choosing for his subject the rise and fall of civilization in general, and Johnson County in particular. He was frequently applauded during the remarks." (The ALVARADO BULLETIN) This beautiful structure burned on April 15, 1912, the same day the TITANIC sank. Almost all of the valuable county records were saved. (Dr. Jack Burton)

In 1864 Renfro returned to Johnson County. He was the pastor of Bethesda Baptist Church, rancher, and farmer. In 1880 Renfro offered property for use as a townsite adjacent to the railroad, with the stipulation that he be allowed to name the new community. Offer accepted, Renfro promptly named the town Burleson in honor of his old teacher and friend, Dr. Rufus C. Burleson. (William Clark Griggs, Southwest Museum Services)

## Experiences of a Country Doctor

Dr. U. D. Ezell (Ray McDearmon tells of pioneer Doctor U. D. Ezell in his book *Without the Shedding of Blood.*) of Kimball and Cleburne became a legend for the dangerous crossings of the Brazos River made while serving his patients in southern Johnson and northern Bosque and Hill Counties. "Uncle Doc" Ezell became well known for his ability to help patients whom other doctors had given up as hopeless. As a result of this fame he was called upon to make increasing numbers of calls. J. M. Western of Grandview remembered one such occurrence. *But, now about these risks he took in swimming the river; he did it so many times that it is hard to remember any one event. But on one occasion I had to swim the blasted river with him and I can tell you that incident really stuck in my memory . . . We reached the river just before sundown and found it on a boom. It seemed to me that no horse could swim the thing; but the case at hand demanded our immediate return, so we had to take a chance on crossing the raging stream . . . Since his horse was larger and was a better swimmer, the*

The 1890s Central Public High School in Cleburne. "Our High School is taught on the University Plan, and is second to none in the state. It is one of the approved High Schools whose graduates are admitted to the University of the State of Texas without examination." Professor C. P. Hudson, 1894.
(Nobia Carlock White and Irene Barnes)

The original building of the First Christian Church was constructed around 1880 on West Wardville Street. Sitting on the front porch are Chester, Scott, and Lucian Wilson. (Dr. Jack Burton)

*doctor had me put my nag on the lower side of his. He told me to keep my horse close to his in order that my horse would be protected from the full force of the current. He warned me to keep my horse's head angled up the river so we would not be swept too far down stream. With much snorting and floundering on the part of my pony, we finally reached on the other and*

Above: Johnson County's red brick jail, circa 1883–84, cost $26,000 to build. (Dr. Jack Burton)

City and county law enforcement around 1902 included Charles McClain, town marshal; Frank Long, Sheriff. Law and order in the first few years after the establishment of a town was maintained by the Sheriff and other Johnson County officers, or by the individual citizen's interpretation of the natural law of self-preservation. (Layland Museum, Cleburne, Texas)

Right: The chain gang of convict laborers, guards, and bloodhounds at the Johnson County Farm, Cleburne about 1900. The county farm housed convicts, indigents of the county, wayward girls, and the mentally unstable before state welfare. On 444 acres of land now covered by Lake Pat Cleburne, Johnson County established the "poor farm" in 1885 with A. F. Johnson serving as superintendent. The land was purchased for $10 an acre from M. L. Kennard and Pid Hart, farmers along the lush Nolan River. Maintenance costs for board and clothing for the twelve to twenty-five inmates averaged $7.50 per month. The farm raised stock and crops which provided most of its own support. Prisoners were housed in a grim stone jail and were chained at night and when they worked during the day. A news article from February 1903 tells of two men who subdued an officer and were pursued ten miles across the county by law officers and the county's bloodhound pack before being caught near Egan. The operation of the County Farm was discontinued in 1947, and the inmate record book was lost or destroyed. The establishment of the state prison system, welfare benefits, and institutions for the mentally ill made the county system obsolete. (V. L. "George" Pierson)

*clambered up the steep bank. We were soaked through, and the March wind seemed to chill us to the bone. On we rode through cedar brakes, across creeks, and ravines, and over rocky hills until we reached my home.*

Ed Pyeatt of Rio Vista relates this story. *[W]e found the Brazos on a big rise . . . and prepared to wait for the durn thing to run down so we could cross it . . . While the river was at its most dangerous stage Sol called my attention to a horseman who had approached the river on the far side, and seemed to be preparing to attempt a crossing. He looked the situation over, carefully, rode a few yards up the stream; and right into the flood the*

Members of the Cleburne Volunteer Fire Company pose during an exercise about 1895. The two firemen operating the hose are Lorance Scurlock, left, and Mabry Thomas. The first Cleburne fire unit was formed in 1891. Fires which destroyed several buildings about the square in 1881, 1884, and 1886, probably hastened the organization. A venerable fire horse, "Old Tom," is remembered fondly in Cleburne before the advent of motor driven fire equipment in 1913. "Old Tom," was used by the county to pull the road grader; when the fire alarm sounded, he would snort and paw until released. He would then run to the fire station and back into a stall to receive the harness to pull the fire fighting machinery. Two memorable fires are frequently mentioned in Cleburne history: in 1912 the blaze which caused $125,000 damage in the Santa Fe Shops and the 1912 destruction of the 1883 Johnson County Courthouse. (AC)

Nix Baird & Gresham,
DRY GOODS.

NEW YORK OFFICE
57 WALKER ST.

BRANCHES:
GRANBURY, GLEN ROSE,
CLIFTON.

Cleburne, Texas,_____ 189

Sold to _____

In 1879 H. C. Gresham, W. R. Nix, and A. C. Baird were clerks at J. S. Taylor's fancy dry goods store. In 1886 they established Nix, Baird, and Gresham Dry Goods & Clothing Store. This firm set a new pace in volume business. It was not unusual to sell a leading article at one-half the cost to attract trade. (Irene Barnes and Nobia Carlock White)

Nix Baird Gresham Letterhead(JCA)

*dang fool rode, while me and Sol stood there frozen in horror! He kept his horse's head turned slightly up stream . . . On he came, carefully dodging floating logs, while horse and rider gradually drifted down stream; But all the while they were coming closer to the west bank . . . We began to think, now that the fellow might make it across the stream; but we thought he must surely be crazy to take such a risk. As he came nearer, we saw that the man was Dr. Ezell, who was returning from a call near Blum. He had strapped his medicine bag up close around his neck to keep it dry and to keep from losing it . . . So accurately had he judged the rate of the current that he landed some thirty yards down stream form where he started, and near the only place where his horse could climb up the steep bank . . . Although we*

*were scared stiff, the doctor appeared quite calm. As his horse made its way, slowly and painfully, up the steep bank, the doctor helloed to us and exclaimed, "She's as rough as hell isn't she boys?" We agreed with his diagnosis . . .*

Doc Ezell bred a special stable full of tall horses that he also found could swim, thus providing himself with mounts suitable for his work. Ezell's services were in such demand that when exhausted, he resorted to sleeping in a graveyard where people would not think to look for him. He would slap his horse on the rump to send it home and lay down to sleep on a slab monument. However he had a skeleton in his closet. It was customary for a doctor to keep a skeleton for study in his practice, and Ezell kept one in his office's closet. Some time after a studying apprentice left town, Ezell found that his skeleton was missing—in all likelihood having left with the apprentice. "Uncle Doc," solved the problem in a scandalous manner. As a boy he had witnessed vigilantes lynch a murderer from a tree in Pogue's pasture. One night at one a.m., Doc went to the place where as a boy he had seen the corpse hanging from a limb, dug up the unmarked grave, and used the skeleton for fifty years as a study specimen. For years locals wondered who would have robbed the grave by the big oak tree.

## The Coming Attraction

A poster boy walked his rounds pasting colorful banners on the sides of barns, buildings, shacks, and on wooden sidewalk signs. The sounds on the streets began to hint that something was up. The word was out, whether the children could read or not; they knew what the pictures meant. They ran to their parents with excitement. Screams and squeals shouted the big news, "The circus is coming to town!"

There was great anticipation of which show would get here first. The first to arrive would get the kids' savings and do the best financially.

In the 1850s the Johnson County Commissioners created a $100 license for "the display of such" menageries. Among the purveyors of diversions and amusements who visited Johnson County were Buffalo Bill's Wild West Show, Wild West Ropers with Booger Red, and Buckskin Bill's Wild West Show. These shows came to portray the "Wild West" in a place that had been the wild west only a few years before.

### Step Right Up—

The heyday of the "Medicine Man" in America was the last two decades of the 1800s. A "Medicine Show"

Ringling Brothers Circus parading on the north side of The Square, Cleburne circa 1896. According to T. U. Taylor, the circus would parade around the town square and the town's people would follow the circus to the fairgrounds.(Jack Burton)

was the circus, the showboat, the magic show, the minstrel musical comedy show, the wild west show and the preacher of damnation all rolled into one. The "medicine man" was a unique entrepreneur of the 1800s, and the traveling medicine shows were very popular.

Living on West Heard Street in Cleburne was a ventriloquist medicine man named Doc Breeding who had created a "dummy" for use in attracting and persuading his crowd. The best known medicine man in Johnson County was Doc Smith. Cleburne was the home base of his well-known North Central Texas "Medicine Show" called the King-K Medicine Company. George "Doc" Smith was our unique local version of the classic "Medicine Man of the Old West."

Doc Smith moved to Texas after 1880 from Howard County, Arkansas. On April 15, 1893, he invented the King-K formula and began to market the concoction in Cleburne. In the "Board of Trade Saloon" on the east side of the courthouse square a deal was struck

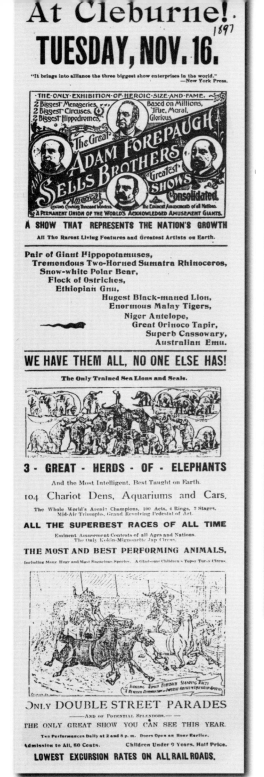

1897 Circus Ad. "At Cleburne! Tuesday, Nov. 16, 1897." Notice a rare "flock of Ostriches and Emus," which now roam the pastures of Johnson County. Faye Burton recalls Mr. Pat Munan who drove a wagon around town advertising the circus and other events. He had the posters on each side of the wagon and would be ringing a bell which hung on the wagon's tung.(AC)

between Doc and one of the owners, W. H. F. Moss, to sell King-K over the counter.

Doc Smith listed his occupation as "Medicine Man" on the 1900 U.S. Census in Johnson County. Although Doc had no formal education as a Doctor of Medicine, he certainly deserved an honorary doctorate in human psychology, earned from the "good ol' boys" around the courthouse and market square. Under the name of the King-K Medicine Company, Doc sold "King-K" and Tonka Wonka as well as the nationally known patent medicine of the day, Swamp Root. Doc parlayed his own "King-K Medicines" from wagons, doorways, corners, reunions, fiddle contests, fairs, and to crowds gathered around blacksmith shops.

## Show Day

In Texas towns, Saturday was the day everyone went to town to trade and do business. Doc would assemble the King-K Fiddle Band to play along the crowded streets. His trunk full of miraculous spirits took front and center stage, as the fiddle band would stroke their strings. The harmonious sound became irresistible to Doc's unwary, soon-to-be customers as the melodies brought back many fond memories. A crowd would gather and some would begin to dance. Ben Williams would do the calling. Doc used a megaphone so the crowd could hear. He may have stopped the dance just as he thought the crowd was beginning to tire as though to give them a rest. Then he would slyly ask them about their apparent "aches and pains." Those aches and pains might be the sign of some serious malady—why, just last week a man with a similar pain dropped dead on Chambers Street—if that man had been a regular user of King-K, he would be dancing here with us today. Friends, my special formula guar-

antees you will 'feel no pain and it will cure anything' and it's only fifty cents a bottle! Doc would get a bottle, and take a drink, then smile with satisfaction. Then he would splash some on his hands and rub it in. *Now don't leave, the band is getting ready to start up again,* Doc implored, as an assistant in blackface, Hunter Gassoway, acted as a clown. This clown called "Sambo" would go into the crowd and sell medicine calling out, *One more sold, Doctor, another bottle gone, more medicine, Doctor.* If business wasn't good, the bottles went "two for the price of one." A second blackface assistant, called "Buck-Wing Dancer," would dance while Doc Smith or one of the others played the fiddle "and the band played on."

At a reunion of old settlers in Glen Rose the HERALD declared that:

*Any one who has not lost the last microbe of enjoyment* [would have commendations for] t*he King-K Medicine Company. They played both day and night and always to standing room only.* However, a Glen Rose HERALD subscriber, who had lost that last microbe, chastised their "concerts," grumbling:

*But that King-K outfit, I can't see how mothers can sit under such an uproar of folly and shame with their little children by their side, and they are the hope of our country . . .* [The place was] *a dumping ground for those that want to get drunk and raise trouble. We should set better examples for our children and let all our efforts be to raise the moral standard and not lower it . . . we could see a great deal of deviltry in the whole thing.*

However, their performance in 1900 at a fiddle contest in the Johnson County Courthouse was held "under the auspices of 'The King's Daughters.' " At this gathering, the "King-K" Fiddle Band played again and was rated by the Cleburne paper accordingly:

*By this time the fiddlers were getting warmed up to their work and some old fellows in the audience were getting young again as they remembered how they had danced all night to the same old tunes and then gone home with the girls in the morning. It was Immense! Everybody had already got their fifty cents worth and there was more, and the best, to follow: for every fiddler had kept his favorite tune for the supreme test.*

Doc's patent medicines and fiddling made him a living for many years. Doc had formulas for "King-K Liniment, Salve, Tooth Powders, and Soap." Many records survived and were handed down through the family. Invoices from Doc's wholesale suppliers confirm the alleged alcohol content; the patent medicine also

Above: J. C. Brown letterhead. (JCA)

Left: The first Brown's Opera House was built in 1877, on the corner of East Chambers and South Anglin. John C. Brown was the "high sheriff" of Johnson County who hung Sam Myers, Jr., in 1880. In 1900 this grand version of the Brown's Opera House was constructed of brick from Easterwood brick yards, on East Buffalo Creek, and included cast iron arched lentils. The lower two floors of the building are still standing. Tickets cost ten, twenty, and thirty cents. Touring acts presented included the Donnelly-Hatfield Magnificent Minstrels; a lecture by Henry Ward Beecher entitled, "The Reign of the Common Man"; The Mandolin and Glee Clubs from the University of Texas; and Miss Lottie Kendall in "The Telephone Girl," one night only. The building was declared unsafe for habitation by large crowds in 1911, because the stamping of feet had caused the walls to weave and the floor to quiver in a dangerous way. (Wanda Erickson)

Left: Myrtle Corbin, the four-legged woman, was from Cleburne and is considered by circus historians more unusual than Frank Lentini who was "the acknowledged king of freaks." Lentini could kick balls the length of a circus tent with his third leg and use it as a rudder while swimming. Myrtle toured with the circus from the 1880s to 1910s. Her unusual two extra legs made her famous among performers in circus history. She toured both Europe and America with Barnum and is featured in a number of circus history books. She was married and had four girls and a boy. (Circus World Museum, Baraboo, Wisconsin)

Below: Wild West Ropers, an early 1900s wild west show, included Booger Red, considered by some to have been the all-time best bronc rider. On one of Red's visits to Cleburne, he was down on his luck so he sold his personal set of mounted longhorns to a local jeweler. (Courtesy of the Cleburne Public Library)

The Texas
Wild West Ropers

A man about town, George Cuthbert "Doc" Smith, (September 1849–September 1924). "Doc" was born in Loudoun County, Virginia, and came to Texas after 1880. He married Alpis Anna Filgo on July 28, 1889, in Cleburne. The Smith Family lived in Cleburne from the 1880s to 1920. A colorful character of the community, "Doc Smith" was described as witty, rather fussy, and very creative. He sold locally and also took his "Medicine Show" on the road around North Central Texas. Family letters show his childrens' great anticipation of his return from these "road trips" when he would bring trinkets, coins, stories, and hugs! Doc may have apprenticed in a medicine show during his younger years. He did business under the King-K Medicine Company name during the period from 1893 to 1915, selling "King-K Liniment, King-K Salve, King-K Tooth Powders, and King-K Soap." (Patricia Smith Boatright Collection)

Aplis Anna Filgo Smith, wife of George C. "Doc" Smith, circa 1888. The King K. Medicine Company provided the Smith Family with the latest fashions and finer amenities of the day. (Patricia Smith Boatright Collection)

contained opium and chloroform! (It is no wonder King-K relieved pain.) Doc's advertisments also showed his medicine could cure asthma, snake bites, burns, stings, colds and female troubles. And King-K was a very effective insecticide—when "set out" for screw flies, it "Kills them instantly." Since it could cure lock

jaw for horses, one would assume it would certainly "loosen things up" for humans when properly mixed.

Nothing that fun and useful could last forever and soon the "writing was on the wall," or on the sidewalk in Doc's case. His career as a street vending medicine man was soon to be overshadowed by larger issues of the day. In 1906 Congress passed the Pure Food and Drug Act which curtailed the unregulated manufacturing of patent medicines. His show would come to an end soon after 1914–1915, when Cleburne revised its civil and criminal ordinances. Until that time, all that was required for Doc to set up a gathering was an inexpensive license to sell on the streets. In 1915 assembling people on the street or market square "for the purpose of offering to sell them medicines" was a misdemeanor with a fine of up to $200 according to Article 113,

Above: King-K Medicine Company Band on the front steps of the Carnegie Library after 1906. His fiddle band went to work while Ben Williams called dances to lure in the customers. The members of the fiddle band over the years included his partner J. Y. Cason, along with Jack St. Clair, Sam, Charlie, and John Peacock. Around the turn of the century, local prohibition ebbed and flowed along with alcohol, as a result of frequently close wet-dry elections. During one of these dry spells, the Board of Trade Saloon put up a sign reading "King-K Office" after buying over eight hundred bottles of Doc's spirits. Doc Smith sued and had the sign removed. In 1905 Cleburne finally went dry, which may have helped his business for a time. With the saloons closed, his "medicines" may have provided the quick fix needed for the recurring problem of dry throats. In addition to the necessary alcohol content, Doc's special King-K formula included the pain relievers opium and chloroform at no extra cost in the standard fifty cents per bottle price. (Patricia Smith Boatright Collection)

Left: Flyer for King-K contains testimonials and mixing instructions for the cure-all. The flyer also served as the bottle wrapper which was finished off with a cork stopper and sealed with the proper amount of revenue stamps. By mixing different strengths, you could drink Doc's medicine for consumption (tuberculosis), rub it on your arthritis, use as a horse liniment, or at full strength, use it to kill biting flies. "NOTICE: be sure to follow directions closely!!" (Patricia Smith Boatright Collection)

The King-K Medicine Show attracts a large crowd on the Courthouse lawn, circa 1895. At the upper left the two blackfaced assistants can be seen on the back of a buckboard "float" while the banjo is played by Mr. J. Y. Cason, one of Doc's partners. In front of the crowd wearing black hats, one of the Peacock Brothers can be seen beside the buckboard. Note the saddle with the large Spanish-styled saddle horn at the lower left and the cord wood stacked on the wagons with what appears to be auctioneers standing on top. Detail of an unusual photograph in front of Johnson County's 1883 courthouse. (Dr. Jack Burton)

Section 1. Doc's unique profession had been criminalized and from that day until now, schemes to sell "medicines" on the street have continued to be frowned upon by local authorities. In 1919 the U.S. Congress voted National Prohibition, and Doc Smith died five years later with Prohibition still in effect. One wonders if he was still mixing the special recipe for his old cus-tomers during those final years. Can you picture Doc mixing up a special batch in his bathtub?

## Building a Better Place

"Chambers Street from the square to the Depot will soon be a solid row of business houses. Let the good work continue. Cleburne can stand it and it makes The Review happy." (1891) Downtown the city blocks were filling up. During the 1880s and 1890s rows of homes were lining up on the streets that radiated from downtown. On Cleburne's North Anglin and North Main Streets homes were built in the grand Victorian styles. These palacial homes over the years would enviously be referred to as "Silk Stocking Row" by the townsfolk. The Prairie Street and Featherstone area also featured some mansions beginning about 1900.

Above: A delivery man awaits your finishing needs at the J. Ganong & Gay Paint Company, 116 North Main, Cleburne, around 1904. Paint, wallpaper, and mirror replacement are this company's specialities. (Layland Museum, Cleburne, Texas)

Left: The interior of a paint and wallpaper shop reveals numerous sample books for wallpaper selection. (AC)

Above: Builders assemble needed materials for delivery from A. C. Barber Lumber in anticipation of the day's projects. Barber and Company, on East Willingham, along the railroad tracks, stocked a full line of builders' materials. (Layland Museum, Cleburne, Texas)

Right: Finishing artisans pose before a newly completed coal-burning fireplace which was common in Johnson County after the railroads arrived. (AC)

The home of M. M. Pittman under construction in 1900. These laborers pose in front of their nearly completed masterpiece. This home at 723 North Main on the southwest corner at Williams was torn down about 1959, to make way for the Cleburne Shopping Center. Since 1901, M. M. Pittman had been the owner and operator of a major soft grain milling company in Cleburne with most of the grain grown and sold locally. The mill manufactured "Big I" flour at the rate of one hundred barrels daily. (AC)

Pittman's Mill in 1905, where he made flour, meal, bran, and chops. His brand names were "Big A Patent" and "Queen of Cleburne,—Best Flour in the World." He would trade ground meal to farmers for their field corn on a daily basis. (Wanda Erickson)

Above: The Stratton home, 521 North Anglin Street, Cleburne, later known as the Goldsmith home, was built in 1893. (Pat & Martha Culpepper)

Right: This group may be the Shakespeare Club, founded in 1896 by Mrs. C. W. Mertz. The original officers were Mrs. C. W. Mertz, president; Mrs. W. H. Stratton, vice president; Mrs. T. P. West, secretary; Mrs. Eva Dickson, treasurer; and Mrs. C. P. Hudson, leader. In 1908 the club divided into the Bible Study Club and Shakespeare Club. The time of meetings was changed from afternoon to evening and gentlemen were admitted as members. The club was always exclusive, the membership having been limited to a small group entertained in the home. Only Mrs. R. A. Poole (front row, third from left) and a relative of Mrs. Poole's (on her left), along with Mrs. George Etter (middle row, second from left) have been identified in this picture. (AC)

Opposite page top: The home of Dr. and Mrs. W. P. Alexander at 523 North Main Street was built in 1892 in the Georgian style. The home was razed in the late 1970s, after the death of "Mary Q." A demolition worker found a beautiful crazy quilt top pieced from silks and brocades. It was hand embroidered with flowers, birds, and animals and each lady's initials. The wrecker took it from a closet with some old sheets and was about to throw it down a well when he was asked to stop. The quilt top is now framed and on display in the Anglin Queen Anne Guesthouse as a valuable work of art. (Layland Museum, Cleburne, Texas)

Opposite page bottom: Dr. William P. Alexander (d. 1933), Mary Quincy, and Mrs. Lou Alexander. Dr. Alexander arrived in 1885 buying Dr. Deal's Drug store. After "solid paying patients demanded his full attention," he sold it to Mr. Fain who later sold the store to Mr. Crow. The ladies of the Alexander family were noted for a tradition of highly accomplished hand embroidery. A sampling of which may be seen here on the dress of "Mary Q.," the survivor of two daughters. Willie Dell Culpepper remembered Lou and her mother, Mrs. Baker, as always having their "hand work" with them in their laps wherever they went. (Layland Museum, Cleburne, Texas)

Below: Looking down North Anglin Street and North Main in Cleburne, Texas. (AC)

Skipping Ladies. "Ah . . . the Victorian life." If you look closely you may see a resemblance to Homerette Huey. (AC)

Above: The Conway family home was 509 North Anglin Street, Cleburne. John Conway owned a lumber company and was able to select the finest materials on the market. He continued to build and make major additions to this home yearly—perhaps as many as seven. (Theatre Arts Collection, Harry Ransom Humanities Research Center, The University of Texas at Austin)

Right: Mayor Conway seated (left front wearing glasses) and his wife Tommye Johnson Conway (standing in back row beside lady in white) in their home. (Theatre Arts Collection, Harry Ransom Humanities Research Center, The University of Texas at Austin)

Above: The Hale family pose in front of their home across the street from The Conways. They invited Gordon Conway over for donkey rides. (Theatre Arts Collection, Harry Ransom Humanities Research Center, The University of Texas at Austin)

Right: Gordon Conway in a canoe baby carriage. (Theatre Arts Collection, Harry Ransom Humanities Research Center, The University of Texas at Austin)

Below: Gordon Conway and the Hale children with their donkey. (Theatre Arts Collection, Harry Ransom Humanities Research Center, The University of Texas at Austin)

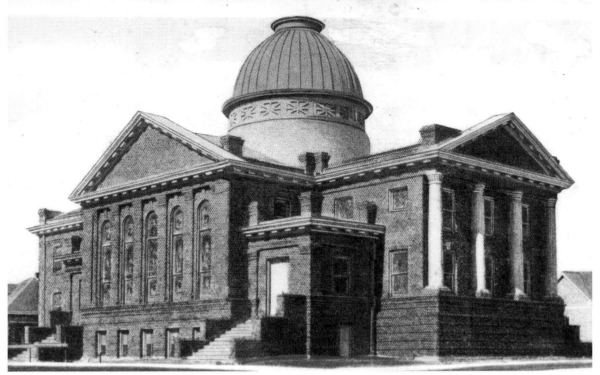

Above: The building of the East Henderson Street Baptist Church was initiated in 1900 and completed in two years. The magnificent structure was built one brick at a time with the masons taking the brick right out of a homemade kiln set up on the property. Clay for the brick was obtained a few blocks from the site along East Buffalo Creek. (AC)

Below: The First Presbyterian Church was erected in 1904 during the ministry of the Reverend John V. McCall. The church lot was bought with funds raised by the women of the congregation, organized in 1875 as the Presbyterian Sewing Society and later known as the Aid Society. They held ice cream socials, bazaars, and gave dinners to buy the property. (AC)

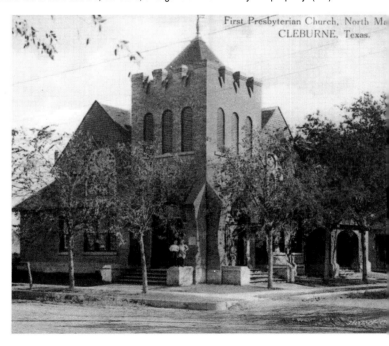

Above: Main Street Methodist Church, constructed in 1902 at the northwest corner of Main and Brown, was described as a beautiful white brick structure. Its interior sanctuary was gold leafed and additional lighting was provided by a skylight. A pipe organ was installed in 1908. An outstanding feature was its stunning stained glass and its corner entrance topped by a towering box spire. (AC)

First Baptist Church.                                    CLEBURNE, Texas.

Above: The First Baptist Church was constructed in 1900. The church pews and windows now in use are the same ones originally placed in this building. (AC)

Below: The Church of the Holy Comforter (Episcopal) was built in 1893 under the leadership of the Reverend W.W. Patrick. A parish hall was added in 1905 and, at one time, housed a boys' school. The doors of the church were painted red as a symbol of the "fire of love," the gift of the Holy Spirit the Comforter promised and given by Jesus. (Layland Museum, Cleburne, Texas)

Above: The High Altar of the Church of the Holy Comforter was installed in 1905. This classic altar with a triptych reredos rising behind is the center of the church's design. Carved from oak, it features romanesque pillars underneath the table and gothic decorations above the three niches in the reredos. The candlesticks and the altar rail were used in the original church, as were the metal uprights of the altar rail. (Layland Museum, Cleburne, Texas)

Above: George Etter built a "stick-style" Victorian home at 614 North Anglin around 1879. In 1899 George deeded land next to the family home to his son, Frank Etter. Frank built a Queen Anne home at 610 North Anglin. The photo is of the George Etter Family in 1880. In the front row, left to right are: Annie, George (father), Clavindia (mother), and Frank. In the back row are: Letha, Clarence, Ethel, and Arthur. (Anna Faye Etter)

Left: Members of the Modern Priscilla Club were accompanied by their families when they attended socials held at the homes of members. Charles Eyster and Mrs. F. G. Beamish were winners in a game in which pictures of prominent men—politicians, authors, etc.— were placed for the guests to name. The winners were those who named correctly the largest number of celebrities and each received a pair of silk hose. (Layland Museum, Cleburne, Texas)

Below: Gordon Conway as a child with Mrs. Conway and other ladies on the front porch of their home at 509 North Anglin Street, Cleburne. (Theatre Arts Collection, Harry Ransom Humanities Research Center, The University of Texas at Austin)

Above: According to the history of the First United Methodist Church, Mr. and Mrs. R. L. Bartley were the first couple married in the church. The seating on the north side of the church was for men, south side for women and the center section for young people and strangers. (Layland Museum, Cleburne, Texas)

Above: Mrs. Davidson, Allie-Wood Johnson, Gordon Conway, and Mrs. J. C. Conway, circa 1895. At the Conway home, 509 North Anglin Street, Cleburne, south porch. The reverse of the photo has the notation: "Mrs. Davidson, Allerwood, Gordon and myself. Aunt Tom's [Tommye Conway] house in Cleburne where Gordon was born." (Theatre Arts Collection, Harry Ransom Humanities Research Center, The University of Texas at Austin)

Right: "The elegant residence of Mrs. John Catlett Conway at 509 North Anglin Street was the site of a Porch Dance Party in August 1897 featuring 'dreamy music, scintillating electric lights,' together with the magnificent costumes of the ladies and gentlemen, and making the dance an occasion long to be remembered." CLEBURNE CHRONICLE (Theatre Arts Collection, Harry Ransom Humanities Research Center, The University of Texas at Austin)

Above: Residence collage of Cleburne, Texas. Circa 1895. ("The Enterprise Edition" for the Texas State Fair in Dallas.) The three residences on the left still remain on North Anglin Street in 1998. 1. J.C. Conway, 509 North Anglin; 2. C.W. Mertz, 723 North Anglin; 3. W.H. Stratton, 521 North Anglin. (AC)

Left: "Ladies canvass North Anglin Street. The ladies of the neighborhood are seeking funds to have the street sprinkled with water daily to settle the dust. Mrs. C. W. Mertz and Mrs. C. B. Stratton are leaders in the drive for contributions. They say there is now more driving on Anglin Street than any other in the city and that improving it will make it even more accessible." Circa 1903. (Theatre Arts Collection, Harry Ransom Humanities Research Center, The University of Texas at Austin)

Mrs. Frances Dickson Abernathy (1881?–196?) The youngest daughter of Campbell Dickson and Lucy Ellen Tracy. Frances was a teacher who became one of Johnson County's most prolific local history writers and researchers. Her mother, Lucy Tracy Dickson, died when she was a young woman taking away the opportunity to know her mother as the "older children knew her." This yearning for knowledge of her mother's life became a driving force in her life. In 1936 she wrote, "I have found a tender joy in going through old letters and diaries, in recalling the stories that so fascinated me in my childhood and that still hold their charm for me now, and in living again the days that seem at once a very short time ago and a very long time ago." (Cleburne Public Library)

## Pen Education

Johnson County's first school was held in a small log building near Alvarado erected by Samuel Myers, Jackson Bradley, and Abraham Futhey as early as 1852. During the earliest years the community of settlers supplied the food, plowed the fields, and herded the animals of the teacher. Among the early teachers at Myers's school were W. T. Wise, Miss Harris, and E. M. Heath. From that humble log school grew and developed the public school system in Johnson County.

On August 22, 1854, the county was divided and organized into school districts as directed by law. In 1884 the commissioners made major changes to conform to an 1876 state law requiring a community school system with a special school tax. Johnson county set a rate of twenty-five cents per one hundred dollars valuation to supplement the state school fund. About 1902–1903, a new change caused each town to set up its own school district expanding the number of districts.

In Cleburne, the biggest accomplishment began in 1868, with a revival meeting held on the grounds where the old Cleburne High School stands today by the Reverend W. A. Mason, a Baptist minister. He began an educational institution named the Cleburne Institute which later developed into the public schools of Cleburne.

Rev. Mason, elected the first pastor of the First Baptist Church when it was established, envisioned a college to be built on the site of this revival. At the end of the meeting he began cultivating interest and support for the project. The college was fostered by the Alvarado Baptist Association, and the Reverend J. R. Clark came to Cleburne to head it. The land was given by Col. B. J. Chambers and the college was established in 1869.

The frame structure (25 x 40 feet) grew from 10 to 100 pupils in a few months. By 1872, a brick building was built, but during the 1880s the building was declared unsafe. In the spring of 1883, the Cleburne Public School System was organized with Frank Johnson as the first superintendent. A public school was located where the college had been, but it burned and the frame Fulton Building was erected. This building burned, and the old Cleburne High School building was erected. Three ward schools were under construction at one time in the spring of 1890: Adams, J. N. Long, and Irving schools.

Peyton Irving came to Cleburne in September 1877. He organized and established the Irving Select School for Young Ladies (page 157) with an enrollment at first limited to twenty-five. Flourishing for about twenty years where the Main Street Presbyterian Church later stood, a larger building was erected on North Anglin Street where the Irving School stands today.

Superintendant S. N. Marrs told of an 1892–1893 public school controversy in Cleburne which divided the town and brought down the city's government. There was a progressive movement at the time to shorten the actual time children attended school by reducing the noon recess from one and one-half hours to three-quarters of an hour. This was endorsed by the mayor and council who daily conducted city business on the first floor of the public school building. The same mayor was the ex-officio chairman of the school board and the council appointed the school's trustees. Those who opposed this innovation, which would keep the children away from the city office/public school, were

Bertha L. Cason, about 1896, was the daughter of James Y. and Anna V. Cason, residing at 804 South Wilhite, Cleburne. George "Doc" Smith and James Cason invested in Cleburne real estate near Chambers and Douglas Streets, selling lots to interested home builders. (Patricia Smith Boatright Collection)

Phillip Huey was the child of a farming family. His mother, Daisy Hooker, married W. G. Huey in 1893. Phillip had one brother, Paul Huey. Cotton was the main crop in the 1890s, but grain was raised too. They had jersey cows, horses, mules, sheep, hogs, and fowl. One of the barns was constructed in 1870, and a windmill was erected in 1900. Little boys didn't start wearing pants until they could walk. Henry Collier recalls wearing little boys' dresses until he was four or five years old. His first pants were homemade and came only to his knees. (AC)

aroused to fight the decision. Among them were some attorneys who found that early in the city's organization, the city had voted to set up an elected rather than an appointed school board. With this controversy opened, the city election of April 1892, saw Mayor B. F. Frymier replaced by John H. Boyd. In 1893 there were two tickets placed in the running for school board: administration and anti-administration. An "old-time election" ensued, with banners, placards, and carriges for either side. The old administration lost by only one hundred votes out of one thousand; bad feelings were felt on all sides as the city vote changed the entire school administration. There were many who were willing to stand for principle and made sacrifices to lay the foundation of our schools today.

In 1903, Booker T. Washington School was organized with a first graduating class in 1904 of two students, Felix Garrett and Louis Price. The original building was a two-story frame located south of the present structure on the edge of the campus; it was spacious with four or five classrooms on the first floor and an auditorium on the second floor. This was during the early years of organized education in the State of Texas, and such a building was the pride of the entire black community. The original structure burned in 1930.

The school was closed in 1965, after the Federal and Supreme Courts ruled segregation unconstitutional in 1954. The old building still stands at 100 Mansfield Road as a memorial to the school that was the heart and soul of the well-defined black community in East Cleburne.

Right: The children of Dr. L. L. Harris on South Robinson, Cleburne were Lowell (standing in cart), Nell, Clayton (sitting), Marie, and Ruth (standing) with a Studebaker cart, circa 1910-1911. (Sandra Harris Osborne)

Below: The Rigby boys, Robert and Isom, came to Antioch, Texas, in 1880. They lived near each other on farms, and each had a large family—mostly boys. Bob and his wife Ann raised seven boys: Charlie, L. D. (Pug), Robert, Luther, Bradley, Homer, and John; and two girls: Mattie and Lillie. These are some of the Rigby boys shooting marbles outside the school. (Layland Museum, Cleburne, Texas)

Right: Gordon Conway, the daughter of Mayor John Catlett and Tommye Johnson Conway contemplating her future at the age of three in 1896. Gordon Conway later became a famous fashion illustrator and motion picture and theater costume designer. (Theatre Arts Collection, Harry Ransom Humanities Research Center, The University of Texas at Austin)

Below: Gordon Conway eating a watermelon in her backyard, 509 North Anglin, circa 1897. (Theatre Arts Collection, Harry Ransom Humanities Research Center, The University of Texas at Austin)

Above: KEENERS KORNUCOPIAS delivering ice cream. (AC)

Left: Gordon Conway with domestic housekeeper's child near the street at 509 North Anglin Street, Cleburne. (Theatre Arts Collection, Harry Ransom Humanities Research Center, The University of Texas at Austin)

Above: In 1877 Peyton Irving established the Irving Select School for Young Ladies. The school prospered and enrollment grew. Mr. Irving moved the school to 1100 North Anglin Street. He constructed a large two-story frame building with classrooms on the lower floor and dormitories on the second floor. Girls from the rural areas boarded here. (Layland Museum, Cleburne, Texas)

Right: "LOST HER COW—Mrs. H. F. Oliver has lost her milch cow. The brute was left in the front yard to graze Wednesday night and yesterday morning was gone and no trace of her has yet been discovered. She is a large brown cow, dehorned and has a rope about her neck."

"RODE A COW—A boy riding a cow about the public square was one of Cleburne's attractions yesterday afternoon." NEWS BRIEFS, August 7, 1902 (AC)

Right: Adams Elementary School was erected in 1892 as a wooden structure and was then called South Ward. The school was named for Judge F. E. Adams who was known to take an unusual interest in the school and teachers. The school was a two-story structure with three rooms on each floor. At first, they didn't have desks, but used chairs and put their books under them. The 6th graders had gardens. The boys' garden was west side; the girls' on the east. They raised vegetables and sold them to neighbors. The money was used to buy pictures for the room. The school had a fence around it with no gate. (Layland Museum, Cleburne, Texas)

Right: The children of the Adams Elementary school climbed the fence each day. They ate lunch outside under the big trees in the shade. (Layland Museum, Cleburne, Texas)

Below: A typical, modern 1890s classroom consisted of desks, blackboards, wall maps, globes, and rock samples. A Rio Vista student recalls most large schools had coal burning stoves to heat the building. Usually the principal was a man, and he would go early and fire up the stoves. Pupils loved to be selected to bring the coal in old scuttles (buckets) from the coal house. They also enjoyed gathering the erasers and going outside to pound the chalk dust off. (Layland Museum, Cleburne, Texas)

Primary classroom. "When I was a boy in school, Mr. Barnett was the only teacher that whipped me, and it was a real hard one. It was the only whipping I ever got in my life. The reason he whipped me was 'cause the class was reciting history, and I was playing with Miss Fannie Blair's long, pretty, curly hair and pulled it a little too hard and she jumped, so he whipped me for it," Joseph McClure. (Layland Museum, Cleburne, Texas)

Above: In 1893 Alta Vista College was transferred to the ownership of Red Oak Presbytery and became Red Oak Academy near Burleson, equivalent to a junior college. Rev. L. C. Collier was named president. Rev. Collier is in the fourth row, at the end with his hat on his arm. There were boardinghouses for girls and boys. The oldest student on record was a man of forty-nine; the youngest, a girl fifteen. (Ron Geiser, The Apothecary Shop, Burleson)

Right: "Batter, up!" Students at recess square off for a work-up game of baseball at Union Hill School, circa 1909. Located two miles east of Joshua, the one-room school served that community until 1916 when Union Hill and Marystown consolidated their systems and built a new school. During the 1898 school year, Peyton Irving reported, "our one-room building is furnished with new desks and well equipped with black boards, wall maps and globes; there are 29 pupils, and the work was good." (Don and Lucille Jackson)

In 1891, John W. Hirt and John W. Miller started a meat market, added a slaughter house, and soon had a thriving business. The Hirt and Miller Meat Market was located at 109 North Anglin in Cleburne. Mr. Hirt on his horse seems to have just come in off the range. Cattle would be brought on the hoof from Hirt's Ranch and slaughtered at the store. J. Lee Filgo on delivery buggy stands ready to bring your order. Also pictured are Jim Miller (center with apron), Auburn Cheek, Roger Collins, and Dub Collins (hand on wagon). (AC)

## Fast Food

The gardener from Keene comes to Cleburne about six o-clock in the morning driving his peddling hack loaded with tomatoes, beans, okra, black-eyed peas, field roasting ears, peaches, plums, cantaloupes, watermelons, and a good variety of bunched root vegetables. He arrives at the Santa Fe Railroad station and drops off a load of twelve dozen cantaloupes with the cooks at the kitchen door of Fred Harvey's eating place. With him under the shadow of a Coca-Cola umbrella sits his almost ten-year-old son shaking the reins of the

Mckenzie Produce-Wagons. (Anna Faye Etter)

Cleburne Ice & Cold Storage Company drivers with their teams of mules begin the day's work at the Cleburne Ice & Cold Storage Company in Cleburne. In 1892 the plant had the capacity of five tons per day. Large amounts of ice were purchased by the Santa Fe Railroad for icing down refrigerated produce and meat shipments. The young man at left stands beside a 300-pound block of ice, the weight at which ice was produced using ammonia as the refrigerant. Home delivery saw 25 pounds of ice for 10 cents, 100 pounds for 40 cents. (Layland Museum, Cleburne, Texas)

Inset: Cleburne Ice & Cold Storage Company ticket. (AC)

Brewer Meat Market on South Main, Cleburne, circa 1907. Meat was delivered every hour so that customers who had no refrigeration would receive fresh, good meat. (Layland Museum, Cleburne, Texas)

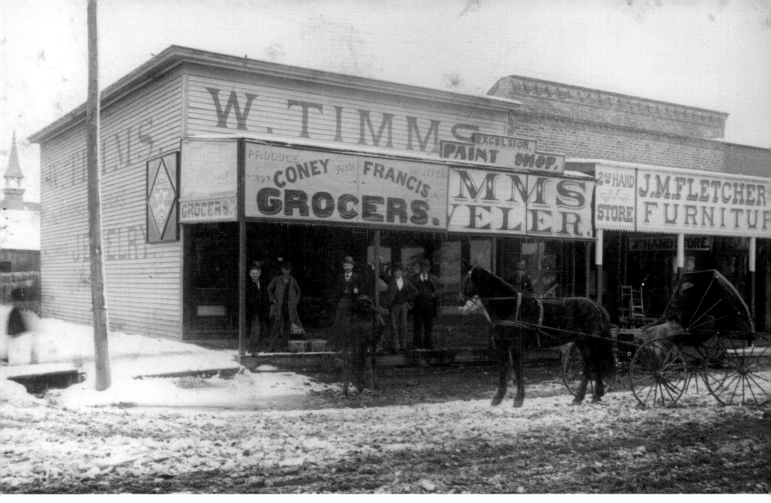

harnessed mules. They drive by the boardinghouses and restaurants and leave them all they want.

By that time the dwellings were stirring, so they transfer to North Main and take the street, house to house, all the way up to the twelve hundred block and then transfer to North Anglin and head back towards town. He gives his old brass bell a ding-a-ling as the boy pulls the mules to a stop in front of a house. The housewives and maids call to the family, "Mr. Mattison is here," as the screen door slams shut. The ladies and children walk out to the street as Mr. Mattison throws a tarpaulin back to display the work of many cool mornings and many hot days in the sun, gathered the afternoon before just about sunset—everything in order, and the finest looking and tasting garden goods that can be found. Their kitchen aprons cradled everything that appealed to them always getting a Biblical measurement of packed full and running over. Some impolite new neighbors had run to get there first and being unfamiliar, believed the best articles were always placed on top, so they had been inspecting down through the baskets, then at last looked up with a glance. The ones at the bottom were as good or better that the ones on top. Mr. Mattison was a man of integrity. The whole neighbor-

Top: W. Timms and Company jewelers on the northeast corner of Chambers and Anglin Streets, Cleburne. Witt Wilson, J. H. Styron, and W. Timms were partners in the store. Coney and W. D. Francis operated a grocery in 1894. J. J. Fletcher operated a furniture store in 1882. The Church of the Holy Comforter (Episcopal) church bell tower can be seen in the background. (Dr. Jack Burton)

Bottom: Milk was delivered daily to Mrs. Arthur Etter at 206 Locust St., Cleburne, circa 1900. (Anna Faye Etter)

Cleburne House. Also known as Hotel Cleburne, was located at West Henderson and North Main in Cleburne, Texas. (Layland Museum, Cleburne, Texas)

hood looked forward to his arrival each day, except Saturday when he did not come to town. Often on Mondays male shoppers came out and got advice on gardening and might ask him about his religious convictions and beliefs. He would not discuss his beliefs, but would refer them to what God says in the Bible.

Many seasons and years the old man and his son drove the route, the boy grew up and left one day, but the old man kept coming. Then after twenty-three years the old man came no more. The ladies of Silk Stocking Row were disturbed by the poor quality and high prices of those who tried to take his place. Some of them had to walk, take their buggy or tin lizzie to town to purchase needed groceries at one of the high priced markets. Soon the news came Mr. Mattison was asleep in the Lord; they knew no one would ever take his place.

Many years later, Mattison's boy came back to Texas for the funeral of a friend and was recognized by one of the old customers who said "many of us . . . still miss his visits." She informed him about another peddler who attempted to take his father's place and sold her a basket of beautiful peaches. The ones on the top were beautiful, but the ones on the bottom were small and no good. When confronted, the man remarked: "I don't propose to be a Christian like Mr. Mattison professed to be." Mattison's old customer gave the new peddler a reprimand saying: "I would have you know that Mr. Mattison did not profess to be a Christian. He was a Christian."

## Hogg Returns to Cleburne

Hogg is considered the most important Texan of his time. Historian Eugene C. Barker said of him: "Probably only two other men have left their impression so deeply on the history of Texas as did James Stephen Hogg. Those two were Stephen F. Austin and Sam Houston; and perhaps only Houston affected popular feeling so strong, both favorably and unfavorably."

Govenor James Hogg stayed at the Cleburne House on May 4, 1892. (AC)

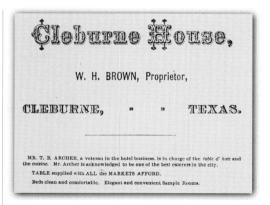

Govenor Hogg's signature on guest register at Cleburne House. Circa 1892 (AC)

Born in 1851, Jim Hogg came to Cleburne in 1868 when he was about seventeen. He hitched a ride hoping to get a start in the newspaper business and possibly see the West. Jack Davis who started the CLEBURNE CHRONICLE had come from Rusk with his family and warned Hogg that he could not pay him. They passed Fort Worth by because the prospects there did not look too good. Davis came to the new town of Cleburne and printed six issues of the paper before he sold it to John Graves. Hogg stayed on with Graves but found the going rough as he and the editor did not get along. Jim Hogg was about to give up when a fire destroyed the print shop and sent Hogg hitching a ride back to East Texas with fifteen cents in his pocket.

Hogg talked with some of those who elected him—the Grangers and the Farmers' Alliance. At his peak in 1892 as governor of the state, he was in the middle of the reorganization of Texas government, which was very popular with the farmers. He appointed E. M. Heath and other locals to state boards, commissions, judgeships, and as delegates. Soon after Hogg was here he contacted and corresponded with the last living signer of the Texas Declaration of Independence from Mexico. W. C. Crawford at the time lived in Alvarado.

Top: Cleburne House ad, circa 1879–80. (Layland Museum, Cleburne, Texas)

Bottom: William Carrol Crawford (1804–1895) was the last living signer of the Texas Declaration of Independence from Mexico. He moved to Alvarado in 1884. Governor Hogg was contacted by Crawford soon after Hogg's visit to Johnson County in 1892.

To his Excellency Governor J. S. Hogg
Dear Sir
. . . we supported you in your last election and will support you again. There are many Strong men in Texas I am proud of them they are my sons I am the father of all Texans. . . . I saw you once when you war a bony young man I hear that you have become corpulent Be strong and guide Texas to Prosperity and God help you for she is a refractory fellow since the year A. D. 1835 I have tried with all my power to guide her in the ways of righteousness God bless Texas and her sons
Very Respectfully your fellow helper W. C. Crawford.
(Star of the Republic Museum, Washington, Texas)

1. M. S. Kahle - Va. Inf
2. C. Y. Kouns - Tex. Inf
3. J. R. Keating - Ga. Inf
4. G. O. Winn - Ga. Inf
5. J. D. Mitchell - Va. Inf
6. J. V. Leatherwood - Ala
7. J. M. Blackwood - Miss
8. H. M. Glass - Co. D. El
9. T. J. Davis - Ga. Ca
10. J. A. Styron - Ala. In

## Civil War Veterans

William A. Fletcher of Hood's Texas Brigade referred to himself and other Confederate veterans as belonging to "a generation of warriors." These veterans had the war wounds and stories to prove it. After the war E. M. Heath traveled over one thousand miles on horseback to return the flag of the First Ohio captured by his company during the battle of Atlanta. The gesture was part of the healing of old wounds.

The Old Soldier's Room in the basement of the courthouse bellowed with the boasts and laughter, as the old men chewed, spat, and puffed away their final years. Their last battles were with pension boards and politicians. They spent their closing years writing letters for comrades' widows and each other to get pensions and placement in Confederate Veteran's Homes. They hounded and threatened ungrateful young politicians for greater benefits and assistance. "Now a few words to the law makers—that they sympathize more with the old tottering veterans and give them larger pensions." Abe Onstott, 1912.

Above: Confederate Veterans Reunion, Burleson 1903. Top Row Standing on the Porch: John Shannon, Wick Tye, N. L. Fairless, William Bransom, D. I. Murphy, Mr. Wilson, Mr. Dickenson, W. M. Ferris. Second Row, l. to r.: R. L. Roberts, unknown, unknown, Mr. East, Mr. Summerlin, Joe Thompson, and at far right seated on the top step another unknown. Third Row, l. to r.: Jimmy McGee, Mr. Roddy, Mr. London, Mr. McNairn, unknown, Mr. Jackson, A. J. Beavers, Y. P. Bowers, and unknown. Front Row, l. to r.: W. E. Pope, unknown, Capt. B. B. Paddock, unknown, Mr. Leveritt, Mr. Rust, Mr. Jackson, and Walter Neeley. (Layland Museum, Cleburne, Texas)

Right: Pat Cleburne Camp No. 88 U.C.V. at 1882–83 Johnson County Courthouse, circa 1895. Local company soldiers were taught to shoot low at the knees. This would immobilize the enemy better than body shots. (Tolbert Mayfield and The Cleburne Dairy Queens)

H. Smith - Tex. Inft.                   21. J. M. Odell - Tex. Cav.                   31. J. L. Morgan - A                   41. W. C. Coney - Ala. Inft.
T. Smith - Tenn. Inft.                  22. J. Upton - Tex. Cav.                     32. J. N. English - Tex. Cav.         42. W. H. Helsey - Ga. Inft.
W. Dalton - Ky. Cav.                    23. J. W. Smyth - Miss. Cav.                33. J. Black McMillian - Scout        43. A. W. Price - 7th. Tex.
M. Heath - Tex. Cav.                    24. H. Hart - Tex. Cav.                      34. H. D. Beckner - 18th. Tex.        44. T. J. Hooker - Miss. Inft.
_y Plummer - Daughter of Camp 25. John McCutchins - Tenn. Inft. 35. J. P. Berry - 23rd. Ga.                    45. Unidentified
H. Griffin - Tex. Cav.                  26. J. C. Morton - La. Inft.                36. J. L. Edmonds - E. 11th            46.
M. Helsey - Scout                       27. M. L. McDowell - Ga. Inft.             37. Jessie B. Jones - Co. I, La.      47.
_ector McNeil - Tex. Co. E              28. O. T. Plummer - Tenn. Inft.            38. J. R. Ransone - Ga. Inft.          48.
_. R. Wilson - 19th Ala.                29. A. M. Cleer - Ala. - Cav.              39. W. H. Comer - Tenn.                49.
_. Scurlock - Wallers Bat.              30. Zeb. Mobly - S. C. Inf.                40. F. M. Adams -                      50.

| 1 | J. J. Murphy | 9 | John Doby | 17 | Stevens | 25 | Mrs. J. R. Ransone | 33 | W. W. Pearce | 41 | J. T. Ford | 49 | R. W. Ferrell |
| 2 | W. D. Choate | 10 | Miss Nannie Doby | 18 | A. J. Richards | 26 | J. R. Featherstone | 34 | W. H. Dickerson | 42 | T. N. Lawson | 50 | John Cheek |
| 3 | W. P. Daves | 11 | Dr. J. D. Osborn | 19 | J. J. Funderburk | 27 | B. J. Armstrong | 35 | J. T. Muse | 43 | J. T. Wright | 51 | H. P. Barnes |
| 4 | W. H. Comer | 12 | E. B. Scott | 20 | M. D. Miller | 28 | James Nicholson | 36 | C. Y. Kouns | 44 | J. D. Allen | 52 | Mrs. H. P. Ba |
| 5 | J. W. Armstrong | 13 | J. H. Kerley | 21 | Joe Goodwin | 29 | A. B. Kanada | 37 | John Jacobs | 45 | Wince Hooker | 53 | Mrs. Hines |
| 6 | | 14 | James Daves | 22 | H. D. Beckner | 30 | Mrs. A. B. Kanada | 38 | C. R. Warren | 46 | Brady Pride | 54 | J. W. Freemar |
| 7 | B. F. Yarbrough | 15 | A. F. Johnson | 23 | D. G. Dalton | 31 | Tom Hooker | 39 | D. S. Wylie | 47 | W. O. Menefee | 55 | A. B. Kidd |
| 8 | G. V. Elwell | 16 | Dick Hearn | 24 | J. R. Ransone | 32 | W. R. Bounds (Capt) | 40 | J. M. Hanson | 48 | J. W. Whittsitt | | |

Above: Pat Cleburne Camp No. 88 U.C.V., circa 1900 posed in front of the Johnson County courthouse where they met for many years in the Old Soldiers Room in the basement. (AC)

Right: Alvarado Civil War veterans' reunion, August 7, 1907, Alvarado, Texas. (Layland Museum, Cleburne, Texas)

Above: Stock Certificate for Pioneers and Old Settlers Association of Johnson County. (Pioneers and Old Settlers Association of Johnson County, Alvarado, Texas)

Right: J. James of Alvarado, Texas. (Pioneer and Old Settlers Association of Johnson County, Alvarado, Texas)

Below: Alvarado parade float with Smith & Welch Furniture ad. (Layland Museum, Cleburne, Texas)

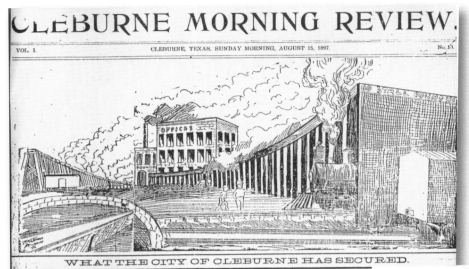

# CLEBURNE MORNING REVIEW.

VOL. 1.     CLEBURNE, TEXAS, SUNDAY MORNING, AUGUST 15, 1897.     No. 13.

**WHAT THE CITY OF CLEBURNE HAS SECURED.**

"Hurrah! The Announcement in the Cleburne *Morning Review* confirmed that on August 13, 1897, the contract for the Santa Fe Shops had been signed between the citizens of Cleburne and the Santa Fe officials, bringing the main shops of that railway to the area. The Santa Fe Shops became the backbone of the economy of Cleburne and Johnson County. As the county's largest employer they provided work for many generations of local citizens and their families. (AC)

---

## Our Entire Line

—OF—

Ladies' Sleeveless Vests ranging from 25c to 50c Close Monday at 15c.

## Nix, Baird & Gresham

## MASS MEETING

Last Night of the Citizens at the Court House.

### AN ENTHUSIASTIC SUCCESS.

The Hall Was Filled to Overflowing and the Speeches, Heartily Applauded—Demonstration Yesterday Morning.

Long before the hour announced for the grand jubilation meeting last night crowds began to pour into the district court room, and at 8:30 o'clock there was not a vacant seat to be had for love or money, while hundreds were obliged to stand in the aisles and halls. Cleburne turned herself inside out for a fact in the matter of attendance, and a more enthusiastic audience probably never gathered together in a city of ten times the population of Cleburne. Brawn and muscle, labor and capi-

tal, intelligence and artistic merit the learned and the unlearned professions all mingled together and whooped her up last night in a spontaneous outburst that showed an ebullition of a feeling overwhelmed with joy at the reception of a boon that makes from its inception the steady growth of Cleburne.

The two bearers of the precious document from Cleburne to Galveston and back home again, with it signed, sealed and delivered, were loudly applauded on their entrance to the hall. Many speeches were made, and they were all good ones, containing as they did, sunbeams of prophetic utterance for the future prosperity of the city.

Mayor Keating, on taking the chair as presiding officer of the meeting, was the recipient of much applause. He said that they had expected to have some instrumental music, but instead they would have some chin music. He said as the chief executive of the city, "I desire to announce to you that at the conclusion of this meeting, Cleburne will be wide open." He further admonished the citizens not to interfere with the rights of others, but to enjoy themselves to their heart's content.

At the conclusion of the mayor's remarks, Judge Ramsey arose amid loud applause and moved that Mr.

Poindexter be requested to tell the meeting the result of the trips. Thereupon that gentleman ascended the platform accompanied by the applause of the audience, and in an eloquent address, told of the signing of the contract, the labors of the committee and predicted the future steady growth of Cleburne.

He did not forget to say a good word for Col. Polk of the Santa Fe, and concluded amid great applause by saying that he was for Cleburne first, last and all the time. According to Mr. Poindexter, the money that will be distributed by the railroad company will more than equal the amount of the cotton crop of three adjoining counties if all the money could be spent here.

At the conclusion of Mr. Poindexter's speech Judge Ramsey enthused the audience with word painting and put them in the best of humor by his witty allusions. He was willing "to weep with those that weep and rejoice with those that rejoice." He placed the credit for the obtaining of the contract not on any one man but on the patriotic citizens of Cleburne that had signed the contract. He advised fraternity, a long pull a strong pull and a pull all together for the benefit of the city. Cal. Polk came in for many complimentary remarks from Judge Ramsey. His advice to the citizens to sink their animosity of whatever nature and stand together for the glory and honor of Cleburne was vociferously applauded.

County Attorney Odell made probably the most eloquent speech of the night. He was in great voice and entered thoroughly into the subject. The applause which greeted his points and oratorical periods was loud and frequent. H. P. Brown wound up the formal speech making and brought down the house by the vigor of his utterances which breathed of patriotism for the city of Cleburne. Mayor Keating, after Mr. Brown had concluded, made a few remarks and advised the audience to turn themselves loose, which they accordingly proceeded to do.

As early as 4:30 o'clock yesterday morning a crowd of at least 400 people assembled in the neighborhood of The Review office, with the intention of going to the depot in a body to welcome home with the contract Colonel Moss and William Poindexter, who were expected in on the 5:45 train from Galveston.

About 5 o'clock The Review received a telephonic communication that the train was five hours late and would not arrive until 11 o'clock. At the latter hour some 3000 or 4000 people gathered at the Santa Fe depot, and as the train from Galveston pulled in it was the recipient of a salvo of cheers that could be heard all over town.

Colonel Moss and Mr. Poindexter, on emerging from a Pullman, were surrounded by a crowd of jubilant citizens and heartily congratulated on their safe return. A speech was called for, and Colonel Moss was lifted bodily on a baggage box and made a short address. Mr. Poindexter followed him in a few well-chosen remarks, and the fire laddies, who had come down in great shape to the depot, took charge of both the guardians of the contract, and placing them high up on the seat of the fire truck, rode them in triumph about the city, amid the plaudits of thousands.

### Meeting of Fire Engineers.

Special to the Review.

Chicago, Aug. 14—Chiefs and subordinate officers of the fire departments of the principal towns of the state rendezvoused this morning at the Auditorium hotel en route to New Haven, Conn., where the twenty-fifth annual convention of the International Association of Fire Engineers opens next week. Too delegation from this state is the largest yet sent to the national gathering.

### Sewing Wanted.

I want work at home, sewing for families, have had much experience in tailor work and general sewing. Residence on West Henderson.

Mrs. M. J. Sanders.

---

# EXTRA.

# Cleburne Morning Review

EXTRA.     CLEBURNE, TEXAS, FRIDAY, AUG. 13, 1897, 3:30 P. M.     EXTRA.

## HURRAH! HURRAH! HURRAH!

### The Contract for the Santa Fe Shops Has Been Signed by the Railway Authorities at Galveston.

### COL. MOSS AND WILLIAM POINDEXTER WILL BRING IT HOME

Tomorrow Morning on the Early Train. A Telegram Received Today and Which Heads This Article, Tells the Tale of the Successful Mission of These Two Gentlemen—Cleburne's Future Prosperity Assured and the People Should Make a Proper Jubilation.

Beach Hotel, Galveston, Texas,
August 13, 1897.

S. B. Allen,

Cleburne, Texas.

Contract signed. We will be at home Saturday morning.

(True copy)     S. E. MOSS.

The contract between the citizens of Cleburne and the Santa Fe officials for the location of the main shops of that railway at this point, has been signed, sealed and delivered, and the precious document in charge of Colonel Moss of the National Bank of Cleburne and the Hon. William Poindexter will be brought back to this city tomorrow morning from Galveston.

Let Cleburne rejoice; let its citizens throw up their hats and hurrah! The preliminaries of the greatest

event that will happen to Cleburne in this generation, are happily and satisfactorily arranged. Now let the brawn and muscle, the brain and intellect, labor and capital of Cleburne all together as one man, unite in the bands of fraternal brotherhood, bury all past differences of whatever nature, and sensible of the great good that is sure to come to this city, extend a fitting reception to the two patriotic citizens who at a personal sacrifice, have devoted themselves with might and main to secure a boon more precious than anything that has happened in the history of this municipality.

Meet them with a multitude; meet them with a brass band! Let their ears be greeted with the enthusiastic huzzahs of a grateful people! Let salutes of artillery echoing on the morning breeze carry to all parts of Texas, the news of the great blessing

that has come, with the dawning of the sun on the oriental horizon, to beautiful Cleburne, the future queen city of North Texas! Bring the children, the youths and the maidens the men and women of a smaller growth, that they may tell to their children and their childrens' children in times to come, how the people of Cleburne turned out to do honor to the men who brought to the city on August 14, 1897, a gift more precious than the fabled gems in the treasuries of royal princes.

Don't let the opportunity pass! Act at once! There is ample time. Engage your music, appoint your reception committee, have your cannon ready! Awake to the importance of the occasion! Let the whole state of Texas know that you are alive and appreciate the efforts of the patriotic guardians of that, which will stamp its identity indelibly on the future of Cleburne, and advance it to the status of an embryo metropolis!

Meet the morning train from Galveston; your shouts of welcome will be more pleasing to the ears of Col. Moss and Mr. Poindexter, than the honeyed flattery of kings or queens. Do them proud and do yourselves proud! Now is the accepted time! Act immediately and make your preparations! Hurrah! Hurrah for Cleburne and the Santa Fe shops! Hurrah for Col. Moss and William Poindexter! Hurrah for the committee having the original arrangements in charge! Hurrah for the citizens who signed the contract! Hurrah for the committee that labored night and day to obtain these signatures! Hurrah for every body! The Santa Fe shops are ours and the future prosperity of the city assured!

**FIRST IN THE FIELD—A COPY OF YESTERDAY'S REVIEW EXTRA.**

---

## Santa Fe Shops

BECAUSE OF CLEBURNE'S WATER AND GEOgraphic location the Gulf, Colorado & Santa Fe Railroad built a roundhouse, a freight depot, and a large two-story brick depot by 1895. The Atchison, Topeka & Santa Fe Railroad purchased the G.C.&S.F. in 1886 but was required to keep the separate corporate entities intact. The Santa Fe railroad system needed a shop facility located centrally that had an abundance of water for the steam engines. Johnson County and Cleburne bid for and received the prize in 1897 by offering the gift of one hundred acres plus the drilling of water wells for the railroad. The town went so far as to buy out an entire neighborhood to make way for the shops through eminent domain. Johnson County was equipped to enter the new century with the largest shops of the Santa Fe system in Texas, one of the largest in the entire South. The shops employed locals from all over the county and attracted many newcomers seeking jobs. The shops became a financial backbone of the local economy and a mainstay for families. One generation followed another in the same line of work, as they developed knowledge and skills as railroad workers.

## Local Engineers

There is something about the hustle and commotion of the steam locomotive that demonstrates the character and excitement of the American industrial spirit. From the power and noise of the moving levers,

The Santa Fe shops yard. Cleburne, circa 1900. (Layland Museum, Cleburne, Texas)

4

# TURN-OF-THE-CENTURY

# JAUNT THROUGH JOHNSON COUNTY

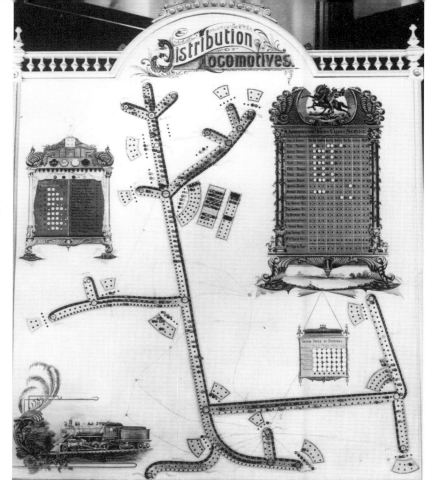

Visual locating system to keep track of the location and disposition of the steam engines on the G.C.&S.F. line. The ornate board showed all of the lines and branches and included the round houses and service facilities of the railroad. (Layland Museum, Cleburne, Texas)

rods and wheels you get the idea that the spirit of the American work ethic has been designed right into it. It fascinates young and old alike from the sound of the first puff of steam or first shrill whistle they heard.

Railroads shops called Johnson County home for over a hundred years. Starting with the MKT in Alvarado in 1881, and its shops a few years later, then the Santa Fe and the T.B.&V. Railroads shops came to Cleburne. By looking at the interior photographs of the shops it is evident that Johnson County workers built and made things. These railroads and their shops were magnets for workers not only throughout the county, but for hundreds and even a thousand miles up and down the tracks.

Spin off creativity from the experience and ingenuity of the designers and engineers was evident as local newspapers published patent applications for new inventions and patents were granted for improvements in existing products.

The modern age required new industries and ways of doing things. By 1900 America was leading the world in certain areas of manufacturing. Local citizens were inspired to built their own versions of these contraptions. Johnson County had more than its share of modern industrial firsts for Texas. Local business-men, mechanics, and engineers completed Texas "firsts" in very important fields.

Teaching car for instructing apprentice engineers. The classroom has multiple steam engine controls including steam gauges, oilers, and airbrake systems for each student. (Layland Museum, Cleburne, Texas)

Left: Master Mechanic Building and viaduct built in 1903, in Cleburne on the west side of the railroad shops. Hundreds of working men walked over this viaduct each day traveling to and from their homes. The viaduct crossed the tracks on the west side of the railroad shops. (Layland Museum, Cleburne, Texas)

Below: Santa Fe Machine Shops, erected 1909 by H. D. McCoy of Cleburne. There were 45 machines (floor side), 75-foot-high ceilings, and 23 stalls in a building 515 feet long. The crane in this facility had a 15-ton capacity. Cleburne, circa 1909. (Layland Museum, Cleburne, Texas)

Right: The Santa Fe Boiler Shop where locomotives were retubed and overhauled. Cleburne, circa 1900. (Layland Museum, Cleburne, Texas)

Below: The assembly lines for rebuilding flat cars and box cars in the yards of the Santa Fe Shops, Cleburne. (Layland Museum, Cleburne, Texas)

Above: Santa Fe Coach Shop and New Garden tracks, where the coaches are located. The first stall with the open doors is where coaches were painted. It was destroyed by fire in 1976. The smoke stack in the background was built in 1929 and is 230 feet high, with 17 feet underground, 14 feet in diameter at the bottom and 7 feet in diameter at the top. Cleburne, circa 1900. (Layland Museum, Cleburne, Texas)

Left: Coach Shop of the Santa Fe Shops, capable of handling the refurbishing and repair of 250 cars a year. Cleburne, circa 1900. (Layland Museum, Cleburne, Texas)

Above: Assembly building of the Santa Fe Shops planing mill. Cleburne, circa 1900. (Layland Museum, Cleburne, Texas)

Left: Painters doing finish work on private car of Adolphus Busch. (AC)

Bottom: "Cleburne Foundry Company & Machine Co. manufacture(s) all kinds of brass castings, pipes, steam and water fittings. Their foundry is 45 by 50, with a wing addition 35 by 40 feet, and they have it filled with first class machinery, employ about a dozen men and draw business from a large territory." 1892 (JCA)

GENERAL MACHINE REPAIRING SUCH AS ENGINES, PUMPS, BOILERS, ETC. FARM, GIN AND MILL MACHINERY MACHINE FORGING AND CASTING IN IRON AND BRASS FURNISHED ON SHORT NOTICE PATTERN MAKING

W. G. HAMILTON Owner.

CLEBURNE, TEXAS. 5-7-1921.

TERMS: 6-1-1921.

Our No. 6040.

Your No. O. O. Chrisman, County Judge.

Shipped By

Sold to Johnson County, O. O. Chrisman, County Judge, Cleburne, Texas.

Above: On the right is the Santa Fe Depot. There was an original frame structure built in 1881. The 2-story brick structure seen here was built in 1894. The second story was removed in 1941–42. It was demolished completely in 1994, a century later, to make way for a bridge over the railroad crossing. The Trinity & Brazos Valley Railroad Company Depot on the left was built in 1903, closed in 1932, and the structure was gutted by fire in 1986. (AC)

Below: The Santa Fe YMCA Building, in Cleburne at the northeast corner of Border and Willingham, was completed in 1899. The YMCA was a central force for morality in the life of the railroad town of Cleburne from the association's beginning in the early 1800s. The original building was constructed in that decade—a wooden structure which cost $10,000. When the first building was completed and the furnace ignited, there was an explosion and the new building burned to the ground. The Santa Fe Railroad immediately replaced it with an elaborate new brick building, three stories high, with 20 bedrooms. The building also contained the secretary's offices, a gym, dressing rooms, library, piano and bowling lanes. (Wanda Erickson)

Civilized dining was the key to the success of entrepreneur Fred Harvey and his Harvey Houses which stretched across the West with the railroads in the early 1900s. The five Allen Brothers set up a model kitchen in Cleburne's Harvey House located in the 500 block of East Henderson in the Santa Fe Depot. It became the pattern for the eating nooks across the West. Fred Harvey's waitresses were known as Harvey Girls. Under strict supervision of a matron, they lived in Harvey Dormitories and were to be in by 10 p.m. They were clean, well-dressed, and attentive to diners. They signed a pledge that they would not marry for a year, but the pledge was often broken as ranch hands and railroaders snapped up the waitresses in marriage. Pictured is the Harvey House kitchen crew, Cleburne, circa 1905. (Layland Museum, Cleburne, Texas)

Above: Horse drawn fire truck, circa 1900. (Layland Museum, Cleburne, Texas)

Left: Cleburne Fire Department. Chief Cashion in center seated in wicker chair. (Layland Museum, Cleburne, Texas)

Below: Blacksmith W. N. Bauman in his repair shop, circa 1900. "Horse shoeing a specialty." Bauman was of German heritage and located his shop on West Henderson in Cleburne. (Martin "Nooner" Griffith)

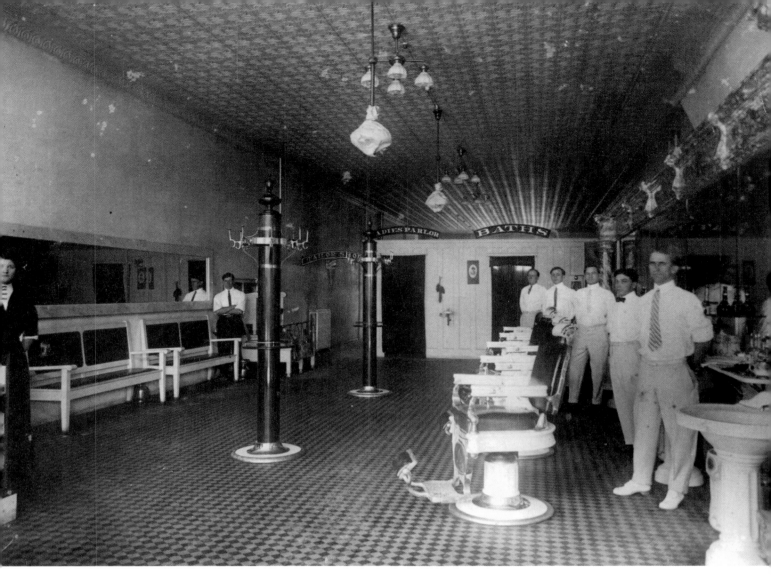

The Peacock Barber Shop which flourished in Cleburne was known to Santa Fe men from Temple to Gainesville. Earlier versions of the shop according to a September 1904 news item were called the Postoffice Barbershop (because it was next door to the post office) and the Famous Barbershop. Located finally at 109 East Henderson and owned by Sam Peacock, the ten-chair facility was a popular spot for daily gossip and political discussion.

The shop offered a hot bath, change of clothes, laundry drop, pedicure, mustache trim and wax, and pants pressed. One could read the latest issue of the Police Gazette, place sports bets, and collect on winnings. From a spacious display, the freshly trimmed and shaved customer could select a cigar of superb quality. Note the display at left in this photo.

It was a full-time job to be a porter in a barber shop. Andrew Odom prepared thirty-two baths one Sunday for customers of the expanded twelve-chair Peacock Barber Shop. Bath water was heated by circulating it around a coal burning stove with an iron jacket. "Yes, the barber shop was a man's domain in the old days," recalls the old bootblack, and while the barbershop had been an Edwardian sanctuary for men, more progressive shops later offered hair preparation facilities for ladies with an entirely separate and partitioned shop for women. (Dr. Jack Burton)

T. Lawrence Jewelry, north side of square, Cleburne. "The old reliable Jeweler of Cleburne. Diamonds, Watches, and Jewelry. Afternoons Specially for Ladies." (Dr. Jack Burton)

1895 Dickson Building, Anglin & Henderson Street, northwest corner, Cleburne. (Dr. Jack Burton)

Farmers & Merchants Bank, Anglin & Chambers Street, northwest corner, Cleburne. "They are putting the ornamental work on the front of the Farmers and Merchants' national bank building and painting the structure this week." August 11, 1893. (Wanda Erickson)

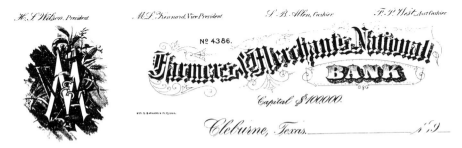

B. F. Bryan Insurance, Cleburne. Many documents and letterheads in the book are from the files of this company which were preserved in the garage of the family. (Layland Museum, Cleburne, Texas)

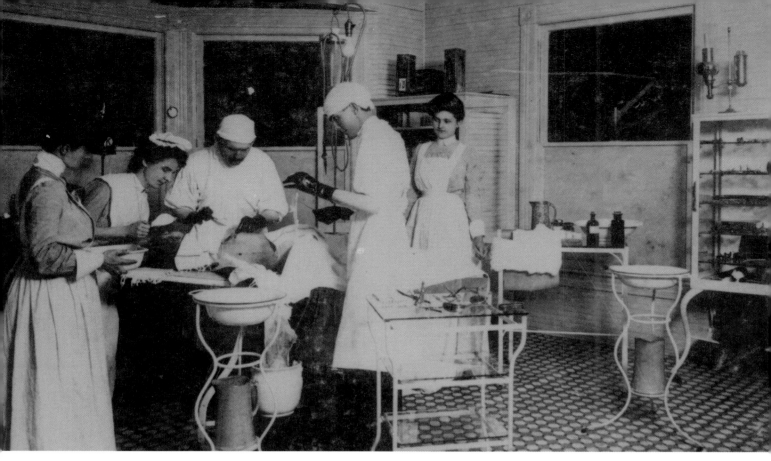

Dr. Robert Lee Yater owned a grocery store and made enough money to go to Baylor Medical School. He also attended Johns Hopkins University for special courses in bacteriology. Dr. Yater and his six brothers built the first hospital in Cleburne at 414 North Main which later burned. Dr. Yater's first office was located above the Wright building. He built a clinic later and Dr. O. T. Smyth occupied that same clinic. (Layland Museum, Cleburne, Texas)

Doctor Yater's Sanatorium, North Main Street, Cleburne. (Wanda Erickson)

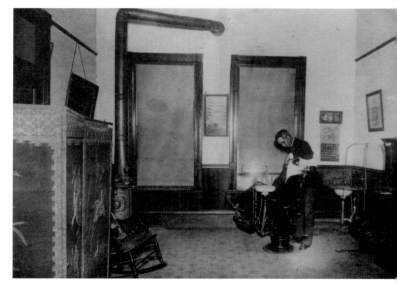

Dr. Gus Clements' dental office, northeast corner of Henderson & Caddo, Cleburne, circa 1902. (Layland Museum, Cleburne, Texas)

A. J. Wright's horse-drawn float in a parade. A. J. Wright, 113–115 South Main Street, Cleburne. (Layland Museum, Cleburne, Texas)

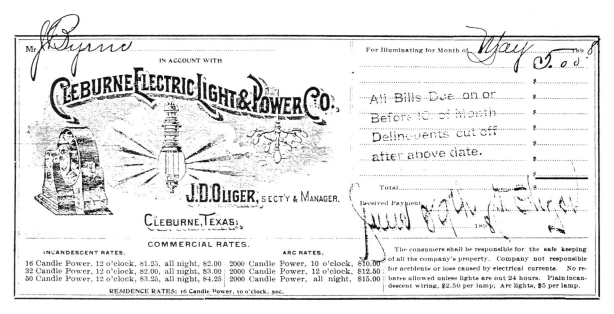

Cleburne Electric Light & Power Company receipt. Cleburne had electric lights in 1888 but the power plant burned in 1892. On August 11, 1893, the papers read, "In a few more weeks see how Cleburne will shine—with electrictt lights." An 1895 promotion reads: "The electric light plant is the source by which the city is made bright by night as the streets of any metropolitan city. It is a fine plant, and is in (the) charge of Mr. Olinger, one of the best known electricians in the South." Cleburne Water, Ice & Lighting Company receipt, circa 1896. (AC)

Above: Overhead view of Cleburne. (Lyman Cronkrite)

Right: Lindgren & Kennedy Photographic Art Gallery, North side of Square, Cleburne. (AC)

FROM LINDGREN & KENNEDY
Photographic
Art Gallery

North Side Square
CLEBURNE,
TEXAS

WE RESPECTFULLY SOLICIT YOUR PATRONAGE
IN ANY GRADE OF COPYING AND ENLARGING
SATISFACTION GUARANTEED IN ALL OUR WORK
DUPLICATES OF THIS PICTURE
AT ANY TIME
AT REDUCED PRICES

In the early 1900s Cleburne had two competing telephone systems when the Cleburne Automatic Telephone Company began operation. This exchange was credited with being the first automatic telephone system in Texas and advertised privacy. "Automatic Secret Service, The Cleburne Telephone Company has the only perfect system, lower rates, and better service; an individual line and secret service for each subscriber." (AC)

## Pioneer Texas Telephones

Telecommunication is basic to our information age. Only six years after Alexander Graham Bell developed his telephone in June of 1875, Cleburne had phone service. These weren't just any phones though, Cleburne was one of the earliest cities in the U.S. to have dial telephones installed. The Automatic Telephone Company installed its dial telephone system in Cleburne in 1882, the same year that Jesse James was said to have been killed. By 1883 there were forty-two subscribers. Thirty years later in 1912, when the Automatic Telephone Company disolved, Cleburne was still the only city in the state that had dial phones. Southwestern Telegraph and Telephone Company opened service in 1897 with rates of $1.50 per month. For many years Cleburne had two phone systems. Many businesses had both phone systems and two phone numbers. Southwestern Telephone and Telegraph Company added long distance in 1904 to the Alvarado Junction, which cost about $2.50 per month. Galveston had the first Texas Telephone service in 1879, and the first Texas long distance line, from Galveston to Houston 1883.

Below: In the oval inset is one of the Automatic Telephones at Shaw Studio. One sits on the counter by the teddy bear. "The first engravings to appear in a Cleburne newspaper were six pictures of the Glen Rose cyclone in 1902. The pictures were taken by Photographer Arch Shaw, and were very clear." (AC)

## A Jaunt Through Johnson County

Here we go on a turn-of-the-century tour through the country towns and communities that grew up in Johnson County.

"In a small town, there's usually not much to see, but what you hear, makes up for it!"

Before the new-fangled contraptions called automobiles came to Johnson County, the favorite form of entertainment on Sundays and holidays was to hire a horse and buggy for a ride over the country. "A young fellow could . . . take his girl riding from one of the then prosperous livery stables for $3.50 a day or $2.50 an afternoon."

Let's go for a trip and visit the towns out in the country. Time travel back to turn-of-the-century Johnson County and see what grew up in the early days.

## Alvarado

Alvarado Panorama, circa 1885. (ALVARADO NEWS)

Top: August 29, 1884, a hook and ladder company was organized in Alvarado by R. M. Chapman and R. H. Coleman. In 1885 the fire department began operating in the first floor of City Hall. The inscription over the entrance proclaimed it as "Alvarado Fire Station No. 1." The tower on top of the building was observation platforms to spot fires. (ALVARADO NEWS)

ALVARADO BANK,

By......................................................

Alvarado, Texas.........................188

| | DOLLARS. | CTS. |
|---|---|---|
| CURRENCY........................ | | |
| SPECIE ............................ | | |
| CHECKS ........................... | | |
| DRAFTS ........................... | | |
| Total.... | | |

Alvarado bank deposit slip, circa 1880s. (JCA)

The Alvarado Methodist Church was completed around 1886–1887. The building is of Victorian architecture, and the interior is of the "Akron Auditorium" style. The auditorium floor is at an angle with the rear higher with semi-circular pews. The chancel area is elevated, the floor plan is representative of the cross. The spire is a landmark in Alvarado. Rev. R. E. Goodrich was pastor from 1903 to 1907. (Dorothy Schwartz)

**Antioch**

Antioch Church, circa 1902. The church (in the background) served as both church and school. It was erected by the men of the community. In bad weather a wagon was used to pick up the children. They would put chairs in the wagon for the children. One day, while going up a steep hill, the chairs turned over and dumped all the children out! (V. L. "George" Pierson)

**Burleson**

Renfro-Clark Home, 128 North Clark Street, Burleson. Built in 1894 by Mrs. H. R. Renfro and her daughter, Mrs. Margaret Annette Baker Clark. (Collection of Historic Burleson)

Dr. Rufus C. Burleson, the first president of Baylor at Waco, was the one who baptized Sam Houston. After coming up out of the icy water and being told by Burleson that all his sins had been washed away, Sam Houston said, "God help the fishes." When the Missouri, Kansas, and Texas Railroad came through Renfro's land they would not give Renfro his asking price. In the contract, Henry held back the privilege of naming the planned town and agreed to the railroad's price. Renfro chose to name the town after Burleson, his teacher, mentor and counselor of many years. (Texas Collection, Baylor University)

Inside the blacksmith shop, from left to right, are: Richard Burns, Lucian Burns, and J. J. Graham. (Ron Geiser, The Apothecary Shop, Burleson)

Richard Henry Burns's Blacksmith Shop. Uncle Dick wearing apron and holding plow sweep; his son, Lucian, standing behind him. Burns Blacksmith Shop was established in Burleson around 1886. Uncle Dick's two sons, Lucian (Loosh) and Elisha (Lish) spent a great deal of time assisting their father. (Ron Geiser, The Apothecary Shop, Burleson)

Panorama of Burleson taken from atop the feed elevator on the east side of the tracks. The Big Four Furniture Store is located at South Main, Burleson. The business was established by Charles Taylor in 1899 as a general merchandise store. The original name was "Armstrong, Norwood, & Taylor," representing the Armstrong brothers, Charles Taylor, and Robert L. Norwood. The name did not last long. People would say, "I've got to go to Armstrong, Norwood & Taylor," and someone else would say, "Oh, you mean the Big Four?" The name change occurred in 1905. (Frank G. Norwood through Community Bank)

First Methodist Church of Burleson was built in 1895 on the southern corner (Ellison and Dobson) of the present church grounds. This photo shows the one-room structure as it was after Sunday School rooms had been added. The church was the site of civic meetings and the organization of the Burleson Chamber of Commerce. (Ron Geiser, The Apothecary Shop, Burleson)

# Cuba

Dr. Larkin Leonidas Harris poses with his horse and buggy, Mrs. Harris stands on the front porch, and Catherine Goldman Smith stands with the horse by the fence. Dr. Harris began his practice in Cuba near Sandflat in 1893. He was joined by his brother Dr. R. L. Harris in 1896. The doctor had a separate house for his office and wrote and filled his own prescriptions. He accepted vegetables, meat, or services as payment, because cash was scarce.

Dr. L. L. Harris made his first house calls on a mule, then a horse, a horse and buggy, and finally an automobile about 1910. The doctor performed extensive surgery. In 1912 he performed an emergency surgery on 13-year-old Lillie Barnes for a ruptured appendix. Dr. L. L., assisted by his brother, Dr. R. L., and Dr. Shaw, had the patient placed in her sister's home on the dining table for the operation. Lillie was kept tightly wrapped in a blanket afterwards to keep her from moving. She was in bed seventy-two days and lived to be over eighty years old. (Sandra Harris Osborne)

Dr. L. L. Harris and his brother, Dr. R. L. Harris, served their entire medical careers in Johnson County. Sometimes as many as forty relatives and friends would gather at their home on Sunday afternoons for a prayer service and the singing of hymns accompanied by Dr. L. L. on the organ. The family home had a large barn, windmill, croquet field, and a millhouse.

Shown here in late 1900 are Mrs. Etta (Goldman) Bennett (a sister of Mrs. Harris) holding son George, her husband Louis Bennett, the Harris family including Hugh, Ira, Dr. Larkin, John, Nellie holding Ruth, Arthur, Frank and Catherine (Goldman) Smith (another sister of Mrs. Harris). (Sandra Harris Osborne)

# Egan

Street scene, early Egan, showing support by the local gents during a boxing match. Note Buckskin Bill's Wild West Show Posters on the store. (Alvarado Public Library)

Egan School, February 7, 1906. (Layland Museum, Cleburne, Texas)

Egan country home. The Thompson children, circa 1900. (Layland Museum, Cleburne, Texas)

**Godley**

Street scene, Godley. (Layland Museum, Cleburne, Texas)

**Grandview**

Street scene, Grandview, where crowd has gathered to see speaker dressed as "Buster Brown." (Layland Museum, Cleburne, Texas)

Grandview Store interior. (Melba Swaim)

The school "High Building" in Grandview was built in 1887 and burned 1920. (Layland Museum, Cleburne, Texas)

Frank Harrell home, Grandview, 1900. Pictured are: Frank and Nannie, with children; Mattie, Eldon, Yater, Ethel, and Laura. ( Layland Museum, Cleburne, Texas)

Cotton gin, Grandview. (Melba Swaim)

Bank check from the First National Bank, "Grand View," Texas dated January 26, 1892. (JCA)

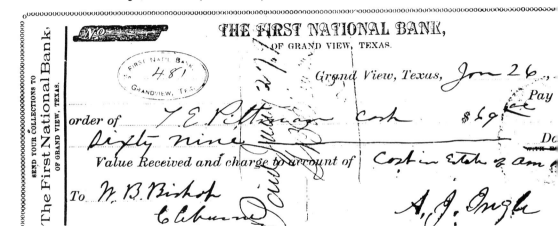

**Joshua**

W. A. Hunter Groceries, Restaurant and Meat Market, Joshua, Texas. (Layland Museum, Cleburne, Texas)

Joe and Sam Hunter holding their horses with Dicie Pearson and Opal Hunter in the foreground of the Hunter family home, Joshua, Texas. (Layland Museum, Cleburne, Texas)

Joshua Cotton Gin. (Don and Lucille Jackson)

# Keene

Above: Keene panorama. Early College Street in Keene looking north towards the college in the background. Photo was taken from the top of the Lone Star Sanitarium, circa 1912. (Southwestern Adventist University)

Left: Arthur Rust standing in front of tent used as a dormitory for boys before "The Home" was built. Mr. Rust was among the first to attend the school at Keene. He rode as a pioneer with R. M. Kilgore to the Keene area to help establish the school where students could learn to live and work for others. Six generations of pioneer Rust's family covering over ninety years, attended the school at Keene. (Southwestern Adventist University)

Cassius Boone Hughes (1859–1921). Professor Hughes spent thirteen of his forty-six years in education in Keene. (Southwestern Adventist University)

Keene students with banner. (Southwestern Adventist University)

Graves store and Post Office in Keene. Pictured are: Harry Reynolds, Claud Gage, E. S. Graves, and George Findley. The building on the left later became W. O. Belz grocery store. (Southwestern Adventist University)

Texas Tract Society of Seventh Day Adventist in Keene. The Seventh Day Adventist have always carried on their own publishing work to disseminate their unique religious beliefs. Almost as soon as Keene was founded, they opened a printing house. The Seventh Day Adventist still operate a much-respected graphic printing facility with the latest four-color printing machines in Keene. This print shop, along with cottage industries, provided work for willing students through the years. (Southwestern Adventist University)

The class of 1901 in Keene. Left to right, front row, are: Leona Wisler, Myrtle Kirk, Dausy Sutherland, Alice Bayliss, Selma Schramm, Bessie Newell, and Katie Beeler. Second row: Mrs. Young, Willie Lambeth, Bertie Taylor, Nellie Stoner, Mrs. Mintie Bodwell, Mrs. G. F. Jones, and Mrs. Walter Jones. Third row: Mrs. Taylor, Leila Falls, Mrs. Kilgore, Ada Phillips, Rena Stephenson, and Mae Williams. Fourth row: C. R. Jones, George Sutherland, Cara Taylor, Ernest Taylor, Grant Abodwell, Lamont Jones, and G. F. Jones. (Southwestern Adventist University)

Dr. C. C. Cooke Family of Keene. Front row, left to right: Elsie Cooke Clothier, Grandpa Cooke, Felix Cooke, Grandma Cooke, Olive Marvin, Emma Cooke, Mary Brandom (holding Abel) Carl, Grandma holding Esther Cooke Anderson, and Aunt Emma holding Esther's twin Harrell. Back row: Haskell, Fred, Charles Lane (Haskell's twin), and Cooke Lewis Brandom. Circa 1902-04. (Don & Lucille Jackson)

The first train of the Dallas, Cleburne, and Southwestern Railroad pulled into the depot at Keene on December 20, 1902. Just when this train was called "Old Betsy" is not known. But no local train has gathered more nostalgia than "Old Betsy." She merits having a main thoroughfare named after her. Old Betsy was quickly woven into the life and existence of the college town of Keene. It was the only way students had of coming and going.

Old Betsy was pulled by a typical coal burning steam engine of those days. The one set of equipment consisted of the small engine and its coal-car, a wooden baggage car, and the quite commodius passenger coach with its upholstered seats that would flip either way. Whatever freight cars switched off from Cleburne for Egan or Keene, made up the rest of the train, usually three or four cars. One round trip was made each day from Cleburne to Egan. (Southwestern Adventist University)

"The Home" also known as North Hall, was occupied by both girls and boys until 1908. Old assembly hall in background. (Southwestern Adventist University.)

Keene Depot, Keene, Texas. "Old Betsy" and the Depot were the scenes of many special occasions. The conductor on "Old Betsy" would often go though the train as it neared Keene crying "The Holy City." (AC)

## Klondyke

An aerial view of Klondyke Ranch, Johnson County. In 1881 Tom Childress purchased land and built the lovely Klondyke Ranch House. He also built three artesian wells and a rustic summer house and walks. Folklore says he struck gold in the Klondyke Gold Rush. In 1901 he sold the ranch to B. B. Sellers. Sellers built a race track and raised race horses. (Layland Museum, Cleburne, Texas)

## Lillian

Street scene, Lillian. (Lyman Cronkrite)

Lillian Gin. (Lyman Cronkrite)

## Marystown

The country home of John Robert and Malinda (Lightfoot) Carlock, circa 1890. In the front row are: Robert E. "Babe" Lee, Rumina, Mary "Callie" California, John Stonewall Jackson, Marion "Frank" Francis, and Grandma Comfort Lightfoot. In the back row are: William "Base" Arthur (hired hand), John Robert (in chair), and Malinda Carlock. John Robert Carlock first came to Texas in 1856 and he joined a cattle drive to California. In 1871 he moved just east of Joshua (Marystown) where he farmed and ranched until his death in 1915. (Don and Lucille Jackson)

Marystown school, 1906.
(Nobia Carlock White and Irene Barnes)

## Nathan

Professor W. G. Slaton came to Johnson County in 1889. Slaton and his brother, Henry T. Slaton, donated the land and founded the Slaton Chapel and Friendship School in 1893. It was located nine miles from Cleburne and served the black community of Nathan. Professor Slaton organized and directed all of the school activities. He was also the principal of the black school in Grandview. Professor Slaton and his wife, Eula, had ten children. Standing in the back row, are: Lillie B. "Aunt O.," Johnny "Duck," Paul, Mattie, Charlie, Claudia, Ella, and Bryan. Sitting are: Eula (Nana) Ann Bell Slaton, and Professor W. G. Slaton, circa 1908, Nathan. (Charlee McNeil)

## Rio Vista

Cooper Brothers Hardware, Rio Vista. (Layland Museum, Cleburne, Texas)

## Union Hill

Mary "Etta" (Walker) Briley, Calvin, and William J. "Billy" Briley in the Union Hill Community, circa 1908. The Brileys came to Johnson County around 1890 and settled in Union Hill. Jim and Etta Briley lived on a farm adjoining the one on which Jim's mother, Mary Briley, lived. April 21, 1898, Jim died of appendicitis in the early morning. Mary, his mother, died of influenza in the afternoon of that same day. Etta Briley married Jim's brother June 20, 1898. They continued to live on the farm and raised Jim's sons. (Don and Lucille Jackson)

Davidson family, Union Hill, circa 1910. Left to right, are: Myrtle, Eula, John F., Bertha, Reed, W. B. Davidson, and Callie (Carlock) Davidson. The children grew up in the Union Hill community. (Don and Lucille Jackson)

**Venus**

On west side of the square, Venus, circa 1910, showing: L. P. Sanders Furniture, the movie house, Simpson Confectionery, pool hall, novelty-groceries, Dr. J. T. Shyles office, and the hardware store. (Lyman Cronkrite)

G.C.&S.F. Depot, Venus, circa 1912. (Layland Museum, Cleburne, Texas)

First Baptist Church of Venus, circa 1912, was organized on August 23, 1896, following a revival by L. S. Knight. (Betty Trussell)

The Illinois & Great North Railway Depot, circa 1913, located east of Venus. (Betty Trussell)

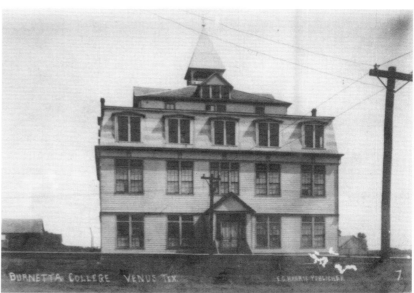

Burnetta College in Venus was a four-story frame building. The school was named "Burnetta College" in honor of Mrs. Burnetta Barnes. Burnetta College opened its first term September 7, 1896, as a thirty-five-room college and dormitory. Around nine years later, the college was turned into a public school. (Betty Trussell)

Venus Post Office interior, circa 1910. (AC)

## "Harrah!
## For Those That Have Come and Gone"

And so our picture storybook comes to an end. We look back on all that we discovered during the writing of this book. We are astounded by what those heroic pioneers were able to accomplish in only a generation or two. Sadly, little of what they considered their favorite and familiar places remain for us to see today, as they have vanished in the mist of time.

As the old frontier veterans arrived at the end of their trail of years, these surviving pioneers became whimsical. They conveyed the phenomenal contrast that they observed between the new and the old times—the amazing changes that had taken place during their lifetime—and they lamented the passing of the Old West.

Confederate Veteran Joseph McClure of Alvarado was born in 1844. He lived through those wild adventurous frontier years of Johnson County as an orphaned boy. Many of the experiences we have told from the frontier years were his. In 1920 the seventy-five-year-old McClure, looking back on those times, ends his memoirs exclaiming, "I say, Harrah! for those that have come and gone. Don't you wish you had been there?"

Thank you Joseph, thank you and all the others for sharing your stories and lending us your pictures. We treasure them all. They allow us to understand how we got here, what we've done, and for a few moments, as Frances Abernathy wrote, "To live again the days so long ago."

And for those of you who have photographs and stories, wherever you are—take them to your local historic preservation group, genealogical society, or museum and allow them to copy what you have and please place the names and dates on the back of the pictures with a pencil.

The Johnson County Heritage Foundation is preserving local Texas history. If you have any folklore, stories, photographs, or documents you would be willing to share, please contact us at:

Johnson County Heritage Foundation
P.O. Box 101
Cleburne, Texas 76031-0101

"He only deserves to be remembered by posterity who treasures up and preserves the memory of his ancestors."—Edmund Burke

### Printed Sources


Abernathy, Frances Dickson. "The Building of Johnson County and the Settlement of the Communities of the Eastern Portion of the County." Master's Thesis, University of Texas, Austin, 1936.

_____. "Campbell Dickson and Lucy Ellen Tracy." Cleburne, Texas, 1935.

Adams, Andy. The Log of a Cowboy. University of Nebraska Press, 1903.

Allin, Jack. The Truth about Cleburne and Johnson County, 1905.

Andrus, Pearl. Juana: Spanish Girl in Central Texas. Austin: Eakin Press, 1981.

Anonymous. (One who must not now be known). Jesse James, His life and Startling Adventures. E. E. Barclay & Co. 1883, 1966 facsimile.

Bailey, Ellis. A History of Hill County, Texas. Waco: Texian Press, 1966.

Bellah, Lynn. Phillip Nolan. Reprint. Cleburne, Texas: Perkins and Son Printing Company, reprint 1984.

Block, Viola. History of Johnson County and Surrounding Areas. Waco: Texian Press, 1970.

Bonanza. Guns and Gunfighters. Los Angeles: Peterson Publishing Co., 1982.

Broder, Patricia Janis. Shadows on Glass, The Indian World of Ben Wittick. Savage, M.D.: Rowan & Littlefield, 1990.

Brune, Gunnar. Springs of Texas. Fort Worth, Texas: Branch-Smith, Inc., 1981.

Buck, Irving A. Cleburne and His Command, Ed. by Thomas R. Hay, Jackson, Tennessee: McCowant-Mercer Press, 1959.

Buel, J. W., Wild Bill. St. Louis, Mo.: W. S. Bryan Publisher: n.d.

Burleson Historical Committee. Burleson—The First One Hundred Years. Dallas: Taylor Publishing Company, 1981.

Campbell, Randolph B. and Richard G. Lowe. Wealth and Power in Antebellum Texas. College Station: Texas A&M University Press, 1939.

Carlton, Jack. It Took Their Kind. Waco: Texian Press, 1994.

Carrell, Ina Mae. One Hundred Years of Godley History, 1883–1983. Cleburne, Texas: Bennett's Printing, n.d.

Carter, Cecile Elkins. Caddo Indians, Where We Come From. Norman: University of Oklahoma Press, 1995.

Chidsey, Donald Barr. The Great Conspiracy. New York: Crown Publishers, Inc. 1969.

Chorlian, Ruth Whitehead. The Long Trail of the Texas Longhorns. Austin: Eakin Press, 1986.

Cleveland, Agnes Morley. Satan's Paradise. Boston: Houghton Mifflin Co., 1952.

Clissold, Stephen. The Barbary Slaves. Marboro Books Corp., 1977.

Conger, Roger N. A Pictorial History of Waco. Waco: Texian Press, 1964.

Coolidge, Dane. The Cowboys. Tucson: The University of Arizona Press, 1937.

Culley, John H. Cattle, Horses & Men. Tucson: The University of Arizona Press, 1940.

Cushman, Ralph B. Jesse Chisholm. Austin: Eakin Press, 1992.

Cutbirth, Ruby Nichols. Ed Nichols Rode a Horse. Dallas: Texas Folklore Society and University Press, 1943.

Daniel, Clifton. Chronicle of America. Austin: Chronicle Publications, n.d.

Dary, David. Seeking Pleasure in the Old West. New York: Alfred A. Knopf: Inc., 1995.

Day, James M. Jacob DeCordova, Land Merchant of Texas. Waco: Texian Press, 1962.

DeCordova, Jacob. Lecture on Texas. Philadelphia: Ernest Crozet, 1858.

Dobie, Frank J. Cow People. Boston: Little, Brown and Company, 1964.

_____. Tales of Old-Time Texas. Boston: Little, Brown and Company, 1977.

_____. The Longhorns. Austin: University of Texas Press, 1979, reprint.1985.

Drago, Harry Sinclair. Wild, Woolly, & Wicked. New York: Bramhall House, n.d.

Durham, Phillip and Everett L. Jones. The Negro Cowboys. University of Nebraska, 1965.

Eckhardt, Charley. The Lost San Saba Mines. Austin: Texas Monthly Press, 1982.

Elliot, Raymond and Mildred Padon. Of a People and a Creek. Cleburne, Texas: Bennett Printing, 1979.

Elman, Robert. Badmen of the West. Secaucus, N.J.: Castle Books (The Ridge Press), 1974.

Exley, Jo Ella. Texas Tears and Texas Sunshine. College Station: Texas A & M Press, 1985.

Frantz Joe B. and Julian Ernest Choate. The American Cowboy. Norman: University of Oklahoma Press, 1955.

Enterprize Publishing Company. Enterprize Souvenir Edition of Johnson County. Cleburne, Texas, 1895.

Gard, Wayne. The Chisolm Trail. Norman: University of Oklahoma Press, 1954.

_____. Sam Bass. Boston: Houghton Mifflin Co., 1936.

Garner, J. W. A Memorial and Biographical History of Johnson and Hill Counties, Texas—The Lone Star State. Chicago: Lewis Publishing Company, 1892.

Gibson, Arrell M. The Chickasaws. Norman: University of Oklahoma Press, 1971.

Glad, Paul W. McKinley, Bryan, and the People. J. B. Lippincott Co., 1964.

Granbury Junior Woman's Club. Hood County History in Picture and Story. Fort Worth: Historical Publishers, 1978.

Griggs, William Clark. Parson Henry Renfro. Austin: University of Texas Press, 1994.

Haley, James Evetts. The XIT Ranch of Texas. Norman: University of Oklahoma Press, 1953.

Handbook of Texas. 3 vols. Austin: Texas State Historical Society, 1952, 1976.

Hill County Historical Commission. A History of Hill County, Texas 1853–1980. Waco: Texian Press, 1980.

Historical Advisory Committee. "Rio Vista in Review 1884–1984." 1978.

Horan, James D. The Authentic Wild West; The Gunfighters. New York: Crown Publishers, Inc., 1976.

_____. The Authentic Wild West; The Outlaws. New York: Crown Publishers, Inc., 1977.

Horan, James D. and Paul Sann. Pictorial History of the Wild West. New York: Crown Publishers (Bonanza Books), 1954.

Hudson, Wilson M. Why the Chisholm Trail Forks. University of Texas Press: Austin, 1956.

Hunter, J. Marvin. The Traildrivers of Texas. Austin: University of Texas Press, reprint 1985.

Hyer, Julien. The Land of Beginning Again. Atlanta: Tupper & Love Inc.: 1952.

Irving, Washington. A Tour on the Prairies. London: John Murray, 1835. Time-Life, Classics of the Old West, reprint, n.d.

Jackson, Helen Hunt. A Century of Dishonor. New York: Indian Head Books, 1881, reprint 1993.

Jenkins, John H. Basic Texas Books: An Annotated Bibliography of Selected Works for a Research Library. Rev. ed. Austin: Texas State Historical Association, 1983, 1988.

Joshua Historical Committee. Joshua: As It Was and Is 1853–1976. Cleburne, Texas: Bennett Printing Co., 1977.

Joshua Historical Book Committee. Joshua As It Was and Is, Volume II Centennial Edition, 1881-1981. Cleburne, Texas: Bennett Printing Company, 1981.

Kelly, Charles. The Outlaw Trail, A History of Butch Cassidy and the "Wild Bunch." New York: Bonanza Books, reprint 1958.

Kendall, George Wilkins. Narrative of the Texan Santa Fe Expedition. 2 vols. New York: Harper and Brothers, 1844.

Kimball, Justin F. Our City-Dallas, Kessler Plan Association of Dallas, Dallas, 1927.

Klos, George. "Our people could not distinguish one tribe from another." Southwestern Historical Quarterly, April 1994.

Knight, Oliver. Fort Worth, Outpost on the Trinity. Fort Worth: Texas Christian University Press, reprint 1990.

Lale, Cissy Stewart. Fort Worth: Outpost on the Trinity. Fort Worth: Texas Christian University Press, 1990.

Lavender, David. The Great West. New York: American Heritage Publishing Co., 1982.

Lucius, Beebe. "Purveyor to the West," (Fred Harvey) American Heritage, February 1967. Vol. XVIII, No. 2.

Maloney, Vance J. The Story of Comanche Peak, Landmark of Hood County. Private Printing, 1970.

Mayhill, Mildred P. The Kiowas. Norman: University of Oklahoma Press, 1962.

McCoy, Joseph G. Historic Sketches of the Cattle trade of the West and Southwest. University of Nebraska Press, 1874, 1939, reprint 1985.

McDearmon, Ray. Without the Shedding of Blood. The Story of Dr. U. D. Ezell and of Pioneer Life at Old Kimball. San Antonio: The Naylor Co., 1953.

Meinig, D.W. Imperial Texas. Austin: University of Texas Press, 1969.

Miltenberger, Rev. Gordon. The Church of the Holy Comforter: The History of the Episcopal Church in Cleburne, Johnson County, Texas. n.p., 1971.

Mims, Mollie Gallop Bradbury. The History of Johnson County, Texas. Curtis Media Corp.: Dallas, 1985, 1993.

Morgan, Andrea Gurasich. Land: A History of the Texas General Land Office. Austin: Texas General Land Office, 1992

Moseman's Illustrated Guide, C. M. Moseman and Brother, New York City, 1892.

New Handbook of Texas. 6 vols. Austin: Texas State Historical Association, 1996.

Newcomb, W. W. The Indians of Texas: New Handbook of Texas. Austin: University Press, 1961.

Nunn, W. C. Somervell: Story of A Texas County. Fort Worth: TCU Press, 1975.

The Old West, Time Life Books, Various Editors, Alexandria, Virginia, 26 vol. series.

Pirtle, Caleb. Fort Worth:The Civilized West. Tulsa: Continental Heritage Press, 1980.

Padon, Mildred. The History of Cleburne and Johnson. Cleburne, Texas: Layland Museum, 1992.

Pertulla, Timothy K. The Caddo Nation. Austin: University of Texas Press, 1992.

Pool, William C. Bosque Territory, Kyle, Texas, Chaparral Press. 1964.

Radde Rebecca D. Bosque Primer. 1976.

Redford, Robert. The Outlaw Trail. New York: Grosset & Dunlap Publishers: New York, 1976, 1978.

Richardson, Rupert N. Comanche Barrier to South Plains Settlement. Abilene: Hardin-Simmons University, 1991.

Roemer, Ferdinand. Texas. Waco: Texian Press, reprint 1967.

Rollings, Willard H. The Commanche. New York: Chelsea House Publishers, 1989.

Sanders, Leonard and Ronnie C. Tyler. How Fort Worth ,Became the Texasmost City. Fort Worth: Amon Carter Museum of Western Arts, 1973.

Schmidly, David J. Texas Mammals East of the Balcones Fault Zone. College Station: Texas A&M Press, 1983.

Scifres, Charles J. Brush Management. Texas A&M University Press, 1980.

Selcer, Richard F. The Fort That Became a City. Fort Worth: Texas Christian University Press, 1995.

Smith, F. Todd. The Caddos, the Wichitas, and the United States, 1846–1901. College Station: University A&M University Press, 1996.

Sonnichsen, Charles L. Outlaw: Bill Mitchell alias Baldy Russell. Sage Books, 1965.

Southwestern Adventist College and S.A.C. Alumni Association. Lest We Forget. Southwestern Colorgraphics: Keene, Texas, 1985.

Swanton, John R. The Indian tribes of North America. Washington: Smithsonian Institution Press, 1974.

Taylor, T. U. Fifty Years on Forty Acres. Austin: Alec Book Co., 1938.

Taylor, T. U. Jesse Chisholm. Frontier Times. Bandera, Texas, 1939.

_____. Frontier Times. Various articles.

Texas Almanac (1904), page 216.

Terrell, J. C. Reminiscences of the Early Days of Fort Worth. Fort Worth: Texas Printing Co., 1906.

Tidwell, Jerry. Hood County Historical Highlights. Granbury, Texas: Hood County News Publisher, 1993

Tyler, Ronnie C. and Lawrence R. Murphy. The Slave Narratives of Texas. Austin: Encino Press, 1974.

Utley, Robert M. The Indian Frontier of the American West 1846–1890. Albuquerque: University of New Mexico Press, 1984.

Vincent, James U. "Johnson County, A Pen Picture of General Robert Tombs with Glimpses of the Mental Characteristics of the Hons. A. H. Stephens and Benjamin H. Hill." Louisville, Kentucky Courier–Journal, Job Printing Company, 1886.

Waldman, Carl. Atlas of the North American Indian. New York: Facts on File Publications, 1985.

Wallace, Patricia Ward. Our Land Our Lives. Norfolk: The Donning Company, 1986.

Wallace, Ernest and E. A. Hoebel. The Comanches: Lords of the South Plains. Norman: University of Oklahoma Press, 1952, 1986.

Weems, John Edward. Death Song, The Last of the Indian Wars. Indian Head Books, n.p. 1991.

_____. Men Without Countries. Boston: Houghton Mifflin Company, 1969.

Weston, Jack. The Real American Cowboy. New York: New Amsterdam Books, 1985.

Wilbarger, J. W. Indian Depredations in Texas. Austin: Hutchings Printing House, 1889

Williams, J. W. Old Texas Trails. Burnet, Texas: Eakin Press, 1979.

Wilson, Maurine T. and Jack Jackson. Phillip Nolan and Texas Expeditions to the Unkown Land, 1791–1801. Waco: Texian Press, 1987.

Winton, W. M. The Geology of Johnson County. Austin: Bureau of Economic Geology, 1922.

Worcester, Don. The Chisholm Trail. University of Nebraska Press, 1980.

Wortham, Louis J. History of Texas. Fort Worth, Texas: Wortham-Molyneaux Co., 1924.

Yoakum, H. History of Texas From Its First Settlement to Its Annexation to the United States. New York City, 1856.


### Newspapers, Periodicals, Magazine Collections, and Directories


Alvarado Bulletin, Jan. 13, 1882–Dec. 21, 1883. Microfilm, Cleburne Public Library

The Alvarado Post.

Alvarado Weekly Bulletin, Jan. 4, 1884–Sept. 11, 1891. Microfilm, Cleburne Public Library.

Burleson Star.

The Century Magazine. 1888–1889.

Cleburne Bulletin.

Cleburne Chronicle, Oct. 21, 1868–Sept. 17, 1874. Microfilm, Cleburne Public Library.

Cleburne City Directories, 1899–1905. Layland Museum, Cleburne, Texas.

Cleburne City Directories, 1907–1911. Dan Leach.

Cleburne City Directories, 1900–1947. Cleburne Public Library.

Cleburne Daily Enterprise, Nov. 6, 1894–Jan. 31, 1923. Microfilm, Cleburne Public Library.

The Cleburne Eagle, John & Tina Harrison.

Cleburne Morning Review, May 25, 1905–Dec. 31, 1934. Microfilm, Cleburne Public Library.

Cleburne Times Review, 1928–1998. Suzanne Wright, Rob Fraser, Bill Rice.

Dallas Morning News.

The Enterprise, July 1, 1890–Jan. 24, 1893. Microfilm, Cleburne Public Library.

Fort Worth Gazette.

Fort Worth Star-Telegram.

Galveston Chronicle.

Galveston News.

Joshua Tribune.

Keene Reporter.

Waco Daily Examiner.

The Weekly Enterprise, Cleburne, Texas. Feb. 18, 1893–June 19, 1894. Microfilm, Cleburne Public Library.


### Manuscripts, Collections, and Unpublished Sources


Abernathy, Frances Dickson. "Campbell Dickson and Lucy Ellen Tracy." Manuscript, Cleburne, Texas, 1935.

_____. "The Building of Johnson County and the Settlement of the Communities of the Eastern Portion of the County," Master's thesis, University of Texas, 1936.

_____. "Scrapbook of Johnson County, 1870–1963." Cleburne, Texas.

_____. "Scrapbook of Johnson County, Vol. 2." Cleburne, Texas.

Billingsley Memoirs (Aaron). Alvarado Public Library. Alvarado, Texas.

Billingsley Memoirs (John). Alvarado Public Library. Cleburne, Texas.

Boatright, Patricia Smith. "Doc Smith." Personal collection.

Bosque County Collection, Elizabeth Torrence. Meridian, Texas.

Bosque Memorial Museum, Clifton, Texas.

Bryant, C. H. "History of Johnson County." Master's thesis. Waco: Baylor University, 1931.

Burleson Historical Society. Burleson Heritage Calendar, 1994 and 1995.

Burton, Faye. "Early Cleburne Memoirs." Manuscript.

Carlton, W. E. "Jack." Oral interview, Junell, Oct. 16, 1994.

Cavasos, Juana. File, Glen Rose Somervell County Public Library.

Clayton, Grace. Senior class term paper.

Cleburne, City of. Tax Roll, 1914, vol. 1.

_____. "Contagious and Infectious Diseases of Cleburne, Texas, 1886–1946. Dan Leach Collection.

_____. Civil and Criminal Ordinances, 1914–15. Dan Leach Collection.

Cleburne High School. Essays on Local History by Senior History Class, 1909, Layland Museum.

Crook, Albert. "Early families of S.W. Johnson County." Manuscript, 1938.

_____. "Goatneck & Camp Creek Area." Manuscript.

Crook, Albert. "In the Shadow of the Longhorn. An Autobiography by J. A. Crook." Manuscript.

_____. "Reminiscences of Albert Crook." Manuscript.

Elliott, Raymond. "A Sprig of Grass." Manuscript.

Greenstein, Ruth

Guinn, Ernest. "A History of Cleburne." Master's thesis, University of Texas, n.d.

Hejl, Susan, Gordon Conway File

Hill College, Confederate Research Center.

Historic Burleson Foundation, Inc.

Hughes, Junior. Junior Historian Award-winning Themes 1985-86. Burleson, Texas.

Irvine, Laura J. "Sketch of Johnson County, Texas," American Sketch.

Jetsel, Pam. "Head 'Em Off at The Past." Newsletter.

John, Elizabeth A. H. "Inside the Comancheria, 1785: The Diary of Pedro Vial and Francisco Xavier Chaves," n.d.

Johnson County Brands. Cleburne Public Library.

Johnson County Genealogical Society, Cleburne, Texas. Tangled Roots.

Johnson County Heritage Foundation.

Johnson County Historical Commission.

Johnson County Historical Markers.

Johnson County Records: County Surveyor, Commissioners Court, County Clerk, District Court, Probate Court.

Johnson County Tax Rolls, 1855–1910, 1911, 1912. Microfilm, Cleburne Public Library.

Johnson County, Texas, 1860, 1870, 1880, 1890 Census. Microfilm, Cleburne Public Library.

Kitchens, Peggy

Leach, Dorothy. "Barnards' Indian Trading Post." Draft of subject marker, Somervell County Historical Commisssion, 1996.

Lemens, Bill. Personal collection.

Maxon, Peter Flagg. 1912–13 Johnson County Courthouse, National Register of Historic Places Registration Form, 1988.

_____. Letters and deed records on the Little Hoss Ranch and the Indian-Wels massacre.

McClure, Joseph. "Memoirs." Alvarado Public Library.

McKee, Shirley. "Grandview Mystery Girl." Article.

McLeroy, J. "The D. C. Ned Clayton I Remember." Manuscript. n.d.

Moore, Erlynne Lily Ewing. Scrapbooks. 1972.

Moore, Karl H. "History of Johnson County Baptist Church." Dissertation, n.d.

Murphy, George L. "Scrap Book of Johnson County History," n.d.

National Register Archives.

Osborn, William. "A Corporate History of the Gulf, Colorado and Santa Fe Railroad." Manuscript.

Peters, Doris. "The Y.M.C.A. of Cleburne." Manuscript.

Pioneers and Old Settlers Reunion Association of Johnson County, Texas

Public Records, including deeds, wills, marriages of:
Bosque County, Texas
Dallas County, Texas
Hill County, Texas
Hood County, Texas
Johnson County, Texas
Somervell County, Texas
Tarrant County, Texas

Research Files: Alvarado Public Library; Cleburne Public Library; Denver Public Library; Western History Department, Fort Worth Public Library; Glen Rose Somervell County Public Library, The University of Texas at Austin, University of Texas at Arlington.

Save Old Cleburne.

Shropshire Civil War Letters and Artifacts. On loan to Hill College Confederate Museum. Dan Leach Collection.

Sparkman, Sue. "The Menefee Family, 1620–1955,"n.d.

Star of Republic Museum, Washington, Texas.

Texas Historical Commission. Letters, files.

Texas General Land Office.

Texas State Archives.

Texas State Historical Association.

U.S. Army Military History Institute, Department of Army.

Utley, Sandra. "Phoebe Whitham" article

Wooten, Dudley G. "A Complete History of Texas Schools and Colleges," Dallas, Texas, 1899.

Young, Dan. "A Calendar of Johnson County History." 1981.

**Oral Interviews by Dan Leach:**

Boatright, Pat. 1994–1997.

Carlton, W. E. "Jack" 1986–1996.

Cavasos, Rose Mary 1993.

Culpepper, Willie Dell 1971–1994.

Earl, Larence. 1995, 1996.

Earl, T. W. 1995–1996.

Gertzenkorn, Victor and Ida Glenn 1971–1975.

Kimbro, Dr. Robert and Tommie, 1972–1998.

Lemens, Bill. October 1994, January 19, 1995, May 1995.

Moore, Erlynne Lily Ewing 1971–1979.

McCall, Mabel 1978–96.

McLean, Jo Dell, 1976–92.

McNeil, Charlee 1994–96.

Norwood, Gracie 1994.

Pearson, J. Hunter, 1992.

Ragsdale, Mrs. 1972–75.

Sullivan, Lowell. 1995.

Vaughn, Millie 1973–96.

**Photo Credits**

Alvarado Public Library

Angel: Ralph, Albert, Mary Grace, and Lois

Arney, John and Fredda

Bailey, Jim. Historic Burleson

Barnes, Irene

Baylor University, The Texas Collection

Bell, Marie

Bennett's Printing

Benson, Mrs. E. P.

Boatright, Patricia Smith

Bob's Antiques, Santa Fe Hotel

Burton, Dr. Jack

Carter House Museum, Franklin, Tennessee

Cleburne Public Library

Cronkrite, Lyman

Danner, E. H. Museum of Telephony, Erlinda Cline, Curator, San Antonio, Texas.

Denver Public Library, Western History Department

Earl, Lawrence

Earl, T. W.

Erickson, Wanda

Estes, Bobby

Estrada, Robert, Santa Fe, New Mexico

Etter, Mrs. Anna Faye

Genealogy/Local History Unit, Fort Worth Public Library

Gieser, Ron, Apothecary Shop

Griffith, Nooner

Griggs, William C.

Hopper, Gay and Helen

Jackson, Don and Lucille

Kleschnick, Ann

Knox, Tom

Lane, Otis

Layland Museum, Julie Baker, Curator, Cleburne, Texas

Layland Plumbing, the Layland and Hadley families

Leach, Ben and Helen

Leach, Dan, author's collection

Lemens, Bill

Linscott, Ralph and Ola Finley, Cleburne Antique Mall

McNeil, Charlee

Meador, Gary

Mims, Mollie Gallop Bradbury

Mitchell, Bob

Morris, Travis and Vivian

Morton, Jack, Cactus Jack's Boot Country, Alvarado, Texas

Neeley, Linda

North, Mrs. Frank

Norwood, Gracie

Oklahoma Historical Society, Cowen, Photographic Archivist

Osborne, Sandra Harris

Peters, Ed and Doris

Pollock, Ron and Susie

San Angelo, Texas,

Schwartz, Dorothy

Seals, Opal

Silver Horse Gallery, Donna Davidson

Sladovnik, Joe Ann McClure

Somervell County Historical Commisssion

Southwest Museum Services, William C. Griggs

Southwestern Adventist University, Advancement, Museum of Student Life, Mary Ann Hadley

The Smithsonian Institution, National Anthropological Archives, Paula Fleming, Photo Archivist

Swain, Melva

Texas State Library, Archives Division

The Texas Sports Hall of Fame, Waco, Texas

The University of Oklahoma, Western History Collections

The University of Texas at Arlington, Special Collections

The University of Texas at Austin, The Center for American History, The Harry Ransom Research Center, Architectural Drawings Collection

Theatre Arts Collection, Harry Ransom Humanities Research Center, The University of Texas at Austin

Torrence, Elizabeth, Bosque County Collection, Meridian, Texas

Trussel, Bettie, Bettie's Antiques

White, Nobia Carlock

Zimmerman, Nina (Carye King)

**Key to Illustration Abreviations**

(AC) Author's Collection

(JCA) Johnson County Archives

(JCR) Johnson County Records

**Businesses and Individuals**

Badgett, Jim, Burleson, Texas

Bailey, Jim and Betty, One Main Place, Burleson, Texas

Bennett's Printing and Office Supply, Cleburne, Texas

**The Black and White Works, Lynn Mayes**
3027 Lackland Road, Fort Worth, TX 76116
817/731-4001

Geiser, Ron, Apothecary Shop, Burleson, Texas

Studio II, Bob Force, Cleburne, Texas

T's Photo Quik, Cleburne, Texas

# BIBLIOGRAPHY

# INDEX

# JOHNSON CO.

Prepared from Records in Land Office.
June 1, 1871, and
PHOTO-LITHOGRAPHED FOR
SPENCE & McGILL,
REAL ESTATE AGENTS,
AUSTIN, TEXAS.

1871 Spence & McGill (Texas General Land Office)